Cracking the SAP Certification Test

Application Associate Financial Accounting with SAP ERP 6.0

H.G. NZABANITA
SAP SERIES

SAP SERIES – Volume 1

CRACKING THE SAP CERTIFCATION TEST, Application Associate – Financial Accounting with SAP ERP 6.0
H. G. NZABANITA, May 2014

Image courtesy of ddpavumba / FreeDigitalPhotos.net

Table of Contents

Foreword

SAP is the world leader of Enterprise Resource Planning (ERP) software. It has been chosen by many top companies in different industries, as a reliable tool for running their businesses. A good knowledge of SAP has led many consultants to brilliant careers in the IT industry.
Becoming a certified SAP consultant will not automatically provide you a job. However, a combination of theoretical knowledge and practical experience is a solid foundation for numerous career prospects.

This book has been written to provide consultants the essential knowledge needed to successfully take the test for the SAP Certified Application Associate – Financial Accounting with SAP ERP 6.0.

The content is meant to be covered within a relatively short timeframe, and includes three full-length practice tests that will build your confidence as you review the material. Although, we all have different learning styles, it is suggested to read the book from cover to cover at least five times. Depending on your current SAP knowledge, you may need to read it more times or fewer times. According to a popular saying "repetition is the mother of learning". Your performance on the practice tests is supposed to help you assess your level of readiness, and determine whether you have a good grasp of the essential knowledge. Typically, the entire book can be covered in five days without pressure, and the sixth day can be set aside for a practice test. With this game plan, you can be prepared to successfully take the certification test in a month.

The test answer sections point to the pages where the material covers the knowledge needed to answer specific questions.
Your feedback is appreciated for the improvement of future editions of this publication and future titles. Although we cannot commit to answer all messages, we will endeavor to take into consideration all suggestions. Messages should be addressed to **support@sapseries.com**.

Inquiries: support@sapseries.com

Chapter 1 - SAP ERP Overview

Introduction to SAP ERP

From a technology perspective SAP ERP is built on SAP Netweaver, the application and integration platform **most suitable for Enterprise Services Architecture (ESA) using web services** technology.

The central component of the Application Platform is the SAP Web Application Server (SAP Web AS), which provides:
• Operating System and DB independence
• Multilevel architecture
• JAVA and ABAP environment (open environment)
• Basic functions for the majority of SAP systems
• High scalability

The functions of the different SAP systems are divided in two categories:
• **Basis functions** which are very similar across various SAP systems are provided through Web AS.
• **Application functions** which vary depending on systems.

Advantages of SAP Netweaver:
  ▢ Openness and Extendibility
  ▢ Immediate Integration
  ▢ Lower Total Cost of Ownership (TCO)
  ▢ Clear Roadmap

SAP ERP is a solution within mySAP Business Suite. Other solutions in the Business Suite include:
  ▢ SAP CRM
  ▢ SAP PLM
  ▢ SAP SRM
  ▢ SAP SCM
The processes enabled by each solution are outlined in a **Solution map**.

Organizational Levels

Prior to implementing the System, a company's enterprise structure should be mapped to SAP applications using organizational units that reflect the enterprise structure in terms of legal and business purposes. A table of organizational units can be outlined as follows:

Client: is the overall highest level unit. It is meant to reflect the enterprise group.

Company Code: represents an independent unit that is legally required to produce a balance sheet, as the main organizational element of Financial Accounting.

Controlling Area: is a self- contained organizational structure where costs and revenues are allocated and managed. It portrays a separate unit for cost accounting.

Plant: is the central organizational unit for production planning and of logistics.

Storage Location: portrays a unit for Inventory management.

Sales Area: is a combination of Sales organization, Distribution Channel, Division.

Sales Organization: is the main organizational element that handles terms of sale offered to customers.

Purchasing Organization: is a unit that handles purchases for all plants in a country. A country can only have a single Purchasing organization.

Organizational units need to be linked to achieve integration and to reflect the entire enterprise structure in SAP ERP. The links are defined during customization.
It is **possible to change the assignment of organizational units**, company code, business area, or profit center in the course of a given fiscal year, **if the conditions here below are met**:
• The currency of the new company code is identical to the currency of the old company code.
• Only planning data has been posted in the fiscal year.
• The cost center is not assigned to a fixed asset, work center, or HR master data.

Master Data

This is data used on a long-term basis and shared by several business processes to prevent data redundancy. Master data is created **centrally for use by all applications** and all authorized users. From an organizational perspective the information in **master data is organized into views** which are assigned to different organizational elements.

For instance, customer master has three views: (1) at client level: General data, (2) at Company Code level: Financial Accounting data, (3) at Sales Area level: Sales data.

Transactions are application programs that execute business processes in the System, such as creating customer orders, approving leave requests, etc.

A **document** is a data record that is created by performing a transaction. It stores pre-defined information from the master data and the related organizational elements.

Reporting

Data Warehouse Concepts:
A **Data Warehouse** stores combined information.

OLAP - online analytical processing is an analysis tool that is optimized for **query in the informative environment**.

OLTP - online transaction processing: is optimized for **transaction processes in the operative environment**. It is suitable for integrated application modules such as external data, materials management, production planning, sales and distribution, financial accounting.

Operative environment versus informative environment - an operative environment **focuses on the business strategy**, driven by business processes based on customers, products and orders. The informative environment **focuses on knowledge** obtained from the data warehouse after data extraction and transformation. The inherent knowledge becomes the foundation for the business strategy.

SAP BW - supports the analysis of data from SAP operative applications and other business applications including external data sources such as databases, online services, Internet.

BW enables Online Analytical Processing (OLAP) to stage extensive volumes of operative and historical data. OLAP technology supports multi-dimensional analyses from various business perspectives.

SAP BW is implemented by using **preconfigured objects from its Business Content**. These objects include InfoCubes, queries, key figures and characteristics. The **Business Explorer** (BEx) component avails **extensive analysis options**.

Introduction to SAP NetWeaver

Application versus Component

A component is considered the smallest software unit that can be produced, delivered, installed, and maintained on an individual level. Components are the building blocks for a solution. Typical components include SAP ECC, SAP SCM or SAP NetWeaver Portal, etc.

The core applications of the SAP Business Suite are: SAP ERP, SAP PLM, SAP SRM, SAP SCM.

• **Industry Applications**:
  - Discrete industries: Aerospace & Defense, Automotive, Engineering-Construction & Operations, High Tech, Industrial Machinery & Components
  - Process industries: Chemicals, Life Sciences, Mill Products, Mining, Oil & Gas
  - Consumer Industries: Consumer Products, Retail, Wholesale Distribution
  - Service industries: Media, Professional Services, Telecommunications, Transport & Logistics, Utilities
  - Public services: Defense & Security, Healthcare, Higher Education & Research, Public Sector
  - Financial services: Banking, Insurance

- **Enhancement Packages** are modules of new or enhanced business functionality for the SAP Business Suite, and SAP Netweaver. They are deployable without service interruption, and enable continuous innovation for all core applications of the SAP Business Suite.

SAP NetWeaver used as an Application Server (AS)

SAP NetWeaver integrates and connects people including information and business processes across technologies and companies, to expedite adjustment to rapid change. It also guarantees the reliability, scalability and safety of a company's business processes.

SAP NetWeaver uses a solution method called **IT practices** to implement IT processes. IT practices rely on a set of key IT activities, that are performed with the integrated components of the platform, which focus on the **IT and business goals** of a company, rather than on the **system and its technological components**.

According to the naming convention for all SAP Netweaver components, every component always starts with "SAP Netweaver".

SAP Netweaver's main function is to provide:
- **People integration** – using Multichannel access, and Portal, Collaboration
- **Information integration** – using Business Intelligence, Knowledge Management, and Master Data Management
- **Process Integration** – using Integration Broker, and Business Process Management
- **Application Platform** – for J2EE, ABAP, DB and OS Abstraction
- □ Lifecycle Management
- □ Composite Application Framework

The Architecture of SAP NetWeaver AS

Three or more tiers can be used in the SAP Business Suite environment to support complex client/server configurations.

An **instance** is an administrative unit that incorporates SAP system components in order to offer one or more services. An instance runs on a physical computer; however, multiple instances can run on a single computer. An instance is identified by **a system** ID (SID) and an **instance number**. A common **instance profile** can be used to define settings for all the components of the instance. The terms instance and Application server are interchangeable.

Installation options for SAP NetWeaver AS include:
• AS ABAP system
• AS Java system
• AS ABAP and Java system

AS ABAP Processes

AS ABAP runs processes on three different layers (presentation, application and database layers). The (ABAP) **dispatcher** is the main process of AS ABAP. It manages resources for applications written in ABAP in conjunction with the operating system.

The **Automation** of routine tasks is achieved though SAP **background processing,** a method that optimizes the use of computing resources by assigning to the system reports and programs for execution without straining any dialog resources.

AS Java Processes

AS Java runs processes on three different layers (presentation, application and database layer).

HTTP requests from user web browsers are received by the **Java dispatcher** that forwards them to the server process of an instance.

The processes of AS Java along with the database schema form the **Java cluster**. The cluster threads of AS Java **are multithreaded**, whereas the processes of AS ABAP are not. This enables AS Java servers to process **multiple user requests in parallel**.

Inquiries: support@sapseries.com

SAP Systems Software Development

ABAP developers have the ability to perform various changes in an SAP system. Developers need to understand the **data structure**, the **development** and **transport processes** of SAP systems to successfully perform system modifications.

Understanding the **data structures** requires a good grasp of the following terminology:
• Client-specific data
• Cross-client customizing
• Repository objects

A **client** is a self-contained unit from a business, organizational and data viewpoint. A client has a distinct business data environment, including distinct master and transaction data, and distinct user data. The data in a client is said to be **client-specific**.

Customizing is the process used to tailor the SAP standard system, to meet a company's specific requirements, by mapping its organizational structures and processes to the SAP ERP system. Customizing is thereby said to be **client specific**.

Customizing or customization is achieved by making additional one-time settings besides **client-specific customizing** settings, which are valid for all clients in the same SAP system. These common one-time settings are referred to as **cross-client customizing** settings. Customizing and customization are used interchangeably hereafter.

Every object that is accessible through the ABAP Workbench is stored in a central **cross-client** location called the **Repository**, which stores:
• All Dictionary objects (tables, data elements, domains)
• ABAP programs
• Menus
• Screens

The Three-System Landscape

SAP Systems have a three-system landscape that offers a **stable test environment** where developers can make System changes and perform testing without affecting the Repository.

A two-system landscape would require that testing be performed in the development environment, and thereby interfere with development activities.

A three system landscape provides distinct systems designated for:
• Development
• Quality Assurance
• Production

Importing Transport Requests

A transport request contains logically related objects resulting from customization or development in SAP environments. The objects are supposed to be transported as a single block; therefore they are saved together in a transport.

The System where the transport was created is the source; it exports the transport. The System that needs to receive the transport is the target, it will import it. Transports need to be released before they can be moved from one system to the other. No additional changes can be made to a transport, once it is released.

A transport request is labelled by an alphanumeric ID that normally starts with a **"K9" prefix**, followed by five other characters. Transport requests can be imported into the target system one by one, or as a single group that contains several transport requests.

Objects should first be imported **by type**, then **by the order** of the transport requests in the import queue. Furthermore, **dictionary objects** should always **precede other repository objects**, such as programs. The order of the transport requests in the different import queues should always be consistent between all systems (Quality Assurance and Production).

SAP Systems Implementation and Installation

Before proceeding with an SAP System installation and implementation, it is essential to consider:
• Supported hardware and software versions
• Hardware requirements (main memory, CPU, I/O capacity, etc.)
• Supported platforms (refer to the Product Availability Matrix – PAM)

- Sizing (based on an estimate of the hardware requirements for the System)
- Load Balancing (based on the best distribution of users among the instances of SAP)
- Availability (high availability for all SAP systems is required with single points of failure)
- Digression: Adaptive Computing (that enables dynamic assignment of hardware resources to application services as needed).
- Installation Tools and Utilities (based on SAPInst, SAP's standard installation tool)
- Digression: SAP Rapid Installer (installation and configuration tool that complements SAPInst, needs to be compatible with the envisioned systems).

SAP Systems Maintenance

Maintenance activities mainly involve **updating the Runtime System** and the **Repository**. The **Runtime System** includes the SAP System and the Database/operating system.

The **Repository** contains a range of objects that are subject to regular updates. Basically there are two main types of updates:

- Updates **initiated by SAP** (such as SAP Note corrections, Support packages, Enhancement packages and upgrades)
- Updates **initiated by the customer** (for example transports).

SAP Notes are normally meant to provide solutions for **known problems within ABAP**-based software components. A tool referred to as the "**SAP Note Assistant**" can import corrections systemically. Nevertheless, the SAP Note Assistant cannot perform changes on table definitions.

Support packages are combinations of corrections for software components **related to a designated release level**. These are available for ABAP-based and Java-based components. An SAP Solution Manager tool, known as the "Maintenance Optimizer" is used to download Support Package stacks.

SAP enhancement packages deliver new developments and enhancements **for current SAP ERP systems**. The business function of the developments and enhancements must be activated after installation in order to take effect. SAP enhancement packages differ from Support Packages.

Upgrades are changes **applied to older SAP** ERP versions, to bring them up to date. The upgrade process **replaces all repository objects** (programs, table definitions, etc.) including the **runtime environment**.
There are three main types of upgrade procedures:

1. **Technical upgrade**: for future compatibility of SAP Systems and risk reduction.
2. **Functional upgrade**: provides limited functional enhancements and reduction of TCO (total cost of ownership).
3. **Strategic upgrade**: sets the ground for intra-enterprise structural changes and the implementation of new strategic business processes

Communication and Integration

A Remote Function Call (RFC) is the most important interface in SAP environments. RFCs are able to **call functions in SAP systems and in non-SAP systems**.

Other **essential interface technologies** used by SAP systems:

- **ALE**: Application Link Enabling
- **BAPI**: Business Application Programming Interface
- **EDI**: Electronic Data Interchange
- SOAP: Simple Object Access Protocol
- TCP/IP: Transmission Control Protocol / Internet Protocol
- XML: Extensible Markup Language

Business Programming Interfaces more known as BAPI's are **special RFC** modules. **A BAPI** is a standardized interface that provides internal and external access to processes and data of business application systems. BAPIs are **used to integrate third-party applications and components in the Business Framework**.

BAPIs are **defined as methods for business objects** in the **Business Object Repository (BOR)**. Nevertheless, they are initially created similarly to other function modules in the **Function Builder**, prior to definition in the BOR. A BAPI can **only be assigned to a single business object**.

Each **business object in the Business Object Repository (BOR) can have several methods** based on one or many BAPI implementations.

BAPIs can be used for:
• Linking business processes that encompass ALE based systems.
• Integration of different solutions within the framework of the SAP Business Suite.
• Connecting an SAP system to the Internet.
• SAP Business Workflows.
• Connecting to external programs.

Cross-System Business Processes

A cross-system business process occurs when a business process **involves different systems or companies**. In such conditions **a link is required** to connect the distinct systems. **Application Linking Enabling (ALE)** is an option for exchanging data between different systems located at **the same company site**, or **different systems operated by distinct companies**. The data is actually **transferred using RFC** based on a predefined format.

The connection uses synchronous and asynchronous communication, instead of a central database, and provides a secure and consistent data transfer.

ALE is designed to support the **implementation and operation of distributed SAP applications,** for environments that include **centralized and decentralized tasks.** The integration of applications is based on message exchange.

Web Services

Web Services are essentially flexible combined modular function programs used as software interfaces.

The **transformation of remote-capable function modules from the Function Builder** is the foundation for developing Web Services. There are two options to call-up a Web service:

▢ From an **ABAP program**
▢ From a **Business Server Page**

Service-Oriented Architecture (SOA)

The **SOA** framework **merges data and application functions** in order to **create reusable enterprise services**.

Enterprise services focus on **the larger business logic** to handle complete industry-specific processes that involve multiple individual small steps, while Web services focus on **detail functions within applications** or enterprise services.

The only **difference between SOA and ALE**; is that **SOA is based on open standards**. Therefore, it provides additional options for connecting SAP system functions with third-party Web Service functions through the Internet.

SAP Service Marketplace

The SAP Service Marketplace is a free service geared towards SAP customers and partners to provide a central web access point to all SAP services. Customers need to register to obtain access to the service. The homepage site can be personalized based on different topics, depending on customer needs. The services provided on the SAP Service Marketplace include:

• Current messages
• Note database
• Applications for developer keys
• Training information
• SAP software change registration
• Service requests
• Corrections
• Problem messages

SAP Developer Network (SDN)

The SAP Developer Network provides online content intended for developers and consultants in relation with SAP Netweaver areas. Services of the SAP Developer Network cover:

- Technical reviews and articles
- eLearning material
- An online forum
- A newsletter
- Netweaver business content
- Webinars
- Download zones

Solution Manager

Solution Manager is **a standalone component of SAP Netweaver** that is delivered to customers at no additional cost. It can be used to service all SAP technologies, **to integrate non-SAP products** and to provide a single point of access from where a solution that incorporates **systems in various landscapes can be managed**. Netweaver is not meant to replace any software products at a customer site, but to complement existing software, by adding value through:

- Increased reliability of the IT solution
- Reduced implementation costs
- Operations and change management projects
- Leveraged IT investments
- Reduced time for experiencing system benefits

Objective of SAP Solution Manager

Solution Manager is a tool designed to help manage the complete SAP solution throughout the entire lifecycle. It is supposed to be the central place in a landscape where all information regarding a solution is gathered throughout all phases of the lifecycle. Solution Manager provides everything needed to manage an SAP solution.

Typically **Solution Manager brings**:

  □ Guaranteed reliability
  □ Reduction of total cost of ownership
  □ Increased return on investment

Solution Manager's approach is distinguished by:

- **Integration**: Solution Manager brings all information for SAP solutions and third-party applications of a solution into a single spot.
- **Life-cycle orientation**: Solution Manager provides a structure whereby **tools**, **content** and a common **gateway** can be used for central management throughout the entire lifecycle. It also provides a framework for the approval of change requests, creation of blueprints for the solution, configuration and testing business processes, transfer of knowledge to end-users, execution of changes and upgrades, etc.

- **Business-process orientation**: Solution Manager provides an end-to-end view of each business process that encompasses all incorporated systems and interfaces, and serves as a link between business processes and the underlying IT infrastructure. Hence, when a problem occurs on a sever customers are able to identify the exact step affected in a business process.

Advantages of Solution Manager

SAP Solution Manager acts as a tool, content and a gateway:
- **Tool** perspective: Solution Manager is primarily a tool to facilitate enhanced implementation and operation of an SAP solution. It contains functionality that is used to monitor systems and processes, and carry out support desk within a context where messages can easily be handled. As a tool Solution Manager can be used to:
  - □ Document
  - □ Implement
  - □ Train
  - □ Test a deployment
  - □ Support and maintain
  - □ Monitor and optimize
  - □ Control change
  - □ Manage incidents

- **Content** perspective: Solution Manager stores a wide range of content including:
  - □ Methodologies
  - □ Roadmaps (upgrade methodology, solution management, etc.)
  - □ Service procedures for solution optimization
  - □ Best practice documents

- **Gateway** perspective: Solution Manager serves as a gateway to SAP for:
  - □ SAP Active Global support (to access SAP notes to solve a problem)
  - □ SAP Development
  - □ Service delivery platform

Solution Manager offers online services for quick browsing and ordering services, while providing a rapid connection to SAP Active Global Support for access to Notes that widely cover details for addressing solution problems.

In a nutshell, **SAP Solution Manager provides the following benefits**:
- More leverage from IT investments
- Reduced cost of implementation
- More reliable IT solutions
- Faster ROI (return on investment)
- Reduced cost of operation

Scenarios:

The functionality of **SAP Solution Manager can be used in various scenarios**:
- Implementation and distribution
- Support desk
- Monitoring
- Service delivery
- Upgrade
- Change request management

1. **Implementation and Distribution**

   The implementation and Distribution functionality supports:
   - Complete implementation of new or additional systems
   - Global roll-out
   - Solution manager
   - Testing
   - Training
   - Support desk

   Solution Manager can be used for the implementation of new or additional ERP, CRM, SCM, SRM scenarios:

   • The **implementation** can be optimized for any project covering all the implementation process steps and activities including project preparation, business blueprint, configuration, integration of non-ABAP and non-SAP components, etc.

   The three **main areas of the implementation Roadmap** include:

        □ Viewing/Text area
        □ Roadmap structure Attachments area
        □ IMG area

• **Global Roll**-out caters for global standardization and harmonization of scenarios.
• Solution Manager has a customization synchronization feature to help **synchronize Customizing** across the entire landscape.
• The **Testing** environment spans management and execution of tests in diversified landscapes. In addition, automated testing (using eCATT or CATT) can be integrated in test execution. Cross-component tests are also supported through a single point of access to the entire system landscape. There is a **central storage for all testing material and test results**.
• **Training** is fully supported through **E-learning management**, which is used to educate end-users on new or changed processes. E-learning courses are referred to as **learning maps**. The "**Knowledge Transfer Optimization**" service is used to deliver best practices for the identification of the most suitable training strategy based on e-learning. Solution Manager's SAP Tutor tool can be used to create simulations of the actual functionality that end-users will work with, therefore providing a training environment that is a perfect replica of the real environment.
• **Support Desk** is included to address problems that occur during projects and in daily operations.

2. Support Desk

The Support Desk functionality of SAP Solution Manager assists customers in the efficient management of solution support. It is mainly targeted towards **customers who have large IT organizations.** It provides an oversight of the technical IT landscape and all associated core business processes, including end-to-end incident management. **It is most suitable for**:

        □ Reporting incidents.
        □ Searching for a solution.
        □ Forwarding problems to SAP support.
        □ Finding solutions in a customer's solution database.

3. Monitoring

Provides the status of the technical infrastructure, and therefore shows the status of a solution. This is performed through **central monitoring of systems**, business processes and interfaces. Monitoring essentially pertains to the **operation phase** of a solution. The **advantages of using monitoring** are summarized here below:

- It provides a central point of access to all monitoring details.
- It helps prevent complex situations through constant monitoring.
- Expedites problem resolution (by using the automatic notification functionality).
- Enables integration of SAP solutions with third party systems, based on open standards.

Monitoring is provided through:
- Service Level Management
- Landscape reporting
- Central System Administration

- Service Level Management – has a complete range of **features for service level management**, reporting to administrators and customers. Benefits provided by the service level management functionality include:
  - Alleviation of service level management.
  - Single report recapitulation for numerous systems.
  - Strategic decision support.
  - Recommending optimizations.

SAP EarlyWatch Alert is a diagnosis service that is used for monitoring SAP and non-SAP systems. Availability of **SAP EarlyWatch Alert** is a prerequisite for the use of Service Level Reporting.
Service Level Reporting provides solution measurements for key performance indicators (KPI) and conveys the results of the agreed service goals.
The System satellite performs a weekly data capture that is transmitted to the SAP Solution Manager. The data capture inlcudes details for:
- General component status
- System configuration
- Hardware
- Performance development
- Average response times

□ Current system load
□ Critical error messages and process interruptions
□ Database administration

• **Landscape Reporting** – offers a complete listing of hardware and software components within the landscape. Benefits provided are:
□ Instant reports on current solution.
□ Detailed list view of hosts, databases, systems, software components and support package levels.
□ Consolidation of maintenance efforts for standardization of patch levels.

• **Central System Administration** – caters for the definition of task lists that pertain to all the required activities and their respective frequencies. Feature usefulness is based on:
□ Automation of support for periodic and sporadic administration tasks, such as background jobs, security audit logs, database backup execution, system performance details, etc.
□ Time savings (resulting from the central access systems administration).
□ Automatic log of activities.
□ Comprehensive reporting for the entire solution.

On the other hand, the **concept of Solution Monitoring** is defined by the following **three components**:
□ Business process monitoring
□ System monitoring
□ Service level management

4. Service Delivery

Service Delivery enables authorized users to setup and improve service and support processes for all SAP technologies. Self-services offer significant transferable knowledge to employees through planned training sessions. Company reliance on SAP consultants for service delivery can easily be reduced by performing **self-services.**

Service delivery is provided through:
□ SAP Active Global Support

□ SAP IT Service and Application Management
□ Service Proposals and Ordering Process

• **SAP Active Global Support** – Solution Support Services:
SAP Active Global Support enables the enhancement of business processes, by taking advantage of innovations, continuous adaptation to the eco-system, reduction of TCO and reduction of ROI. SAP Active Global Support ensures that core business processes remain functional even after technology updates and migration packages have been installed.

• **SAP IT Service and Application Management**:
SAP IT Service and Application Management is the methodology and process model of Life-Cycle Management for SAP solutions. It extends the ASAP implementation methodology to all facets of IT Operations and IT Service Management. SAP IT Service and Application Management offers an end-to-end description of the key operating and management processes that need to be observed throughout the entire lifetime of a solution.

• **Service Proposals and Ordering Process**:
SAP Solution Manager gathers information on a landscape to suggest adequate services and best practice documents for optimizing the management of the related solutions. Solution Manager provides a direct link to the service catalogue in SAP Marketplace from where services can be ordered.

5. **Upgrade**

The upgrade scenario pertains to continuous improvement of an IT solution. Multiple forms of support are available for upgrade projects, and minimization of related costs and risks. These cover:

□ Definition and configuration of future SAP ERP solutions.
□ Guaranteeing configuration correctness (through testing).
□ Delta training for end users (through E-learning management).
□ Handling eventual upgrade problems (through the Support Desk).

The **Upgrade scenario** addresses key **issues that are common to most SAP upgrades**:
□ Adjustment of current functionality for the new release
□ Implementation of the new functionality
□ Organization and execution of testing
□ Minimization of system downtime
□ End-user training

□ Project management

6. Change Request Management

Change Request Management is used to manage change, from the time a change request is created, until the transport and activation of the change in a productive system (end-to-end). Upgrades are one type of change. Therefore, most processes involved in the Change Request Management scenario are very similar to the ones in the upgrade scenario above. The technical Scope of Change Request Management covers:
　　□ Importation of SAP Support Packages
　　□ Implementation of SAP notes
　　□ Modification of adjustments
　　□ Installation of add-ons
　　□ Implementation of an Upgrade
　　□ Change scenarios, processes and process steps
　　□ Implementation of new SAP products and Add-Ons
　　□ Change and enhancement of customer-owned developments
　　□ Change of Customizing
　　□ Master data additions and changes
　　□ Organizational data additions and changes

The main goal of change management is to enable performance of changes economically within a timely manner and with minimal risk. SAP Solution Manager is delivered with three pre-configured Change Request Management scenarios:

• **Hot Fixes** are critical changes that require immediate customer attention, for instance the implementation of SAP.
• **Regular housekeeping activities** normally happen every 3 to 6 months, and include application of SAP patches. SAP support packages and change packages are applied systemically through Support Desk activities.
• **Business changes** cover the implementation of new business processes, or upgrades that lead to fully documented implementations or upgrade projects. Project plans are defined in cProjects when a change request is categorized as a Project task in the Support Desk of Solution Manager.

Solution Manager in Project Preparation

ASAP (Accelerated SAP) is a methodology meant to enable **successful implementations of SAP solutions across multiple industries and customer environments**.
The **ASAP methodology is based on five project phases**:
- (1) Project Preparation
- (2) Business Blueprint
- (3) Realization
- (4) Final Preparation
- (5) Go Live & Support

Project Preparation
In relation with the Project Preparation phase, Solution Manager is used to setup the following:
□ Upload roadmaps
□ Define statuses
□ Define projects
□ Define high level scope
□ Key word categories
□ Project Team authorization profiles
□ Document management (in order to leverage the scope from different projects)
□ Project issue management
□ System landscape

SAP delivers ASAP roadmaps through:
> □ SAP Service Marketplace
> □ SAP Solution Manager
> □ SAP Roadmap composer (this is a consulting internal toolset)

Activities related to the project definition:
> □ Definition of project data
> □ Assignment of project team members
> □ Definition of project standards

Business Blueprint
The **Business Blueprint is managed in SAP Solution Manager** by:
> □ Detailed scoping
> □ Capturing document requirements
> □ Document version control
> □ Storing all requirement documentation

     □ Effective status management
     □ Providing a direct link to SAP documentation

In relation with the Business Blueprint phase, Solution Manager offers a graphical view of the reference structure, and is used to leverage the scope from different projects, generate the business blueprint and handle issue management.

Some of the tasks that will be addressed during this phase cover:
□ Business process requirements
□ Business process models
□ Developments (such as reports, interfaces, conversions, enhancements, forms and workflows – RICEFW)
□ Other documents
□ Business process transactions

Realization

The main activities enabled by Solution Manager in the **Realization phase** include:
□ Accessing IMG and configuring the solution
□ Capturing configuration documentation
□ Keeping configuration in sync with various systems
□ RICEFW development
□ Documenting test cases
□ Planning and performing unit testing
□ Planning and performing cycle testing
□ Planning and executing integration testing
□ Storing and managing training documents

Prior to any development it is essential to identify the business processes that will address the gaps defined during business blueprinting. In addition, it is important to define customer created transactions, user exists and miscellaneous reports pertaining to the business process.

Final Preparation

Activities performed in Solution Manager during the **Final Preparation phase** include:
□ Stress testing
□ Pre-go live SAP services
□ Setting-up operations support

Go Live & Support

Activities performed in Solution Manager during the **Go Live and Support phase**:
□ Recording lessons learned
□ Handing over the Solution
□ Project closeout report

Chapter 2 - Introduction to SAP Financials

Accounting structures for Companies

SAP ERP has a system hierarchy with different levels. The **client** is the highest level in the hierarchy. Any data or specifications that need to be valid for **all organizational units** must be entered at the **client level**.

Several functional units are referred to as organizational units. These functional units need to be mapped to a company's organizational structure in order to represent the corporate organization in SAP. The functional units can be listed as follows:

☐ **Company Code:** this is the **minimum structure required** in a SAP client. It reflects an independent legal accounting entity for which a fully-balanced set of financial statements must be prepared by law. Company codes are created for external purposes. Depending on organizational structure or other criteria, **multiple company codes** can be used to represent a **company**.

The best way to create a company code is to copy an existing company code using the "copy company code" function, because all related company code-specific parameters will also be copied. Changes can later be made to the new company code as needed. This approach copies the following data from the source company code:

    ☐ Definition
    ☐ Global Parameters
    ☐ Customizing tables
    ☐ General ledger accounts (if needed)

□ Account determination

Defining a company code requires:
    □ A four character company code key for identification
    □ Company name
    □ City
    □ Country
    □ Currency
    □ Language
    □ Address

Other important considerations for company code creation include:
The **address data** is needed for correspondence purposes and evaluation of reports. A **currency** must be defined for **each company code**, because **accounts are managed in the company code currency**. Any other currencies used for the company are considered as foreign.
A **language key** is required for the system to create texts in the correct language systemically. The system needs a **country key** to differentiate **the home country** from the foreign countries.

A **country template** can also be used to create new company codes for the country of reference. Country-specific company code templates are created with the **country installation program,** which in addition creates country-specific templates for controlling areas, plants, purchasing organizations, sales organizations, credit control areas and financial management areas.

An authorized user can also define a company code and perform the configuration **without using any reference company code**.

    • **Segment:** segments are organizational units available in the new General Ledger for SAP ERP ECC 5.0 and above. A segment is used as a **dimension for reporting purposes**.

The **company code** and the **segment** are the **most important** organizational elements in Financial Accounting.

    • **Business Area:** Business areas **optional structures** that can be used to **represent separate cross-company areas of operation** for the evaluation of divisional transaction figures beyond company boundaries. A business area **cannot be directly assigned** to a **company code**. Company codes are created for internal purposes.

It is **possible to assign a business area by**:
□ Plant and item division
□ Sales area
□ Sales organization, distribution channel, and item division

The only entry needed to **define a business area** is a four digit alphanumeric key for identification along with a short description.

International Accounting Standards (IAS) makes the following distinction between **business segments and geographical segments**:

• A **business segment** represents a sub-activity of a manufacturing or service company, where the risks and revenues are different from those in other business segments.
• A **geographical segment** is determined based on risks and revenues that differ from other geographical segments, such as political or economic conditions.

However, US-GAAP, defines a segment as a distinct part of a company that incurs costs, and generates revenue, and has its own financial data pertaining to profit making and resource usage.

> • **Profit Center** - in New General Ledger Accounting, profit centers are **used as dimensions for reporting purposes.** Profit centers are areas of responsibility oriented towards profit making. Creating fully-balanced sets of financial statements for profit centers is a standard option in Financial Accounting. Prior to ECC 5.0 Profit Center Accounting was only available in Controlling.
>
> **Profit centers can be used** to represent:
> □ Organizational units in a company code (divided by function).
> □ Specific lines of business (divided by product).
> □ Geographical locations (divided by region or location).

There is a **segment field** in each Profit Center master data. Postings are made systemically to segments, when postings are applied to the corresponding profit center.

During manual G/L entries the profit center or partner profit center can be specified by the user, whereas, in the **case of primary cost elements**, the profit center or partner profit center is **derived systemically from the cost-relevant account assignment.**

It is **not possible** to enter a profit center **manually for payables, or receivables and postings generated** systemically.

> • **Controlling Area:** controlling areas are distinct organizational units in cost accounting where costs and revenues can be managed and allocated. **One or more company codes** can be assigned to the **same Controlling area** if they use the **same chart of accounts and fiscal year varian**t. These are the two prerequisites to **perform cross-company code costing** between the companies assigned to the Controlling area. **A company code** can only be **assigned to one Controlling Area**.

When several **company codes are assigned to the same controlling area**, the company codes can all operate in different currencies. On the other hand, **cross-company code costing** is enabled to support **multilevel product cost management across company codes**. However, all the assigned company codes **must** use the same **operational chart of accounts and fiscal year**.

Controlling areas **depend on cost centers to accumulate the various costs** that are managed across company codes. **Cost elements** defined for each individual G/L expense account are used to allocate costs from the matching G/L account.

Cost elements are divided into **primary cost elements and secondary cost elements**. Primary cost elements cannot be used as tracing factors (because this is a CO function). Secondary cost elements are used to allocate overheads, and cannot be used for direct production costs. As opposed to primary cost elements, secondary cost elements are not related to any G/L accounts, and are only used in Management Accounting (CO).

Cost centers can be created based on various criteria such as:
• Functional considerations
• Allocation criteria
• Activities performed
• Physical location
• Management area

Cost center categories are indicators used to assign the same characteristics to similar cost centers. They can be used in cost calculation to control the percentage of overheads that should be applied to a specific cost center category.

Global Parameters include:
- Chart of accounts
- Fiscal year
- Company code defaults

The following **organizational units** are **mandatory in FI**:
- Client
- Fiscal year
- Company code

The Variant Principle

The **variant principle** is a three-step method that SAP uses to ascribe the appropriate properties for one or more objects. To fulfil the steps:
1. Specify the variant
2. Determine values for the variant
3. Assign the variant to the objects

The variant principle can be used in relation with:
- Field status
- Posting periods
- Fiscal years, etc.

The use of variants speeds up the maintenance of similar properties shared by several business objects. **A business object** is a **real world object** such as an invoice, sales order or an employee; that has been **modeled to represent a central business object** in business application systems.

Fiscal Year Options

The **fiscal year variant** stores the **definition of posting periods** and **special periods** that include the **number of periods** and their **respective start and finish dates**. It does not reveal specific opened and closed periods. Fiscal year variants are **managed at the client level.**

When all fiscal years within a fiscal year variant use the same number of periods, and the posting periods always start and end on the same day of the year; the variant is said to be **year-independent**. Two different options can be used to define year-independent fiscal year variants:

1. Calendar year
2. Non-calendar year

For a fiscal year to be defined as the **calendar year**, the posting periods must be equal to the months of the year. Therefore, a fiscal year that is a calendar year has 12 posting periods.

For a fiscal year to be defined as a **non-calendar year**, end dates for each period must be defined for every single posting period. A non-calendar year can have between 1 and 16 posting periods. If a non-calendar year does not start on the 1st of January, the periods of the year that correspond to the former or the coming fiscal year must respectively have an indicator **-1** or **+1** **to indicate the year shift**. The day limit for February should be 29, in order to take into account leap years.

When the **start dates** and **end dates** of the posting periods for a fiscal year differ from the dates of other fiscal years, the fiscal year variant must be defined as **year-specific**.

When one year of a fiscal year **variant has fewer posting periods** than the other periods, it is described as a **shortened fiscal year**. A typical instance where this could apply is when closing has to be carried out before the end of the normal fiscal year.

SAP standard fiscal year variants normally begin with a **K or a V**. Therefore, it is not advised to create any custom fiscal years that start with these letters.

Currencies

A **currency key is required** for the definition of any currency. Nearly all world currencies are already defined in SAP ERP with standard international currency keys. **A validity date can** be assigned to **each currency key.**

Exchange rate maintenance needs to be performed for every combination of two currencies. **Distinct exchange rates** are maintained through **exchange rate types**. A set of different exchange rates is needed for several purposes, including **valuation, conversion, translation, and planning**.

Translation ratios are used to maintain **relationships between currencies** per exchange rate type and currency pairs. Normally **maintenance of translation ratios is only performed once**, whereas **maintenance for exchange rates** is a **continuous task**.

SAP ERP offers a number of **tools** that reduce the demands for exchange rate maintenance, according to exchange rate type. Available tools include:
• **Inversion** (the oldest tool and least used)
• **Base currency**
• **Exchange rate spreads**

There are three exchange rate types, labeled as:
B – for the selling rate
M – for the average rate
G – for the buying rate

Typically a **"base currency"** is used for the **average rate (M),** and the **"exchange rate spreads"** are used to calculate **the buying (G) and selling rates (B)**.

All SAP ERP applications and functions handle exchange rates using direct quotation and/or indirect quotation. The **use of indirect quotation is neither application-specific nor country-specific**.

In **direct quotation** (also known as price quotation), **one unit of foreign currency** is quoted **for the matching local currency** (converting a currency to the company code currency), whereas in **indirect quotation** (also known as quantity or volume quotation), **one unit of local currency** is quoted for **the matching foreign currency** (converting company code currency to a different currency).

Here below is an example where the **local currency is EUR** and the **foreign currency is GBP**
Direct quotation: 1 GBP = 1.20441 EUR
Indirect quotation: 1 EUR = 0.82963 GBP

Worklists can also be used to perform **exchange rate maintenance**. **Advantages** of worklists:

• Maintenance only involves the relevant exchange rates.
• Authorizations for maintenance can be assigned for worklists.
• Maintenance only involves the relevant quotation.
• The range of exchange rates is smaller and more manageable.

• Different worklists can be processed in parallel.

Posting Periods

Selected posting periods can be closed to prevent documents from being posted to an incorrect posting period. The System can accommodate as many open posting periods as needed. Each **posting period variant** has a **range of G/L accounts** that are used to **control posting periods**.

Multiple **company codes** can share a single **posting period variant**, in which case the posting periods can be opened or closed simultaneously. This approach simplifies period maintenance. **Posting period variants are opened and closed manually**. On the other hand, a distinct **positing period variant can be configured for each respective company code**, as needed. This approach provides flexibility in terms of period close, but increases maintenance work. A **posting period variant** always has **at least one line with an entry valid for all accounts.**

Posting periods can be handled differently depending on **account types**, for instance during a certain posting period, postings to customer accounts may be allowed while postings to vendor accounts may not. At the line item level, the system checks the account type of the posting key to ensure that the period is open for the assigned account type.

During period closing, **special periods are opened** to record closing postings. During closing, **two period intervals** must be open at the same time. Therefore, **two period intervals** can be entered in **the posting period table**. Although **as many periods** as needed **can be open concurrently, only two period intervals can be open at the same time**

During month end, **an authorization group** can be **assigned to the first period interval**, to enable users belonging to the latter **to post in the first period interval**.

The posting date entered by the user during document entry is used **determine the posting period and fiscal year** for the document systemically.

Posting Control and Document Structure

SAP ERP works according to the **document principle** whereby a document is saved for every posting. The balance of a document must always amount to **zero before it can be posted**. The document abides as a complete unit in the system until it is archived.

Every document is **distinctly identified by the following fields**:
- Document number
- Company code
- Fiscal year

Documents in Financials have the following characteristics:
- A **document header** (information that applies to the entire document).
- Between **2 and 999 document line items.**

There are two important **control keys for every document**:
- **Document type** for the **document header.**
- **Posting key** for the **line items.**

The **document type controls the document header** and **differentiates the business transaction**s to be posted, such as vendor invoices, customer payments, etc. Document types are **defined at the client level** and are therefore **valid for all company codes**.

Document types also define the following:
- Number ranges for document numbers.
- Account types permitted for postings.

Furthermore **document types define** the following:
- The **field status of the document header** fields "Document Header Text" And "Reference Number".
- Whether invoices are posted based on **the net procedure**.

Important standard **document types:**
Document **type AB** allows postings **to all account types**.
All **other document types limit the types of accounts** you can post to.
Document **type DG**, for instance, allows postings to customer (D) and G/L accounts (S) only.

Inquiries: support@sapseries.com

To transfer billing documents from the SAP ERP billing system, you need one of the following document types:

- **RV**, the default document type for Sales Order Management billing documents (customer invoices).
- **RE**, the default document type for Materials Management billing documents (vendor invoices).

During internal number assignment the system assigns a new number to each document in the Financial Accounting component. In external number assignment, the system transfers the billing document number to the accounting document, as long as this number has not already been assigned.

Document **type ZP** is essentially used by the **payment program** during **automatic postings**.

The **document number range** determines the number range that is usable for the documents that are created during company transactions. The **document number** uniquely identifies each document in a company code within a fiscal year. Therefore, document number ranges can be **freely defined for each company code**. These number ranges **must not overlap**. If a document number range is **defined per fiscal year**, it **can be reused** in the following year. Document **numbers can be assigned internally or externally**.

- **Internal number assignment:** in this approach the system saves the last document number that was taken from the number range in the **Current Number** field and assigns the number following the current number as the next document number.
- **External number assignment:** in this approach the user enters the number of the original document, or the number is assigned systemically from another system. The **numbers may be alphanumeric**.

A single number range can be assigned to multiple document types. The intervals of document number ranges **can be copies from one company code to another**. Furthermore, number range intervals **can be copied from one fiscal year to another**. Report RFBNUM00 can be used to locate gaps in the document number assignment.

Posting keys are **defined at client level**, similarly to document types. Besides the control functions mentioned above, posting keys determine that:

- A line item is connected to a **payment transaction.**

•The posting is **sales-relevant** and the sales figure of the account is to be updated by the transaction.

The **posting key has control functions related to the line items**. It controls:
- □ The **type of account** the line item can be posted to.
- □ Specifies the item **posting as a debit or a credit.**
- □ The **field status** of **additional details.**

The fields displayed during document entry depend on the transaction and the accounts used. These different fields are controlled by the **document field status**. **The account-specific field status** needs to be customized for **general ledger accounts.** The **field status specific to the posting key** needs to be customized **for vendor and customer** accounts. **The field status with the higher priority always applies.**

Exceptions to this rule:
- In relation with business areas, the field status can only be used to indicate whether a field is required or optional, because once business area fields are activated they must be ready for input.
- **Entries in tax fields** are only possible if the G/L **account is relevant for tax**.
- The **"hide"** field status **cannot be used** with the r**equired entry** field status **because** the combination **will result in an error**.

Each group of G/L accounts requires a definition for the **status of every document entry field**. This information is split into **field status groups** for each group of G/L accounts.

Table 3.1 represents a typical scenario that shows how the **text field** will be handled on **the document entry screen based** on the **posting key** and **field status group** combination:

Posting Key	Field Status Group	Document entry screen
Text hidden	Text optional	Hidden
Text optional	Text required	Required entry
Text required	Text hidden	Error

Table 3.1

Field Status Groups are **assigned to the respective G/L accounts** in the general ledger account master records. The **field status groups are summarized in one field status variant**. The **field status variant is later assigned to company codes** in Global Parameters. Postings cannot be made prior to the assignment of a field status variant. When a **document is posted to a sub-ledger** account (such as AR or AP), the **field status group of the reconciliation account is used**.

Sub-ledger accounts do not have a field status group; therefore, sub-ledger postings are **distinguished by using different posting keys**. Therefore, numerous posting keys are available for sub-ledger accounts. Postings in the general ledger are mainly distinguished by different Field Status Groups. Therefore, **only two posting keys** (**40 and 50**) are **needed for G/L postings**. **40** is the standard posting key to **debit** a G/L account, and **50** is the standard posting key to **credit a G/L account**.

It is advisable to use the **standard posting keys as delivered.** Changing the standard keys would affect related tables. However, it is possible to copy and change the standard keys.

Document Parking and Holding Documents

Two options are offered for saving documents without a complete posting in Financial Accounting:
□ **Holding** documents
□ **Parking** documents

• **Holding document** is an option whereby the recorded data is temporarily saved to allow further entries on the same document **at a future time by the same user**. Held documents do not have to be complete, because pertaining **account balances are not updated**, and thence underlying **data is not available for evaluation**. On the other hand, **no document number is assigned**. The **user needs to assign a name to the document** after the hold function is selected. The document can later be retrieved under the same user assigned name for **completion, posting** or **deletion.**

• **Parking documents** allows document entry without a full verification. During document parking, **a document number is assigned systemically based on a document type**, although transaction **figures are not updated**. Parked documents can eventually be **completed, changed, posted or deleted**. This approach enables **two different users to handle the documents**, according to **the dual control principle** (whereby one user makes the entry and another one verifies the entry then posts it). When a **parked document is posted** it retains the document number assigned when it was initially parked. In addition, **workflows can be used to post** multiple parked documents.

Validations and Substitutions

A validation is a function that **verifies whether a value or set of values meet some predefined criteria prior to posting**. Validations are driven by rules defined in Boolean logic. Once a validation rule is defined, syntactic correctness is systemically checked.

A substitution is a function **that replaces entered values with other values**, based on a predefined prerequisite. Substitutions are driven by substitution **rules defined in Boolean logic**. The substituted values are transferred systemically to the defined application component.

The common considerations required to execute a systemically are:

(1) Decide upon **the area of application** where the validation/substitution should apply.
(2) Determine the correct **call-up point** for the validation/substitution.
(3) **Define** the validation/substitution.
(4) **Assign** the validation/substitution to an applicable organizational unit.
(5) **Activate** the validation or substitution.
An application area and a call-up point code must be assigned to each validation, substitution, or rule. The **combination of an application area and a call-up** point determine the **applicable Boolean class**.

Validations, substitutions and rules **are used in an Application Area, which is the general area where the** Validation, Substitution or Rule can be used. **Typical application areas are**:
□ FI Financial Accounting
□ CO Cost Accounting
□ AM Asset Accounting
□ G/L Special Purpose Ledger
□ PS Project System

□ RE Real Estate

The following application areas **only apply to substitutions**:
□ PC Profit Center Accounting
□ GA Allocations (FI-SL)

CS Consolidation accepts **validations only**. Each application has a defined structure that provides access to its fields for substitution.

The **Call-up point** is the **exact place** in the application where a validation or substitution comes into action. A **substitution or validation must be activated for a specific call-up point**.

Validations, substitution, or rules use Boolean classes to establish dimensions and to specify the **message classes** that can be used for **validation messages. Certain field combinations are not possible in validations/substitutions. Messages** are used to display information related to an error when **the prerequisite for a validation/substitution is not met**.

Validation messages can have different meanings, based on a three possible symbols:
□ **W** = warning
□ **E** = error
□ **I** = information

There are **three** possible **call-up points for Validations in FI**:
□ The document header.
□ The document line item.
□ The Entire document (only accepts **numeric fields** used for mathematical calculations).

The **steps to create a validation** are:
□ Prerequisite
□ Check
□ Message

A **substitution** consists of **various two part** steps (999 maximum):
□ Prerequisite
□ Replacement

A **substitution method** needs to be defined for **each field** selected for substitution. Possible **options for substitution methods** include:

□ Constant value
□ Exit
□ Field-field assignment

Rules can be used to summarize complex logic, and are re-usable. Enhanced System performance recommends the use of basic or single-dimension sets, as opposed to long lists of Boolean statements or user exits.

Validations, substitutions and rules **should only be defined in development or testing systems**. Independent rules and sets can be used in contexts that require complex logic, such as cases where more detailed rules and extensive processing are required to represent logical statements in prerequisites and checks.

A **rule can be used in a prerequisite statement, a check, or another rule**. Rules are also used in complex logic, for instance where a validation contains an extensive prerequisite that also has a substitution. The **following elements can be used in the rules** for the **prerequisites** (validation/substitution) and **check** (validations):
□ Logical operator (Boolean terms)
□ Comparison operators
□ Operands

Sets are flexible data structures that are used to **portray arranged amounts and hierarchies**. They are usable in nearly all components of the FI-SL system.

A **multi-dimension set is a combination of sets for several fields**. Multi-dimension sets can be used to execute cross-validation with values that have various characteristics. **Sets are administered and maintained centrally**.

Introduction to Automatic Account Determination

Automatic account determination enables line items to be generated and posted systemically. This can be done for a wide range of transactions including:
• Entering a customer invoice.
• Entering Special G/L transactions.
• Posting a vendor payment.

For **customer invoice entries Automatic account determination** can process:
• Tax on Sales and Purchases (for instance, Output Tax during customer invoice posting, input tax during vendor invoice posting).
• Payables and receivables between company codes (during cross-company code transactions).

In **Special G/L transactions, automatic account determination can process**:
• Bill of exchange charges
• Tax adjustments for a down payment

In **postings for vendor or customer payments, automatic account determination can process**:
• Cash discount
• Backdated Tax calculation for tax on Sales/purchases
• Gains and losses from exchange rate differences
• Unauthorized deduction of cash discounts (a payment slightly differs from the amount due)
• Residual items
• Bank charges

A user can add additional account assignments to generate line items systemically, if a G/L account is marked as adjustable and the appropriate field is defined as optional or required **in the field status group**
Depending on the rules, **the assignment of G/L accounts for a transaction with automatic account assignment** can be based on:

• **Chart of accounts**: account determination needs to be configured separately for each chart of accounts.
• **Valuation area**: account determination can be configured based on the valuation area for some transactions, such as consumption postings.
• **Valuation type**: if split valuation will be used for certain materials, account determination can be configured based on the valuation type.

Chapter 3 – General Ledger Accounting

General Ledger Accounts

Creating a **chart of accounts involves three steps** (as per the variant principle):

1. Define the chart of accounts
2. Define the properties of the chart of accounts
3. Assign the chart of accounts to company codes

The **chart of accounts** is a **variant** that stores the structure and the basic information about G/L accounts. A **chart of** accounts must be **assigned to each relevant company code** based on a particular structure. SAP ERP is delivered with a **sample chart of accounts** that can be tailored to country specific needs.

Typically there are **three kinds of chart of accounts** from a functional perspective:

1. **Operating chart of accounts**: designed for a company's daily activities.
2. **Group chart of accounts**: designed for corporate consolidation purposes.
3. **Country-specific chart of accounts**: designed to meet a country's legal requirements.

Every company code **must have at least an operating chart of accounts**. The use of a **group chart of accounts** has the disadvantage of **not allowing cross-company code controlling**. Company codes related to **different countries can use the same chart of accounts**.

The possible **length of** a **G/L account number** is between **1 and 10 digits**. A G/L account is composed of a **chart of accounts segment** and **company code segment.** On the other hand, **G/L accounts are the master data** used in a chart of accounts. **G/L accounts always use external number assignment**.

When a **chart of accounts** is still incomplete, it **can be blocked** to prevent use until it is ready. The **block** can be performed **at the chart of account level or at the company code level**.

A chart of accounts stores basic information about G/L accounts. The information for an account is summarized in a **chart of accounts segment** that shows:

• Account number (**number intervals for G/L account master records can overlap.** However, you cannot create two G/L accounts with the same code in the same chart of accounts).

• Name of the account (as short and as long text).

• Control field.

• Consolidation fields.

The **chart of accounts segment** consists of several groups of fields grouped under different tabs:

- • Type/Description
- □ Control in chart of accounts
- □ Description
- □ Consolidation data in chart of accounts

- • Keyword/Translation
- □ Keywords in chart of accounts
- □ Translation

- • Information
- □ Information in chart of accounts
- □ G/L texts in chart of accounts

The information entered in the **chart of accounts segment for a G/L account applies to all company codes**; therefore it only needs to be entered once. For instance, the **short text field for a G/L accoun**t **can be changed centrally in the chart of accounts segment**. A G/L account has **two segments, namely a chart of accounts segment and a company code segment**.

Texts entered for the chart of accounts segment are managed by text ID and language, and can be displayed using the report **"Account Assignment manual"**.

Prior to using an account from a designated company code chart of accounts, creating a **company code segment** for the specific account is required. **Accounts** must exist at the **client level before they can be created at the company code level**. The company code segment stores information that only pertains to a particular company code. This information controls the entry of accounting documents and the management of accounting data. The **company code segment** consists of several tabs:

- Control Data
  - □ Account control
  - □ Account management
  - □ Joint venture

- Bank/Interest
  - □ Document creation
  - □ Bank/Financial details
  - □ Interest calculation

- Information
  - □ Information
  - □ G/L account texts

The following **information relevant to each company code needs to be defined**:
□ Currency
□ Taxes
□ Reconciliation account
□ Line item display
□ Sort key
□ Field status group
□ House bank
□ Interest calculation information

In addition, specifications for **balance sheet** or **profit and loss** statement account are required in the chart of accounts segment, as these two types of accounts are handled differently during the closing procedure.

The definitions made during **Chart of Accounts** customization include:
□ Description
□ Maintenance language

□ Length of the G/L account number
□ Blocking/ Unblocking chart of accounts

A user defined **retained earnings account** needs to be associated with expense accounts during G/L account master record creation. **If there is only a single retained earnings** account, the system will automatically use it. If there is **more than one retained earnings** account, the retained earnings account that applies for each profit and loss statement account will need to be selected during G/L account master record creation.

G/L accounts in the chart of accounts can be gathered into different **account groups**, based on user defined criteria **to group similar accounts**. In this regard, the **G/L account group** is a **classifying feature** for G/L master records. An **account group** must be entered **in the chart of accounts segment**. SAP ERP is delivered with predefined account groups that are changeable. **Account groups are chart of account dependent**.

The **G/L Account Group** determines the **number interval** that is **suitable for a G/L account**. In addition, the G/L account group also determines the **fields for the data entry screen** (based on the field status assigned to each account group).

The **display and maintenance of an account's master data** is controlled by a **field status.**
□ Fields that are **not to be used** need the **"Hide" status**.
□ Fields with **values that must not be changed** need **"Display" status.**
□ Fields **that require a value** need the **"Required Entry" status**.
□ Fields where a **value can be stored, but is not required**, need the **"Optional" status**.

The fields for **Account Currency** and **Field Status Group** are **always required** fields. This status cannot be changed. Sometimes **hidden fields may contain values,** and despite being hidden, the System will **still take them into consideration**. The fields displayed in the G/L account master record are **controlled by the account group**, but also by **the transaction used to change the master data**: this is referred to as **transaction-specific control**. Customizing provides a "**Change Master Data**" transaction that can be set to prevent modification of certain fields, after creation of a master record.

The combination of **field status definitions from the account group** and the **transaction** is used to determine the field status to use. The combination with the highest priority is always considered. Starting with the highest, **the priorities for each field status are as follows**:
□ Hide
□ Display
□ Required entry
□ Optional entry

To avoid the use of transaction-specific control, the field status for all **fields should be set to optional**. Since **the optional field status has the lowest priority**, the account group-specific control is always used.

Reconciliation accounts are general ledger accounts used by business partner master records to record all transactions in the sub-ledger. Reconciliation accounts are always updated **in real-time**. It is **not possible to make direct postings to reconciliation accounts**.

The **"Line Item Display"** field is a control field in the company code segment of an account. If line item display was not selected when a G/L account was initially created, report RFSEPA01 can be used to subsequently **activate the line item display** where management by line item display is later needed.

Line item display takes up additional system resources; therefore it should only be used if there is no alternative to view the line items. **Line item display should not be activated for**:
□ **Reconciliation accounts** (because line items are managed in the sub-ledgers).
□ **Revenue accounts** (because line items are managed in Sales order Management).
□ **Material stock accounts** (because line items are managed in Purchasing Management).
□ **Tax accounts**

Items in accounts with **open item management** are referred to as "open" or "cleared". Open item management enables users to identify closed (cleared) and open business transactions. The **balance** for such accounts **is always the total of the open items**. Accounts with open item management **must have line item display activation**. **Open item management is a must for the following accounts**:
• Bank clearing accounts
• Clearing accounts for goods receipt/invoice receipt

- Salary clearing accounts.

Activation or deactivation of open item management is **only possible if** the account has a **zero balance**.

Each **account currency** must be setup as a **local currency** or a **foreign currency**. The local currency is proposed by default upon creation of a G/L account. If the **account currency is the local currency, the account can be posted to in any currency.** The other currencies are translated into the local currency for each line item. **Accounts with a foreign currency** as the account currency **can only be posted to in the designated foreign currency**.

If the **"Only Balances in Local Currency"** checkbox is selected in the master data record, transaction figures for the account will only be managed for amounts converted to the local currency. This field should be selected **for clearing accounts where amounts for clearing should not be subject to postings for exchange rate differences.**
The indicator is required for "**Cash discount**" and "**GR/IR clearing**" accounts. It must **not** be set in reconciliation accounts **for customers or vendors**.
The indicator normally applies to **balance sheet accounts** that are **not managed in foreign currencies** and **not managed on an open item basis**.

Parked Documents

Documents are normally parked to allow additional processing at a later time, prior to posting. These documents should only be deleted in exceptional cases.

The document change rules stored for posted documents do not apply when documents are parked. The following **changes are not feasible** on parked documents:
- **Currency**
- **Document type**
- **Document number**
- **Company code**

Other changes can be made as often as needed. **Feasible changes** include: **dates, amounts, accounts and account assignment objects**. Changes to parked documents can be displayed either before or after posting.

Parked documents can be posted using **standard transactions** or a **selections list**.
Documents that posted successfully will be listed. Parked documents that did not post successfully can be reprocessed. In addition, **creating a batch input session** is another option for **posting parked documents**. The **Workflow** functionality can also be used **to post parked documents**.

Once a parked document becomes a fully posted document:
• A complete Financial Accounting document is created.
• Document change history is recorded.
• The document number remains the same.
• Balances for all associated accounts are updated.
• The parked document is deleted from the System, and replaced by complete FI document.

The "Enjoy" Entry Screen

It is possible to use a single-entry **Enjoy** screen for most postings. Occasionally a traditional complex screen needs to be used. In both cases, G/L account postings are systemically listed in the income statement report, and can also be displayed when querying posted accounts.

The entry screen is divided into the following areas:
• **Work templates**: contain screen variants for account assignment templates, or held documents as references.
• **Header data:** is data that pertains to the whole document. Some of the header data can be in display format only, hidden from the user through editing options.
• **Line item information:** is the area where the line items of the document are entered.
• **Information area:** displays the debit and credit balances by using a traffic light icon.

Postings in Financial Accounting are relayed to Management Accounting through **cost elements** represented by associated expense accounts in the chart of accounts. There are two types of cost elements: **primary cost element** and **secondary cost element**.

Primary cost elements are essentially **copies of Profit & Loss** (revenue and expense) accounts from the financial chart of accounts. **Each P&L account must have a cost element** counterpart. A primary cost element is normally related to a G/L expense account. **Secondary cost elements are only usable in Controlling** for allocation purposes. **Secondary cost elements have no counterparts in the chart of accounts**; therefore they are not defined in FI.

A primary cost element can be created concurrently with a new G/L account. In addition, a cost element **can be accessed from the G/L master** record of an account.

Entries for Enjoy screens need to be made according to the sequence below:
- Initial screen: enter document header and initial screen first line item.
- Item screen: enter first line item, initial screen second line item.
- Item screen: enter second line item, initial screen third line item.
- Additional item screens.

Introduction to Document Splitting

When an invoice has **multiple account assignment objects, such as two different cost centers;** balance sheet and P&L statements can systemically be created for each individual segment. There is no need to manually select **the affected segment** during posting, because it **will be derived systemically from the cost center**.

ERP SAP supports **derivation** of the **segment** from the **profit center**. On the other hand, the profit center can be derived from a cost center, a CO internal order, or a project.

"Enjoy" Screen for AP - Invoice/Credit Memo Entry

A **single screen transaction** can be used to post a **vendor invoice** or a **credit** memo directly **into Accounts Payable**, in the case of a miscellaneous invoice without reference to a purchase order.

The Accounts Payable entry screen includes:
• **Work templates** with selection options for screen variants, account assignment templates, or held documents as references.
• **Header and vendor data** for the entry of document header and vendor line item.

- **G/L account items** for the entry of G/L line items for the document.
- **Information area is** for the display of document balance and **vendor** information.

Operating expenses always require a cost accounting-relevant assignment, such as a cost center or internal order. Therefore, when an item is posted, documents are created in **Management Accounting and Financial Accounting**. Existence of a **primary cost element** in the G/L is a precondition for recording amounts with a cost object.

"Enjoy" Screen for AR - Invoice/Credit Memo Entry

Most of the invoices and credit memos from customers, reach the Accounts Receivable through the integration with the Sales Order Management. Occasionally, there will not be a reference to a sales order, but invoices and credit memos can still be entered using the Enjoy transaction.

The Enjoy document entry screen includes:
- **Work templates** with selection options for screen variants, account assignment templates, or held documents as references.
- **Header and vendor data** for the entry of document header and vendor line item.
- **G/L account items** for the entry of G/L line items for the document.
- **Information area** is for the display of document balance and **customer** information.
Documents in a foreign currency can also be created in the Enjoy invoice/credit memo entry screen (single entry). Foreign currency amounts are translated into the local currency based on the defined exchange rates.

Document Parking and Workflow

SAP Business Workflow is an organizational process with four dimensions. Each dimension prompts a couple of questions:
- Organizational structure (**about who**?)
- Process structure (**applies when? According to what order? Based on what circumstances**?)
- Function (**for what**?)
- Information (**based on which data?**)

The process that needs to be imaged as a workflow will be saved in System parameters through a graphical definition tool. The workflow manager is responsible to perform all the tasks identified during the process definition.

Benefits of using SAP Workflow:
- Supports all company processes within the System.
- Supports communication between business processes operated on different systems.
- Provides to end users all details for carrying out consecutive steps.
- Provides standard workflow templates; for portraying business processes.
- Users can customize the standard workflow templates or create their own.

Workflow Management Architecture

The SAP Business Workflow **has three layers**, which offer significant flexibility.

• The appropriate work: the task to perform during the workflow must be implemented **in the Business Object Repository** as a **method of a business object type**.

• At the appropriate time:

The **process level** depicts the business process in a sequence of separate steps. The **workflow definition** is the total of all process steps. Single steps can make reference to methods of the BOR (Business Object Repository), or can be used to control the process. The **Workflow Builder** is a tool used to maintain the process level.

• To the appropriate processor: The organizational level establishes a link with the **organizational structure**.
■ A group of **potential processors is available for each task** to perform in the workflow.
■ The group of **processors can be controlled by a set of conditions** in the workflow.

Workflow Areas of Application
Workflows **can be used to perform the following tasks**:
□ Post invoices

☐ Release purchase requisitions
☐ Change material masters
☐ Approve leave
☐ Create customer accounts
☐ Delete purchase orders

A **task** is a step within a business process.
The specific process needs to be broken down into **individual tasks** to prepare the definition. The **definition** of the workflow outlines the tasks and the sequence in which they need to be performed.

Tasks show **work items** that are part of the workflow. The **work items** are displayed in the inbox of the **receiver**. Every single **task** needs to be linked with **possible processors**. Processors are the people within a company who are responsible for a specific task. Each **task** can be assigned to **several processors**, but **if one of them starts running a task the other processors will no longer have access to it**.

A workflow is **defined** by entering a **job** in the **workflow definition**. **Responsible processors** should be designated in a **workflow step**. On the other hand, certain processors can be **excluded** from a workflow.

• **User Interface: Inbox in the SAP System**
The Business Workplace has three screen areas:

1- **Selection tree**: the selection tree is located on the left side of the Business Workplace. It is the area from where **work items are selected**.

2- **Worklist**: the worklist appears on the top right of the Business-Workplace screen. The entries are **arranged** systemically **in groups** within the folder. A special folder is included for **overdue work items**. When a user highlights "Inbox" in the selection tree, all the work items and documents contained in this area become visible.

3- **Work item preview**: When a user selects a work item from the work list, it appears in a preview at the bottom right of the screen. Although some functions of the work item display or workflow protocol will not be available, the user will be able **to make decisions** based on the work item preview.

It is possible for a work item to be **directly performed in the worklist**. **The recipient** of a work item is set by the **WebFlow Engine**.

Assignment of Workflow Variants

Variants are also usable within the context of workflows. For instance, a **workflow variant** can be created for **document parking during FI customization**. If a company needs to use a specific workflow, the **workflow variant must be assigned to the relevant company code**. The pertaining **documents will not be released** for a company code that is not associated to the particular workflow variant. A single **workflow variant can be used for several company codes**. On the other hand, **multiple workflow variants** can be assigned to a **single company code**.

There are different release procedures applicable for accounts receivable and accounts payable. The **Release Group** field in the master record of accounts receivable and accounts payable; can be used to control the process. The release group will determine the **release approval path** during processing.

Release procedures include release **approval levels**, which **vary by procedure and by company** code. **A workflow sequence has multiple levels**. Individual release procedures are controlled by **subworkflows**; they act as workflow templates for reference. The first subworkflow (WS10000052) has a single-level release, the second subworkflow (WS10000053) has a two-level release and the third subworkflow (WS10000054) has a three-level release.

Posting Control

Tolerances and Posting Authorizations

The **upper limits** for amounts are **defined per company code (at the company code level)** in "**tolerance groups**". The processing of **payment differences** is controlled is also controlled by tolerance groups.

In tolerance groups **maximum amounts** can be specified for:
- Total amount per document.
- Amount per customer/vendor item.
- Cash discount a user is allowed to offer.

The currency referenced for control purposes is always the **local currency of the company code**.

It is possible to create **as many tolerance groups as needed**. Each user can be attached to a tolerance group. **Users not assigned** to any specific tolerance group, will be included systemically **in the default tolerance group** (represented by **a blank field**).

For security purposes, **special tolerance groups** should be created and assigned to user logons of employees who have **very high and low limits**. On the other hand, **the default tolerance group** (blank field) should always have **the lowest limits possible**.

Actual **tolerance rates** are defined during customization. These include **the maximum and minimum exchange rate variances, maximum and minimum discount rates**, etc.

Default Posting Values

Parameter IDs allow users to store a set of default values for fields with values that rarely change, such as company code, currency, etc. When a transaction is executed, the default values will populate the matching fields systemically.

The sources of values that are **defaulted by the system for document entry** include:
□ User master records
□ Parameter memory
□ System data
□ Account master record
□ Accounting functions

Some of the entry screens for G/L, A/P, or A/R (for instance "Enter G/L account document" screen) have a pushbutton for **editing options** that can be used to configure the screens for the following areas:
• Document entry: Users are allowed to hide fields that do not apply for their work.
• Document display: the List Viewer can be used to select different display options for documents.
• Open items: provides options for line layout displays and for processing open items.

By using the **editing options** to hide fields that require no editing, a user can **prevent unintentional changes** to some fields.

Change Control

Documents that have already been posted in SAP ERP can be changed to some extent, based on various rules; only certain fields can be changed. The change rules can be predefined by the system or be user-specific.

The only **changeable fields in saved documents** are:
● Document header: Only the **reference number** and **text fields** can be changed.
● Line items: The system **does not permit changes to the amount, the posting key, the account,** or any other line item **fields that would affect the reconciliation of a posted document**.

As users make changes to documents, **the System records changes for the following**:
□The field changed
□The new and old values
□ ID of the user who made the change
□The time and date of the change

Document change rules are distinguished based on:
● **Account type**: The account type enables rules to be defined for accounts receivable, accounts payable, or G/L accounts (account types: A, D, K, M, S)
● **Transaction class**: only usable with special G/L transactions, bills of exchange, and down payments.
● **Company code**: a blank company code field implies that the rule applies to every company code.

Field **changes** are not possible unless the following **preconditions** are met:
    □ Posting period open
    □ Line item not cleared
    □ Posting as debit/ posting as credit
    □ No invoice-related credit memo
    □ No credit memo from down payment

Changes for all documents can be displayed by running report RFBABL00.

Document Reversal

G/L documents, customer documents, and vendor documents can be **reversed individually** or in a **mass reversal**. In order to reverse a document, a **reversal reason code is required** to explain the reason for the reversal. The reversal reason code also **determines if the reversal date is allowed to be different** from the date of the original posting. Documents containing **cleared items cannot be reversed**; the **document has to be reset** to allow the reversal.

A document can be reversed by two ways:
□ Normal reversal posting
□ Negative posting

The **normal reversal posting creates an increase** in the transaction figures, while the **negative posting** sets the transaction figures back to their **initial state**.

Most times the System uses the normal reversal posting method. **Negative postings cannot be made unless** the following are met:
● The company code allows negative postings.
● There is a reversal reason code specifically for negative reversal.

Negative postings can also be used to perform transfer postings of incorrect line items. This can only be done with a **document type that purposely allows negative postings**.

Standard SAP delivered reason codes that are normally predefined to **allow negative postings** include reversal reasons **03, 04, 05, 06, 07, RE.**

Exchange Rate Differences

Exchange rate differences are generated **systemically** for **transactions including foreign currencies.** Incorrect postings are prevented by systemic recordings of differences to the **revenue/expense account for exchange rate differences** (as realized gains or losses), indicated during customization.

In addition, **exchange rate differences are posted systemically** during **open items valuation for the financial statements**. These exchange rate differences from valuation are **posted to a separate exchange rate difference accoun**t and to **a financial statement adjustment account**. The valuation for open items, is followed by a systemic **reversal of the balance sheet correction accounts** and a **posting of the balance of the exchange rate difference to the account for realized exchange rate differences**.

Account Determination for Exchange Rate Differences
For tracking purposes, all the reconciliation accounts and the G/L accounts with open item transactions in foreign currency must be linked to a revenue/expense account for realized losses/gains. Therefore, **G/L accounts need to be defined for exchange rate losses or gains**.

The **Gain/Loss account assignment** for exchange rate differences can be determined in various ways:
□ One G/L account can be used **for all currencies and currency types**.
□ One G/L account can be used **per currency and currency type**.
□ One G/L account can be used **per currency**.
□ One G/L account can be used **per currency type**.

Bank Accounting

House Banks

Banks used by a company are defined as **House Banks**. Each bank account is represented by a **combination of House Bank ID and account ID**. The combination is entered in a G/L account that represents the bank account in the G/L.

Every **bank account** must have a **matching G/L account** assigned to it and vice versa. Both accounts must have the **same account currency**. The **description for G/L accounts and House Bank names** in the bank directory **do not have to match**.

Inquiries: support@sapseries.com

A Bank Directory stores addresses and general control data. Each bank used in the system must have a bank master record. Bank master records are **saved centrally in the bank directory**.

There are four different ways to create Bank master data:
• During entry of bank information in the customer/vendor master record, or during customization of House Banks.
• The "Create Bank" transaction in the Accounts Receivable/Payable master data menu.
• Import the bank directory from disk or tape using program RFBVALL_0, Country-Specific Transfer of Bank Data.
• Customers who use the lockbox function can create a batch input session to update customer banking information in the master record systemically.

Bank Master data at the client level includes:
        □ Bank country
        □ Bank key
        □ Address
        □ Control data

House Bank data includes:
        □ Company code
        □ House bank ID
        □ House bank data (Bank country, bank key)
        □ House bk. Comm. Data
        □ DME/EDI data

The payment program uses the **House Bank ID and the Bank Types to determine the bank to be used**.

The following components **drive the House Bank selection** during payment processing:
        □ Ranking order
        □ Value date
        □ Accounts
        □ Amounts
        □ Expenses and charges

The payment program **takes the ranking order** into consideration when determining **the bank to pay from**. Payments will not be processed if a ranking order has not been specified, because the bank account to pay from is picked by the System based on the ranking order.

Master Data for Bank Accounting

The **bank directory stores addresses and control data for all the banks** in use. There are **two main ways to enter bank directory data**:
● Automatic import of the bank directory from diskette, using an import program.
● Manual entry.

Once a bank has been setup in the bank directory, its basic data (name and address of the bank) becomes accessible during entry of the bank information in a customer or vendor master record. In such cases the **only additional entries that will be needed are:**
□ Country of the bank
□ Bank key

House Banks represent the banks where a company code holds accounts. The System uses:
□ A **house bank ID** to identify each bank
□ An **account ID** to identify each account at the bank

The house bank ID and the account ID need to be entered in the G/L master record of the G/L account that represents the bank account in the chart of accounts.

Cash Journal

The Cash Journal is used to **manage cash** in relation with **posting cash receipts and payments in local branches and offices**. **Possibilities** offered include:
● Creation of distinct cash journals for each currency.
● Posting to G/L, customer and vendor accounts.
● Holding multiple cash journals in each company code.
● Freely definable cash journal identification number (a four-digit alphanumeric key).

Every **cash journal account in the G/L must be represented by a distinct cash journal** that is assigned to the corresponding G/L account. The **cash transactions that are saved in the cash journals are regularly transferred to the General Ledge**r using a defined account.

The screen for cash journal transactions **has three sections**:

□ **Data selection** is used to select the time period for the data.
□ **Balance display** shows totals for incoming/outgoing cash, the beginning balance and ending balance.
□ **Accounting transactions** represents the entry area for cash journal transactions.

Setting up **a new Cash Journal for a company code requires entries for the fields here below**:
• The **company code** (that will use the cash journal)
• A **name for the cash journal and a four digit cash journal ID**
• The **G/L accounts** where the cash journal business transactions will post
• The **currency**
• The **document types** for:
    □ G/L account postings
    □ Outgoing payments to vendors
    □ Incoming payments from vendors
    □ Outgoing payments to customers
    □ Incoming payments from customers

Transactions must be setup prior to using business transaction categories, such as Expense (E), etc. **New business transactions can be defined** for the cash journal **in two places**:
□The cash journal itself
□The Implementation Guide (IMG).

Cash Journal Transactions

Cash journal entries are saved in the cash journal sub-ledger. The entries can **be copied, deleted and printe**d. Print forms need to be identified in Customizing. The Cash Journal **can also be used to record checks**.

The Cash Journal **can be used as an alternative to standard A/P and A/R transactions**, in which case it generates document numbers that are distinct from standard FI documents.

A Cash Journal **document can be split** during entry. This is **suitable when a Cash Journal document contains many items with multiple different tax codes or account assignments** intended for cost accounting. Financial Accounting **will still store the split document in a single document**.

The Cash Journal **also processes business transactions related to one-time accounts**. When cash journal entries are made on a one-time account, the dialog box for entry is called systemically.

The Cash Journal can handle **many types of transactions and postings** such as:
□ Revenues
□ Expense
□ Cash transfer from the cash office to the bank
□ Cash transfer from the bank to the cash office
□ Vendor payment receipt/issue
□ Customer payment receipt/issue

Payments (pertaining to customers and vendors) made in the Cash Journal **do not clear the open items**. Clearing occurs in a separate step within accounts payable or accounts receivable, depending on the case.

In addition, **Incoming and outgoing bank payments do not post directly to bank accounts**, but to bank **clearing accounts**. The bank clearing accounts are later cleared when the account statement from the bank is processed.

Posting a check deposit list generates two batch input sessions; a **sub-ledger session** and a **bank posting session**. The two sessions will need to be processed to get linked to the corresponding postings in the General Ledger.

• The **sub-ledger accounting session** normally clears open items for accounts receivable. The offsetting entry is posted to a check clearing account.
• The **bank posting session** posts check amounts to the incoming checks account. The offsetting entry is posted to a check clearing account.

The **bank ledger accounting session** needs to be processed beforehand for the relevant records to be updated. Any payment differences that arise during the sub-ledger accounting session should be handled manually.

Bank statement
Banks use **Account statements** to convey information regarding transactions on a company's bank account. The bank statements can be availed to a company in two different formats:
□ **Form**: in this case the account statement is created manually in SAP ERP.

□ **File**: in this case the file is provided on a data media or it is received through a transfer program (bank-specific).

Transfers: the use of **transfers** depends on each country.

Outgoing transfers: The payment program can create transfers and make postings to an outgoing cash account. The associated open vendor items will be cleared concurrently.

Incoming transfers: The bank ledger accounting session performs postings for incoming cash (Bank to incoming cash), whereas the sub-ledger accounting session clears the paid items from the customer account. The assignment information for the bank statement is **picked from the "Note to payee" field**.

Interest Calculation

There are **two types of interest calculations**:
• **Account balance interest calculation:** whereby a specific **interest rate is applied to the entire balance** of a **G/L account**, or a **customer account** over a particular timeframe.

• **Interest on arrears:** whereby a specific **interest rate is applied to distinct open items** in **accounts receivable** or **accounts payable** at a particular date.

Configuration of Interest Calculation

Interest Calculation Configuration steps include:
□ Interest Calculation Indicator
□ General terms
□ Time-based terms
□ Interest rates
□ Account Determination

The configuration of the interest program covers **settings in five areas**:
    1- The **calculation of interest is determined by the interest calculation type parameters**. The master data of an account (G/L, customer or vendor) must include the appropriate **interest**

calculation indicator for interest to be calculated. An interest calculation indicator **is always linked to an interest calculation type** that indicates if it pertains to **account balance interest** or **interest on arrears (item interest calculation).**

2- **General terms** provide additional parameters regarding the functions of the interest calculation indicator: For instance, **the interest calculation indicator** ⇒ specifies a certain **set of interest terms**.

   The interest calculation frequency ⇒ indicates **how often interest is calculated**. The settlement day ⇒ establishes the **day of the month when interest is calculated**. Calendar type ⇒ determines the **interest calculation base**, such as 30/360, 30/365, actual/360, actual/365.

3- **Time-based terms** define validity dates for the interest rates.

4- **Account determination** designates the accounts where the results from an interest calculation should be posted systemically.

5- **Interest calculation indicators** define the basic parameters that are used to calculate interest. **Account master data** must contain an **interest calculation indicator for interest calculation** to take place on a given account.

Interest can be calculated for customers and vendors who owe the company, but **interest cannot be calculated if a company in return owes money to the same customer or vendor.**

A **distinct interest calculation indicator** is required **for each combination** of interest calculation frequency, calendar type, currency and interest rate.

The creation of a **new interest calculation indicator** requires **a two-character interest indicator** and an **interest calculation type**. A descriptive **name for the interest calculation indicator** is useful but **is not required**.

Different interest rates can be charged based on the items in a given **account**.

Users can also set up **reference interest rates** that include the interest calculation indicators, long and short text descriptions, an effective date, a currency, and a financial center.

For maintenance purposes, each reference interest rate can have a value and a validity date that can be reviewed periodically. Existing **interest rate values are subject to validity dates** recorded. Therefore, interest rates are **date dependent**.

Running the Interest Calculation

There are several options for calculating interest:
* **Item interest calculation (calculate interest on arrears)**:

□ Interest is calculated on cleared items only and posted.
□ Interest is calculated on open and cleared items and posted
□ Interest is calculated on open and cleared items without posting the interest.

* **Account balance interest calculation**:
Accounts considered for interest calculation can be **limited to a particular a range of accounts**, or individual accounts for a company code or a business area.

Interest calculation can be run in a background job. A log can be created for monitoring and troubleshooting purposes. To activate systemic posting of interest from background jobs, the "**Post interest settlements indicator**" needs to be set.

New General Ledger

In a nutshell, New General Ledger Accounting combines functions of classic General Ledger Accounting with the Special Purpose Ledger component. The New G/L is **available as an option** in **older** installations, but for **new installations** it **is always active by default**.

Benefits and functions of the New General Ledger, also known as the **four pillars of New G/L Accounting**:

- The standard System provides an **extended data structure**, whereby customer fields can be added to the G/L in order to meet a wide range of requirements for external accounting using one dataset.
- Offers real-time **document splitting** that enables balance sheets to be created for entities such as Segments. In addition, accounts can be balanced for other objects such as profit center. The **segment field** entity also enables Segment Reporting.
- **Real-time reconciliation** of CO and FI is made possible because Financial Accounting and Controlling are incorporated.
- **Support for multiple ledgers** as an option to portray parallel accounting. Transaction figures are managed for each account and also for each ledger.

The New G/L stores the Functional Area field, which was not the case with the Classic Ledger. Therefore, the **cost of sales ledger 0F** no longer needs to be activated in order to create a profit and loss statement based on **cost-of-sales accounting**.

The Profit Center field and the partner Profit Center field are both maintained in the new G/L, thence enabling management analyses within the General Ledger.

With the New G/L it is possible to display a simplified version of Management Accounting (CO light). The objects available for this purpose are **cost centers** and **cost elements (primary)**.

The **functional area, profit center, cost center and cost element fields are all part of the New G/L totals table** FAG/LFLEXT. They did not exist in the totals table GLT0 of the Classic Ledger.

Functional areas are needed to calculate profits based on the cost-of-sales approach, because they are the containers for overhead costs in Controlling. **Functional areas include**:
- Cost centers which are assigned through the cost center category.
- Orders which are assigned through the order type.
- WBS elements which are assigned through the project type profile.
- Cost objects.
- Profitability segments which are assigned Sales and Distribution.
- Profit centers which are derived through account assignments.

Ledger Definition

The first step in the ledger definition is the activation of the New General Ledger.

The New G/L is activated in Customizing using transaction FAGL_ACTIVATION. However, execution of the transaction normally comes as one of the last steps in a migration project for the implementation of New General Ledger Accounting. The acronym FAGL stands for Financial Accounting General Ledger.

Various changes occur, system-wide upon activation of the New G/L, including changes to applications and Customizing paths. **Some of the classic functions and transactions can no longer be executed. Menu paths for New G/L Accounting are incorporated into existing Customizing paths.** Nevertheless, Classic FI menu paths remain available until the execution of program *RFAGL_SWAP_IMG_OLD* which **hides them**.

The standard System also includes a **leading ledger 0L** and a **totals table FGLFLEXT**. The leading ledger gets many of its "control parameters" from the company code, similarly to the Classic Ledger. In accordance with the **special features of the Leading Ledger**:
• There can only be **a single Leading Ledger** per System.
• Values from the Leading Ledger are the only ones that can be posted to CO in the standard system.

Besides the Leading Ledger, other non-leading ledgers can be defined. **Non-leading ledgers can be setup for currencies and fiscal year variants that differ from the Leading Ledger**. For instance, in order to incorporate companies with different fiscal years in the same Controlling Area; company codes that have the same fiscal year would be created in relation with the Leading Ledger, and company codes that have a different fiscal year would be assigned to non-leading ledgers with the required fiscal year variant.

On the other hand, the **Leading Ledger manages the local currency** for the company code. Control parameters including the fiscal year variant and posting period variant remain unchanged by the activation of the New G/L.

The New Totals Table FAGFLEXT

The totals table of the New General Ledger Accounting (FAGFLEXT) updates more entities than the classic totals table (GLT0).

Customer fields can be added to the totals table – including **predefined SAP fields and new customer fields**. Before any customer fields can be added to the totals table (FAGFLEXT), they need to be **added to the account assignment block**.

Typical **standard fields** currently in Financials are:
- □ Cost Center
- □ Profit Center
- □ Segment

Ledger Group Posting

Direct postings to a ledger group can be used to **prevent occasional deviation of accounting values.** Parallel financial reporting caters for the creation of financial statements according to various accounting rules (such as U.S. GAAP and IAS).

Although **different accounting rules** can be directly modeled in the New General Ledger **to provide an account-based solution**, there is additional functionality that allows different ledgers to be used as an option to save data for different valuation approaches - this is the **ledger solution**. According to SAP **the ledger solution** and the **account-based solution** are **equivalents**. Therefore, the choice depends on customer needs and preference.

The **New Ledger approach** should not to be confused with **the Special Ledgers (FI-SL),** which were used in Release R/3 Enterprise. Special Ledgers do not have comparable functionality and flexibility.

Definition of Non-Leading ledgers

Customers who upgrade to SAP ERP are recommended to **not change the leading view**. **A change of the leading view** should always be **handled as a separate project** altogether. The **use of multiple non-leading ledgers** is a good alternative to represent accounts according to different accounting principles.

The **Leading Ledger** or the New G/L is activated at the **client level**. All **non-leading ledgers** must be **activated in a separate step** for **every company code**. Additional **local currencies and alternate fiscal year variants** can be defined for non-leading ledgers. For instance, a non-leading ledger can be useful when a company needs to model the same company code while using a different fiscal year variant.

The fields that will be updated **based on non-leading ledgers need to be defined**. The defined fields **will be the foundation for determining and assigning needed Scenarios.**

Defining Ledger Groups

The ledger group is an option used to **expedite work** in particular cases. A new ledger group is created systemically for each ledger in the new G/L. The new ledger group **stores the relevant ledger and shares the same name**. The creation of additional ledger groups is **optional**.

Documents are only posted to the selected ledgers. Whether a ledger group only consists of a single or many non-leading ledgers, the **document types** for entry view need to be defined in one ledger during customization.

New General Ledger Scenarios

A scenario portrays the **definition of fields that are updated in the ledgers** (in the G/L view) during a posting.

Customers **cannot define their own scenarios**. SAP ERP has **six predefined scenarios. One or multiple scenarios can be assigned to a ledger, including all six** simultaneously. The scenarios to assign depend on the business aspects that need to be reflected in the General Ledger.

The definition of non-leading ledgers is optional; therefore scenarios do not have to be assigned to non-leading ledgers. On the other hand, a **distinct ledger is not required for each scenario.**

Scenarios predefined by SAP for the New G/L:
- Cost center update (FIN_CCA)
- Preparation for Consolidation (FIN_CONS)

- Business area (FIN_GSBER)
- Profit center update (FIN_PCA)
- Segmentation (FIN_SEGM)
- Cost-of-sales accounting (FIN_UKV)

A specific CO object can be used to derive a related profit center and functional area. If scenarios are not assigned to a ledger, **segment balance sheets cannot be generated.**

Entry View and G/L View of FI Documents

In the New G/L context a **Financial Accounting document always has two views**:
  □ Entry view
  □ General Ledger view

The **entry view** is the way a document appears in the sub-ledgers (AP/AR/AA/ Taxes), which is the same **view that a document has during posting. When document display is selected**, the document will initially be displayed in the entry view.

The **General Ledger view** is the particular way in which a document is displayed in the G/L only. Documents in the general ledger view **are always associated with a particular ledger**.

The Segment Characteristics

The **Segment field** is a standard account assignment object that enables segment reporting, a requirement of international accounting principles. In addition, the segment field **enables the analysis of certain objects below the company code level**.

Other account assignments that have been available prior to the segment field:
  □ Profit Center
  □ Business Area
  □ Profitability segment

The above account assignments have been used to meet various requirements, including segment reporting. The Segment field is a field exclusively designed for segment reporting.

Segment Derivation

The Segment field is incorporated in the master data record of a profit center. Therefore, **postings to profit centers systemically update segment fields**, unless no segment field was designated for a particular profit center. There is no "dummy segment posting" like in the profit center logic, whereby postings that have no specific profit center are posted to a default dummy profit center. Therefore, **if a profit center does not have a segment; it will not have a segment account**.

Segments are derived from profit centers. If a company is not using profit centers, user exits (BAdl) can be used as an alternative derivation approach. The specific user exit for segment derivation is **FAGL_DERIVE_SEGMENT**. Furthermore, **a profit center can be derived, from a cost center, a CO internal order, or a project**.

In order to make **full use of the segment** feature (to post, analyze and display documents), **the following must be done** beforehand:

(1) **Definition of the scenario**: the Segmentation (FIN_SEGM) scenario must be defined for the Leading Ledger; otherwise the segment display will only be possible in the entry view.
(2) **Definition of the segments.**
(3) **Derivation of the segments.**
(4) **Maintenance of the segment field status for FI accounts**: must be defined as an "optional entry" in the field status variants and fields status groups of the matching G/L accounts.
(5) **Maintenance of the field status of the corresponding posting key.**
(6) **Display of the segment field** using the document display layout icon.

Document Splitting

Document splitting is a technique that **enables the creation of financial statements at the profit center and the segment level. It is only applicable for the G/L**, because split documents do not need to be visible in sub-ledgers.

Document Splitting process

Document Splitting has 3 steps:
1 – Passive Split: the effects of passive document splitting depend on the definition of the document splitting characteristic (in Customizing), which contains the applicable splitting processes. Passive document splitting takes into consideration all account assignments for document line items during the split process.

2 - Active (rule-based) Split: in active split document line items are systemically split based on the document splitting rules. The delivered **predefined splitting** rules **can be adjusted** according to customer needs. In this case, entities defined as splitting characteristics are inherited in non-account-assigned posting lines.

3 – Subsequent processes: for clearing purposes the "zero balance indicator" triggers clearing for line items systemically, in order to complete the split. Line item display will show the payment document and the original invoice document as cleared items.

Document splitting relies on two important elements: inheritance and the default account assignment.

Document Splitting Characteristics

Before any document splitting is carried out, **the characteristics** that the splitting will be based upon **must be defined**. Potential document splitting characteristics are: **business areas, profit centers and segments**. Custom defined entities can also be split.

The plus sign (+) related to the **Zero Balance Indicator should always be checked, if characteristics will be used during creation of financial statements**. In this case, the balance of the all pertinent entities will be zero for every posting, and balanced.

Document Splitting Activation and Inheritance

Initially, document splitting is activated client-wide in customizing, then in a separate step it is activated or deactivated for each company code.

Inheritance implies that when a new document is created based on an existing one; the new document systemically adopts the characteristics (business area, segment, etc.) of the original document. Therefore, when a customer invoice is created from a revenue line, the entities (such as a segment) are inherited by the customer and the tax lines in the general ledger view.

Inheritance should normally be active when document splitting is active:
• In the **absence of inheritance**, there would be a **need to define rules for the business** processes, to confirm that the account assignment can be projected or adopted as needed.
• **Activation of inheritance is the sole single requirement for documents to be posted** when document splitting is active.
• Inheritance is carried out online at the item level
• The use of a default account assignment requires a constant to be defined in Customizing.

A **document splitting rule is identified by the key fields** below:
- Document splitting method
- Business transaction
- Business transaction variant

Prior to posting, it is advised to **simulate the entry view and the G/L view in order to analyze potential posting errors**. **The expert mode** can subsequently be used to **view further data details of document splitting**. The expert mode is **an option that provides all the important details on document splitting parameters**, such as the splitting method and the business transaction. It also explains the breakdown of split amounts.

The Splitting Method defines:
•The approach used to split a document
•The specifics for handling each item category in individual business transactions

The standard splitting method delivered with SAP ERP is 0000000012.

The Business Transaction describes the elements of the actual SAP business process that is assigned to a range of item categories.

The Business Transaction Variant is a particular version of a predefined SAP business transaction including its built-in technical model for splitting an actual document.

An **item category is a technical representation of posted line items**. It explains the items that are listed in a document or a business transaction. Item categories classify the accounts for document splitting; they are derived from the account types of the G/L accounts.

A **distinct splitting rule is used to identify the item categories that can be split**, and the applicable base.

During document splitting the **profit center** for the split items is determined systemically.

Advantages of using document splitting include:
● Accelerated close.
● Enhanced data quality.
● Extensibility and flexibility.

Taxes

Tax types supported for calculating, posting, correcting tax, and tax reporting include:
        □ **Tax on sales/purchases**
        □ **US sales tax**
        □ **Additional taxes** (country-specific)
        □ **Withholding tax**

Two types of taxation can be handled in SAP ERP:
• Taxes levied **at a national level** using identical rates.
• Taxes levied **at a state/jurisdictional level**, using rates defined by each state/jurisdiction.

The System:
        □ **Calculates tax amounts**
        □ **Posts to defined tax accounts**
        □ **Performs tax adjustments** (for cash discounts or other forms of deductions)
        □ **Reports on taxes**

The System uses the **base amounts and the tax codes to calculate tax amounts**:

The expense or revenue amount is the **base amount, which can include a cash discount** (tax base is gross) **or exclude a cash discount** (tax base is net).

The **tax code is used in the calculation procedure** to carry out the required taxation functions.

The **tax base amount** must be **the net amount** or the **gross amount** depending on national regulations. The amount to be used for each company code will need to be defined in the System:

• The **Net amount:** deducts the cash discount from the taxable expense or revenue.
• The **Gross amount:** adds the cash discount to taxable expenses or revenue.

Tax on Sales and Purchases

The balance of **output tax** and **input tax** provides the amount for **tax on sales and purchases.**

• The **output tax** is a liability of the company towards the tax authorities, because it is levied on the **net value of goods and is charged to the customer**. Therefore, a company collects the tax amount on behalf of the tax authority.

• **Input tax** is a receivable entitled to the company from the tax authority, because it is **levied on the net invoice amount and is charged to the company** by the vendor. Therefore, a company gets to claim the amount back from the tax authority.

Before a company code can process taxes, a **tax calculation procedure must be assigned to the appropriate country. Pre-configured tax calculation procedures** are delivered for most countries. The **tax calculation procedure stores**:

• **The order of steps** required for the tax calculation procedure
• **Tax types** (also known as **condition types**) that pertain to the country
• **Account key/transaction key** for the automatic account determination for taxes

Condition types are tax calculations that apply for a particular country. The **base amount used with a condition type is supposed to be an expense or a revenue item**.

Tax Codes are used to:
- □ **Verify the tax amou**nt
- □ **Compute the amount of tax**
- □ **Compute additional tax portion**
- □ **Verify the tax type**
- □ **Specify the G/L account**
- □ **Correctly display tax on the tax forms**

The **tax code** entered during document posting is the **main connection to the tax calculation**. Depending on whether a country's tax calculation procedure uses tax jurisdiction codes or not, the tax code is linked to either of these elements:
- □ Country key
- □ Combination of country key and tax jurisdiction code

The tax code stores the tax rates that apply to the tax types within the tax calculation procedure. Normally a tax code only has a single tax rate, but **a tax code may contain several tax rates for different tax types**, because of cases where several tax types need to be applied to a line item. The System normally **uses separate line items to post the tax calculations to a special tax account**. **Tax codes are not tied to any validity dates**, and therefore are **date independent**.

The tax type definition determines if the base amount is "percentage included" or "percentage separate".

Tax Postings

Normally, calculated tax amounts are systemically posted to the relevant accounts.
For sales tax payables or other non-deductible input taxes, a transaction/account key (for instance NVV) distributes the tax amount to the appropriate expense/revenue items.

The following data is needed **to enable automatic account determination for tax amounts**:
- □ **Rules** (to specify the fields for account determination, e.g. tax code or account key)

□ **Posting key** (normally 40 and 50)
□ **Tax accounts** (G/L accounts that record tax amounts)

"Post Automatically Only" must be selected on the G/L Master to prevent manual posting.

Tax accounts (G/L accounts that record tax amounts) are defined by entering the appropriate sign in the **Tax Category** field:

< For input tax
> For output tax

The **tax code properties** will determine whether the account is relevant for **input or output tax**. An entry for the **tax category field is also needed for all the other G/L accounts**:

□ "" (**blank**) not relevant for tax postings
□ **-** (minus sign) only input tax allowed
□ **+** (plus sign) only output tax allowed
□ ***** (asterisk) all tax type allowed
□ **xx** predefined tax code, where "xx" represents the specific tax code

Special Tax Codes

• The **acquisition tax code** is used in countries that have tax exemption, but still need to show tax amounts. The tax amount will be posted to both as a payable and a receivable.
• The **output tax code** is used for tax-exempt deliveries within the European Union (EU). A tax account needs to be assigned to the tax code, although no tax will be posted.

Cross-Company Code Transactions

A **cross-company code transaction** is used **when two or more company codes** are involved in **a single business transaction**. For instance, when:
■ A company code makes purchases on behalf of other company codes (**Central Procurement**)
■ A company code pays invoices on behalf of other company codes (**Central Payment**)
■ A company code makes sales to other company codes

Separate document postings need to be created for each company code: the System will generate automatic line items that will be posted to **clearing accounts**, for payables or receivables; so that the debits and credits for the documents are balanced. Therefore, a **cross-company code transaction has at least two documents.** The documents related to the same cross-company code transaction will be connected by a common **cross-company code transaction number**.

Cross-company code transactions cannot occur unless the company codes use **the same operational charts of accounts**, and the **same fiscal year variant. Cross-company code controlling** requires that all **company codes use identical operational chart of accounts and fiscal year variants**.

The System uses a **combination of the document number of the first company code with the first company code number, and the fiscal year** to create the document **number for the cross-company transaction**. The number is stored in the document header of each individual document created.

The invoiced tax amount is entirely posted to the **company code** where the **first invoice item** is recorded. Therefore, the first invoice item must be posted to the company code where the tax needs to be reflected. For countries that are required by law to post tax amounts in company codes according to expenses incurred, **tax can be distributed proportionately from the first company code** by using a program (report RFBUST10). **Cross-company code transactions are feasible** between **company codes that have different local currencies**.

Each company code involved in cross-company code transactions, must define **clearing accounts** in configuration. The **clearings accounts can be G/L accounts, vendor accounts or customer accounts**. A clearing account should be created **for each possible combination of two company codes,** to cater for cross-company entries between the two company codes. In order to limit the number of clearing accounts, a single company code can be used as the **clearing company code**, in which case clearing accounts will only be needed for every combination of the clearing company code and the other company codes.

For instance, to setup clearing accounts for 4 company codes where each company code will have its own clearing accounts: 4*2= 8 clearing accounts would be needed.

Inquiries: support@sapseries.com

To setup clearing accounts for 4 company codes, that will all use a single clearing company code: 3*2= 6 clearing accounts would be needed.

Open Items and Clearing

Open items are incomplete transactions (such as invoices that have not been paid), that need to be **cleared** for completion. Therefore, **documents containing open items cannot be archived.** A transaction is cleared after a clearing posting has been applied to an item or a group of items and the resulting balance of the items becomes zero.

There are **two basic transactions** that can be used **to clear open items**: "**Account clearing**" and "**Post with clearing**". **Clearing a credit memo with an open invoice** is a typical instance of **account clearing**, whereas posting **a payment for an open invoice which results into a zero balance** is an instance of **posting with clearing**.

"**Posting with clearing**" can be performed for several accounts, account types, and for any currency concurrently. On the other hand, posting with clearing can be carried out **manually or, systemically with the automatic payment program**. The "account clearing" function is usable with any account that is **managed with open items in the G/L and in sub-ledgers**. A **clearing transaction** always creates a **clearing document.** There are instances where a **clearing document may have no line items.**

Items in a G/L account are selected for clearing based on the fields below:
• Reconciliation account number.
• Currency.
• Special G/L indicator.
• Five other user defined fields from the document header or line item (such as assignment field, reference number, etc.).

If the local currency **balance for a group of items amounts to zero**, items will be cleared systemically, and clearing documents will be created for the same. **All accounts subject to automatic clearing need to be defined in Customizing**.

Automatic clearing is NOT possible for:
■ Noted items

- Statistical postings and specific special G/L transactions for bills of exchange
- Down payments where matching amounts for payment clearing items do not exist, or have not been posted
- Items that include withholding tax entries

The **assignment field** of a line item **is filled systemically based on the entry in the "Sort Field"** of the master record during posting. For instance, if the sort key is set to the cost center in a G/L master record, then the assignment field in the general ledger line item will be filled with the number for the cost center once that G/L account is used. The **assignment number** can **be created systemically or manually**.

Document Archiving and Master Records

System performance tends to diminish as data volume increases. Therefore, it is essential to remove data that is no longer needed in the database for daily operations. The data cannot be deleted, because read access to the data may occasionally be needed. Therefore, the data should be transferred to an external storage media, where it can be accessed without affecting daily system resources.

Procedures for **archiving** for Financial Accounting data are **defined according to applicable country regulations**.

Archiving is performed to:
- Improve system response time.
- Reduce system downtime during software upgrades, data backups and data recovery.
- Reduce database administration efforts.
- Comply with country specific storage regulations.

Archiving objects have three **components**:
- Data declaration part (stores characteristics of the pertaining database objects).
- Customizing settings (store archiving specifications for an archiving procedure).
- Programs.

There is an **archiving monitor** that displays detailed information regarding individual archiving sessions. Information options include a progress bar to monitor archive file processing and open alerts. During the archiving procedure **the System performs checks at various levels**:

- Transaction figures
  □ Fiscal years selected for archiving should not have any periods that are still open for posting.
  □ Open purchase orders cannot be archived.
- Master data
  □ Bank accounts are checked for deletion indicators, and whether they are still in use.
  □ G/L accounts are checked for deletion indicators, any existing transaction figures and documents.
  □ Customers/vendors are checked for deletion indicators, any existing transaction figures and documents.

- Documents
  □ Document type runtime is supposed to have been maintained.
  □ Account run time is supposed to have been maintained.
  □ Open item managed accounts are supposed to have been cleared.

Recurring, parked or sample documents are **not considered for the archiving procedure**.
The **archiving process** can be launched through **document management workflows**.

Inquiries: support@sapseries.com

Chapter 4 - Accounts Receivable

Customer and Vendor Accounts

There is an important relationship between the **customer and vendor accounts**. Similarly to G/L accounts, **customer accounts** have two segments in the financial accounting view:

■There is one **segment at the client** level to store **general data** valid for the entire client.
■There is a **segment with company code specific data** at **company code level**.

The account segment is arranged in a set of several pages with different groups of fields. The display of an account can be changed by selecting it on the initial display screen. **Customer account numbers** are assigned at the client level.

Controlling the Field Status:
Information on each screen can be defined in configuration as mandatory, suppressed or optional depending on the company code. The appearance of a customer/vendor master data screen depends on several factors:
  □ **Account group-specific** control
  □ **Transaction-specific** control
  □ **Company code-specific** control

Customer accounts have two segments:
There is one segment at client level that stores **general data**, and can be accessed across the whole organization.

The other segment is at company code level and stores **company code-specific data**. Any company code that intends to do business with a specific customer must **create a company code segment for the specific customer or vendo**r. A customer account will also be created in this process.

Creating a **Sales Area segment** is a precondition for a **Sales Area** to do business with a customer. The Sales Area segment stores sales area-specific data. **Customer payment terms** are recorded in the **Sales Area segment**.

A **Sales Area** is an organizational structure that includes a **sales organization**, a **distribution channel** and a **division**.

Days Sales Outstanding (DSO) and the terms agreed are evaluation types which are **only used for customers. Overdue items evaluation and due date analysis** are available for both **customer and vendor** transactions.

A **complete customer account** has the following three segments:
● General data at the client level
● Company code segment
● Sales Area segment

There are separate functions for maintaining customer master records depending on organizational requirements. Maintenance can be performed **centrally for all areas** or **separately** for Financial Accounting and Sales and Distribution. Central maintenance is a good preventive measure for incorrect master records, incomplete accounts and duplicate master data. When **customer master records are created centrally**, they are **not assigned to any company code**. Company code assignment will occur when a specific company adds to its master data a customer who has already been created centrally.

The following options can help **prevent the creation of duplicate records**:
● Use the **matchcode** before you create a new account.
● Activate the **automatic duplication check.**

The **Reconciliation account field** is located in the company code data segment of the customer master record. Only **a single reconciliation account can be maintained** in a customer master record. In addition, only one number range can be linked to customer Account Group. The **reconciliation account** is used to **link the entire set of sub-ledger accounts to a specific G/L account** in the Chart of Accounts.

Customer and vendor accounts must **always be configured for line item display** and **open item management**.

Bank details in the customer/vendor master data:
The IBAN (International Bank Account Number) is an internationally unique identification number for a particular bank account. It can be entered as part of the bank details for customer master data, and also in the Customizing settings for House Banks. The IBAN can only be entered in a vendor or customer master record with their approval.
Therefore, IBANs cannot be generated systemically and saved for numerous master records. IBANs **have to be entered manually** for each master record.

The **Account Group for vendors/customers controls**:
- The number ranges of the accounts.
- The status of the fields in the master record.
- One-time customer or vendor accounts.

During the creation of customer master records, **an Account Group must be entered on the initial screen**. Once an **Account Group** has been created in Financial Accounting, it **cannot be changed**. However, **in Sales and Distribution** there are times when the **Account Group can be changed** from an ordering address to a ship-to address.

Separate number ranges are established for customer accounts. The range of possible account numbers is split into smaller **number ranges**. Each number range needs to be **defined as internal or external**. Each **number range can be assigned to one or more account groups**. When a range is defined as **internal**, it implies that **numbers are assigned systemically**. When a range is defined as **external**, **the numbers** can only be **assigned manually**.

A one-time account master record **cannot store** any **customer specific information**, because the account is used for more than one customer. Therefore, the **customer-specific fields should be hidden. Customer-specific data** for one-time customers is entered in the **pertaining document** during posting.

Account group-specific control: normally the **field status** is only controlled by the Account Group. Thence all accounts that belong to the same Account Group will have similar **screen layouts**.

Transaction-specific control: sometimes the field status can be dependent on the master data transaction performed through a menu (such as "Create", "Change" or "Display").
The transaction-dependent field status should be **set to "display"** for the "change" transaction **if the field is not to be changed** after it has been created.

Company code-specific control: company code-specific **screen layouts** can also control the field status for fields in the company code segment of customer and vendor master records. For instance, **fields that are not needed in one company code can be hidden, while the same fields can be available for entry in other company codes**.

The System compares the account group-specific field status, the transaction-specific field status and the company code-specific field status, in order to identify the field status that has the highest priority. **To avoid use of the transaction-specific or company code-specific control**, set the field **status for all fields to optional**, in which case the **account group-specific control will always be used**, because the optional field status **has the lowest priority**.

The object pertaining to the **field status of the activity** can be used to **prevent a change of the reconciliation account in the customer's master data**.

In order to **closely track changes on certain fields**, a field in the **customer or vendor** master record can be **defined as "sensitive"**. Therefore, a field change will cause the corresponding customer account to be blocked for payment until a person different from the one who changed the fields, confirms or rejects the changes. The person who approves or rejects the change needs to have appropriate authorizations. This approach is referred to as **dual control**.
The **definition of sensitive fields is not company code-specific**, therefore if a field is defined as sensitive in one company code, the definition will also apply to all other company codes.

A customer can also be a vendor, or vice versa within the same company code. **The payment and the dunning program** can **clear open items** against each other. Clearing open items can be carried out if:
■The vendor account number is entered in the customer account and vice versa.
■ Each company code has chosen to clear open items between customers and vendors.

■ The field "Clearing with Vendor" has been selected in the customer account or the corresponding field in the vendor account, in order to allow clearing.

In addition, an **alternative payer/payee** can be entered in the master record (at the client and company code level), in order to perform various functions. The **entry in the company code segment has higher priority than the entry at client level**:

If the "**Individual Entries**" indicator is selected; information about an individual payer/payee for a customer/vendor can be directly entered during invoice creation, even if there is no previous master record for the individual. If the **alternative payer/payee** is already an existing customer or vendor, the customer/vendor account number can be entered in the master record as a permitted payee/payer.

Automatic Dunning

Dunning is a process whereby, SAP ERP prepares notices systemically for customers who have account balances in arrears. **Dunning can** be used to send **notices to both customers and vendors.**

Parameters are used in the dunning program to determine how it should work. Parameters from a previous dunning run can be used after changing the previous dates.

Four steps are required to perform the **automatic dunning procedure**:
1. Maintain parameters
2. Proposal run
3. Edit dunning proposal
4. Print dunning notices

At the time of the **dunning run**, the System checks the accounts for **overdue items**. It also checks whether **dunning notices need to be sent**, and determines the **dunning levels** to assign accordingly. **Dunning data** is stored in a **dunning proposal**. Normally all items that are **overdue at the date of issue will be dunned**. However, **if line item grace periods have been defined** in the dunning procedure, items that remain **overdue after deduction of the grace days are the only ones that will be dunned.**

A **dunning proposal can be edited, deleted, and redone as many times as needed** to meet actual dunning needs. After completion of a dunning run, **dunning notices can be printed immediately**. Dunning notices are **printed in a single step** and **dunning data is updated** in the master records and related documents.

Dunning Program Configuration

Most settings for the dunning program are defined **in the "dunning procedure"** which is directly accessible from the user interface. The **dunning procedure** determines **how dunning is performed**. **Each account** that needs to be considered in the automatic dunning process must have a dunning procedure, and each **customer or vendor account must have a dunning procedure in the master record**. If a dunning procedure is missing in the master data, a customer cannot be dunned.

One-time-accounts require a **single dunning procedure that is valid for all** one-time customers. The System can accommodate **any number of dunning procedures**. The software is delivered with some predefined dunning procedures which can be used as templates for other procedures. The **dunning** procedure **can process standard and special G/L transactions**.

Configuration of the dunning procedure focuses on the **definition of dunning levels and the dunning charges** that apply for each level.

The **settings for the dunning program** apply to the following categories:
- □ Dunning procedures
- □ Dunning levels
- □ Expenses/charges
- □ Minimum amounts
- □ Dunning texts
- □ Environment

The following **specifications are required for each dunning process**:
- ■ The **key to use** with the dunning procedure.
- ■ A description for the **dunning procedure** that applies.
- ■ The dunning **interval in days.**
- ■ The **minimum days in arrears** after which a dunning notice can be used to an account holder.
- ■ **Grace periods** allowed per line item.
- ■ **Interest calculation indicator** if dunning interest needs to be calculated.

Dunning levels are used to **indicate the highest possible dunning level in a procedure**. The **minimum days in arrears** for an account, represents the **lowest number of days** that applies to **at least one item** in the **account**. When the **minimum days in arrears** are **not** met an **account cannot be dunned**, and a **dunning notice will not be issued**.

If **a single overdue item in an account exceeds** the minimum days in arrears, the **account is subject to dunning.**

When an item's number of days in arrears is **lower or equal to the number of grace days,** the **item is not considered due for a dunning notice**.

When the "**always dun" option** is selected, a dunning notice will be **printed regardless of any changes to the dunning proposal** since the last dunning run (meaning no items have reached a higher dunning level and there are no additional items).

Maintenance specifications required **for each dunning process** cover:
■ Dunning charges depending on the dunning level (**fixed or a percentage of dunned amount**, a minimum amount can be set for the dunning).
■ The Minimum amount or percentage of the overdue items required to reach a dunning level.
■ The minimum amount required before interest is calculated for each dunning level.
■ The name of the form to be used at each dunning level.

Dunning charges are **specified for each country according to dunning levels**. A word processing feature enables printing of charges on the dunning forms. A dunning **charge can be a fixed amount or a percentage** of the dunned amount. If the dunning charge has been defined as a percentage, a fixed amount can still be entered. A **minimum amount can be set for dunning at each level**.

Dunning Texts

The dunning program can be used to generate payment advice notes, dunning notices, and payment forms. The form's layout is described in the SAPscript tool that uses the designated key.

Environment

The **organizational entity** in charge of dunning in a company code is called a **Dunning Area**. The **Company Code Dunning Control screen** is used to specify whether dunning notices should be created **separately by dunning area** or **by company code account**.

In **standard dunning all items at the various dunning levels are dunned with a single dunning notice**. However, a separate dunning notice with a different accompanying text is usable for each dunning level in an account.

Dunning Run Parameters

Two fields are used to identify each dunning program run**:**
□ Run Date
□ Identification

The **parameters** provide the information for the dunning run. Parameters from previous dunning runs can be used, once the dates have been changed. **The parameters indicate the company codes, the accounts and the documents** that should be considered in a dunning run.
The **Run on** field is **mainly used to identify dunning runs**, and **does not have to be the date** of the actual dunning run.

An **additional log** can be activated for the display of eventual errors after completion of a dunning run. Preferably, the log should only be used during testing and training, because it places a heavy load on system resources.

The Dunning Run

A **Dunning run has three steps**:
Step 1: Account Selection: the parameters and configuration are used to check which accounts should be included in the dunning run.
Step 2: Dun Line Items: In this step, overdue line items are selected in the accounts and associated with the relevant dunning levels.
Step 3: Dun Accounts: the system identifies the accounts that need to be dunned for payments, and assigns the required dunning level.

Overdue line items that have a **dunning block** are added systemically to the **blocked items list**. Each **dunning procedure can have between 1 and 9 dunning levels**. Items to be dunned are always assigned a **dunning level based on the days in arrears**.

Dunning procedures that only have **a single dunning level** are referred to as **payment reminders**.

The **last dunning level will trigger the manual dunning procedure**, which eventually ends in the legal dunning procedure. Nevertheless, **the legal dunning procedure does not correspond to any dunning level**; therefore it should not be mistaken for one.

Invoice-related credit memos use the **dunning level of the invoice**, because the **payment terms of a credit memo usually do not apply**, thence the due date considered is either **the due date of the associated invoice** or **the baseline date of the document**.
A **dunning key** can be assigned to an item to **prevent it from exceeding a certain dunning level**.

The total amount of items listed in an account with a specific dunning level, must be greater than a **defined minimum amount**. The **relationship between the total balance and the total open items** for an account must also be greater than the designated **minimum percentage** otherwise; the **items are set to a lower dunning level**.

An **account can only be dunned if at least one item** has reached the **minimum days in arrears per account**. Other **reasons why an account may not be dunned**:
• The account is not included in the parameters range.
• All Items in the account are within the grace period.
• The Item or account is blocked for dunning.
• The Item or account has a payment method for incoming payments but has no payment block.
• The overdue amount is lower than the minimum amount.
• Items can be cleared with overdue items on the credit side.
• None of the items is greater than the minimum days in arrears.
•The dunning data has not changed since the last dunning run and the **"Always dun"** option is not checked.

The **dunning data** (master records and related documents) in the System does **not get updated until the dunning notices are printed**. The two events occur in a single step.

Dunning Proposal Changes

A dunning proposal can **be edited, deleted and redone as many times as needed**, because the **database is not updated until the dunning notices get printed**.

Various **lists can be printed to support the Dunning process**:

- Dunning statistics
- Dunning list
- Blocked accounts
- Blocked line items
- Dunning history

A dunning proposal should always be processed until completion. If the dunning notices were not printed and are no longer needed, the **proposal should be deleted**. Otherwise, all the items selected in the proposal will be blocked from processing in other dunning runs.

The following actions **can be carried out in a current dunning proposal**:
- **Block an account or remove** a dunning block.
- **Block a line** item or **remove** a dunning block.
- **Lower** the dunning level of an item.

The following actions will **not have any effect in a current dunning** proposal:
- Change the dunning and correspondence data of an account in the master record.
- Change a document.

Although the above changes are feasible, **the changes to the dunning data** in the line items or master data **will not have any effect if a dunning proposal has already been created**, **because the records were selected before the proposal was prepared.** For the changes to take effect, the dunning proposal would need to be deleted and redone.

Printing Dunning Notices

The **print program** for the dunning procedure will do the following:
- Group dunning items in a dunning notice according to several rules.
- Generate a dunning notice for every group.
- Enter the dunning date and the dunning level in the dunned items and accounts.

A **sort criterion** is used to determine the **printing sequence** for the Dunning notices. **Items and dunning** notices are grouped together for the same:
- Company code
- Dunning area (if in use)
- Account

Items in **one-time accounts are grouped** in the same dunning notice if they have **similar addresses**.

Different **sort criteria** can be used to group dunning notices. Criteria for **item grouping** include:
● **Dunning by dunning level:**
Is the step whereby a separate dunning notice is printed for each dunning level.
● **Grouping key**:
A grouping key is entered in the customer/vendor account to associate dunning notice items that have identical values in the fields assigned to the grouping key.
● **Decentralized processing**:
Head offices usually receive a single dunning notice from branch offices. A dunning notice will outline all items due. If **Decentralized processing** is selected in the branch accounts; dunning will be processed locally, and the **notices will be sent to branch offices**. Centralized processing is the opposite of decentralized processing.

Dunning Text Control
There are **variables** in the dunning formulas that can be used to control texts in *italics. Standard texts* are provided for entering company code or dunning area data in a company code independent form. The **same dunning form can be used for all dunning levels**.
Dunning texts are stored in designated text modules. For instance, text module 616 is used for dunning level 6.
Dunning Texts need to be assigned to the appropriate form with reference to the dunning Level. The dunning level applied, drives the phrasing and content for the letter to the customer.

A **dunning recipient** can have an **address that is different** from the one used on the dunned account. If a **dunning clerk** is not specified in the master record, the **accounting clerk will be displayed**.
Normally, all **items** are **printed at a higher dunning level** to enable the customer or vendor to have an overview of the overall account balance. Items that have **special dunning keys** can be printed individually.

Correspondence

Periodic **correspondence** can be generated based on various **specifications made in the master data**, such as invoices or account statements. Correspondence can be created online when **manually processing payments or from the line item display**.

Correspondence can be **configured for various purposes**, such as payment differences, etc. The steps for creating correspondence include:

Step 1: Make a **request for the required correspondence**:
The required correspondence type is selected at this stage.

Step 2: Print the **requested correspondence types**:
Correspondence usually prints systemically based on periodic intervals. Occasionally, correspondence types can be printed individually and on demand.

Correspondence Types

A correspondence type stands for a specific type of letter issued by a company. An appropriate correspondence type must be created for every type of letter required.
Correspondence types **can be selected manually** while processing business transactions, **or systemically** based on user defined rules.

Definitions for correspondence types cover the following:
• **The required information**: account number and document number.
• Any additional text needed in the form.
• Intercompany relationships for use across company codes.
•The number of date fields needed.

The following **data details** are required for the various **correspondence types**:
- • Document number for:
- □ Payment Notices
- □ Bill of exchange charges statements
- □ Internal documents
- □ Document extracts
- • Account Number and date for:
- □ Bank statements

- Account number for:
  □ Individual letters

A correspondence type **always has a matching print program**, and **each print program** has a **selection variant** and an associated **SAPScript form**. The actual **correspondence is printed** by **the selection variant**. In order to **print a specific individual text**, the **required print report** must be selected.

Correspondence types can be linked to transactions, to tolerance groups and to reason codes. Correspondence types are linked with transactions based on Customizing definitions for **correspondence types** which are also usable with **specific online functions**.

To link a correspondence type with a tolerance group, a **default correspondence type** should be defined for each **tolerance group**.

To create a particular correspondence with a **reason code**, the two must bear the **same correspondence type**.

In order to **always issue the same correspondence type**, the type must be saved in the **Message Required** field. In order to allow a user to select the correspondence type online, the **message required field should be blank**.

A correspondence monitor with monitoring and editing capabilities provides the following functions:
- Overview of current editing status.
- Setting the counter-confirmation status to 'matched'.
- Carrying out planned correspondence directly from the monitor.
- Generating correspondence that was previously produced.
- Access to IDoc management.
- Access to transaction history.
- Access to optical archive display.

Sales Processes and Distribution

Sales processes are **always based on a sales order**. A **sales inquiry** from a customer is the **initial step** in a sales process; it is formalized with a sales order. The customer order is **created at distribution chain level**. The items ordered **can be supplied by several divisions**.
The **sales order** is a sales order management document that does **not lead to any postings in Financial Accounting**.

After receipt of a customer order, an availability check for the required delivery date is made by the System. A **delivery document** will be created **on the shipping day**. Billing can only occur after the goods have been picked from the warehouse inventory and posted as a goods issue.
The **picking process** is based on the warehouse management functions. A **transport request** must be created **to generate the picking request**. At this point, the requested goods are taken from the warehouse and packed for delivery.

A **goods issue document** is generated in **Purchasing Management** and an **accounting document** is generated in **Financial Accounting** for posting the **goods issue** to the relevant G/L accounts.

The **final step** in the Sales process is **billing**. A billing document is generated in sales order management, then an invoice is printed and sent to the customer. Simultaneously, a financial document is created and posted to receivables, and revenues are posted to the relevant accounts.

Before an accounting document is created the following **changes can be performed** on the billing data:
- Billing date
- Pricing
- Account determination
- Message determination

Once the invoice list is created, the existing reference number in each billing document will be overwritten by the number that identifies the invoice list. Therefore, the invoice list number can be referenced when posting the payment receipt.

Revenue Account Determination

Once a billing document is generated, the revenues, sales deductions, and taxes are posted systemically to the matching accounts in Financial Accounting.

Billing Documents Account Assignment Criteria

Account assignment for determining relevant accounts is performed according to different criteria. The standard system considers the following criteria:

- Chart of accounts
- Sales organization
- Payer's account group
- Material account assignment group
- Account key

Account keys are linked with condition types in the calculation procedures **for postings to the revenue accoun**t, based on specific conditions. Therefore, the parameters in account determination must be reconciled with Financial Accounting and Cost Accounting.

Revenue Account Determination

Revenue account determination (for Sales and Distribution) uses the **condition technique** as the basis for account determination, as opposed to **direct G/L account assignment**. In the condition technique an **account determination procedure** is assigned to G/L accounts **depending on the billing document type**.

The account determination procedure contains **condition types** that are directly **attached to an access sequence**. The access sequence is **a set of individual accesses defined as condition tables**. Each **condition table contains the fields and combination of fields** that are needed to specify **revenue account determination**. Access sequence is basically a search strategy used to **select a valid data entry for a condition type**. There is a **predefined access sequence** for each standard condition type.

The G/L account that records **VAT for Sales uses the matching assignment** defined in Customizing for Financial Accounting, **as opposed to account determination**.

Account Determination for Business Areas and Segments

Before a company chooses to use segment reporting it needs to consider all options:

• Using Business areas for segment reporting:
Business areas are an option for segment reporting, because they enable external reporting beyond the company code. Their use is not compulsory in Financial Accounting.
Different business areas **can make postings to the same G/L account**.
Assignments for Business areas are **determined for each order item based on defined rules**, as opposed to fixed assignments in Customizing.
The rules for determining the business area for a sales area are user definable, **based on three rules**:
□ Business area assignment by plant and item division.
□ Business area assignment by sales area.
□ Business area assignment by sales organization, distribution channel, and item division.

• Using Segments for segment reporting:
The segment field is among the **standard account assignment objects** delivered with SAP ERP. It is suited **for running analyses of objects below the company code level**, to obtain a detailed view of different business activities.

Segments can support **segment reporting requirements** for international accounting principles. The **Business area or Profit center** objects are additional options in this context.

Every posting to a profit center also posts systemically **to the matching segment**.
If a profit center does not have a segment, there will not be any account assignment; because there is no option for a dummy segment posting like in Profit Center Accounting.

By default, the segment is derived from the profit center (although users can develop their own derivation solutions from user exit BAdI: FAGL_DERIVE_SEGMENT). There are various business transactions that do not provide any input field for a segment, the same applies for many standard interfaces; therefore it is recommended to **use segments only where profit centers are used**.

Inquiries: support@sapseries.com

FSCM and Dispute Management

SAP Financial Supply Chain Management (SAP FSCM) enhances cash flow by improving the exchange of information between a company and its business partners, thence reducing the amount of tied capital.

The Dispute Management **feature increases customer profitability and decreases Days Sales Outstanding (DSO)** through:
- Early detection of payment issues.
- Monitoring elements that effect the DSO.
- Decreasing price reductions and underpayments.

From a process perspective, it is used between the invoice stage and customer payment to address dispute issues and payments problems. Using FSCM will help:
- Reduce overall days sales outstanding (DSO) which is the average timeframe for customer's payment, based on the company's annual sales.
- Improve cash flow forecast.
- Expedite dispute resolution through automation.
- Prevent customer relationship problems through enhanced quality management.

Advantages of using FSCM process integration:
- Simple functionality for creating, changing and displaying dispute cases in SAP Dispute Management
- Dispute cases are updated systemically through associated financial transactions
- Items in dispute cases are updated systemically by specific actions in SAP Dispute Management

Overview of Dispute Case Processing:
Disputes are accessed through Transaction code UDM_DISPUTE. The screen has **two main areas**:
- The **Organizer**, on the **left side**: this is where **actions are started.**
- The **results** area, on the right: the information displayed depends on the action performed in the editing area (users can search for dispute cases, list dispute cases, create dispute cases, etc.).

The system has various **role-based views** that are used **to process dispute cases**, in different ways. **Views are definable**. A History option provides rapid access to previously processed dispute cases and objects.

Lockbox

A lockbox is a **service provided by banks to expedite the collection and processing of incoming payments**. **Customers** send their payments and **payment advice notes** to the lockbox then banks use these to generate data files **containing the payers, payment amounts**, and other optional details. Each lockbox holder later receives a data file from the bank.

Payment Advice notes provide details pertaining to an incoming payment, such as: a **customer's MICR number (bank routing number and account number), invoice numbers, payment dates, payment amounts and deductions per invoice including deduction reasons.**

The bank's data file is normally prepared in accordance with the standard format in the banking industry - BAI or BAI2. The BAI format is used to provide basic data, such as the check number, check amount, bank number, and invoice numbers. The main limitation of the BAI format is **not being able to break down the check amount into individual amounts per invoice**.

The BAI2 format provides more information than the BAI format; hence better results during systemic invoice clearing. **Additional data includes the payment and deduction amount per invoice, and a reason code for the deduction**.

The lockbox program **relies on the information provided in the payment advice note to clear open items** on **customer** accounts. Document numbers on the payment advice note are compared with the document numbers in the customer file that contains the open items. Items are cleared systemically only if the data in the payment advice note is correct. Depending on the results of the comparison process, **checks can have four statuses: assigned, partially assigned, on account, not processed.**

Partially assigned – In this case the correct invoices will be cleared, while the payment amount for any incorrect invoices is held on account until it is post processed to clear.

Assigned – this applies to checks that were fully processed, after all payments have been properly matched to invoices on customer accounts.

If a payment cannot be identified either from the customer's MICR number or the document number, it will remain **unprocessed**. Once the payment gets traced to the appropriate customer and invoice, it can be assigned during post processing.

Control Parameters

Control parameters must be recorded **to import the lockbox file** sent by the bank; specifications for the import format are made on the **Autocash Control Parameters** screen. SAP ERP supports the **BAI, BAI2, and ANSI/IDOC formats**. Specifications also need to be made for the **type of postings** that need to be **generated by the lockbox program**.

A lockbox mainly uses data record types 6 and 4:
• Type 6 data records hold the bank MICR number, check number, amount, and invoice numbers at the end of the record.
• Type 4 records represents overflow records for additional invoices that are paid under the same check.
• BAI format: the allowed length needs to be defined for the document numbers (10 in the standard SAP System) and the number of document numbers in record types 6 and 4 of the file. The customer's bank should confirm the format information.

BAI2 format: the authorized length does not need to be defined, because each document number is contained in a separate type 4 data record with the matching payment and deduction amounts. The customer's bank should also confirm the format information.

Posting Data

The **Posting Data for Autocash with Lockbox screen** is used to **define the owner** of the lockbox and the **type of postings that can be generated**. Additional parameters for posting are also defined: The **document types** used to create the posting documents, and the **posting keys**.

Lockbox Import Program

The Main Lockbox Program screen is used to specify where the lockbox data is saved and the processing mode. Specifications should be provided for the file name, the format of the input records, the clearing of payments for open items.

During lockbox configuration, it is possible to **create a batch input session to update new or missing bank details in a customer's master records**. Therefore, it is **not required to fully maintain customer bank details** manually in the master record.

Chapter 5 - Accounts Payable

There is an important relationship between the customer and vendor accounts. Similarly to G/L accounts, **customer/vendor accounts** have two segments in the financial accounting view:

● There is one segment at the **client level**, it stores **general data**.
● There is a segment with **company code specific data** at **company code level**.

The account segment is arranged in a set of several pages with different groups of fields. The display of an account can be changed by selecting it on the initial display screen. **Vendor account numbers are assigned at the client level**.

Controlling the Field Status:
The appearance of a customer/vendor master data screen depends on several factors:
       □ Account group-specific control
       □ Transaction-specific control
       □ Company code-specific control

In SAP ERP, the **most important input fields** are displayed on **one** screen. The **Tree** button provides **access to screen variants**, **account assignment templates**, and **held documents** that can be selected as templates.

Vendor accounts have two segments:
● A segment at client level to store **general data**. This data can be accessed throughout the corporation.

• A segment at company code level to store **company code-specific data**. Any company code that intends to transact business with a specific vendor must create a company code segment for the vendor.

Creating a **Purchasing Area segment** is a precondition for a **Purchasing Area** to do business with a vendor. The Purchasing area segment stores purchasing area-specific data, such as the **vendor terms of payment**. Similarly to the Sales Areas segment for customers, there is a **Purchasing Organization segment** for vendors.

A **complete vendor account** has the following three segments:
□ General data at the client level
□ Company code segment
□ Purchasing organization segment

Maintenance can be performed **centrally for all areas** or **separately** for Financial Accounting and Procurement. Central maintenance is a good preventive measure for incorrect master records, incomplete accounts and duplicate master data.

When **vendor master records are created centrally**, they are **not assigned to any company code**. Company code assignment will occur when a specific company adds to its master data a vendor who has already been created centrally.

Use of the following option can help **prevent the creation of duplicate accounts**:
• Use of the matchcode before creation of a new account.
• Activation of the automatic duplication check.

Vendor accounts must always be configured for **line item display** and **open item management**.

The **Reconciliation account field** is located in the company code data segment of the vendor master record. Only **a single reconciliation account can be maintained** in a vendor master record. In addition, only one number range can be linked to vendor/customer account group. The reconciliation account is **used to link the entire set of sub-ledger accounts to a specific G/L account** for vendors in the Chart of Accounts.

Bank details in the vendor master data:

The IBAN (International Bank Account Number) is an internationally unique identification number for a certain bank account. An IBAN can be recorded as part of the bank details for vendor master data, and in the House Bank Customizing settings. The IBAN can only be entered in a vendor or customer master record after approval from a business partner. Therefore, IBANs for multiple master records cannot be generated and saved systemically; they have to be recorded manually.

The **account group for vendors controls**:
- The number ranges of the accounts
- The status of the fields in the master record
- One-time vendor accounts

During the creation of vendor master records, **an account group must be entered on the initial scree**n. Once the account group has been created in Financial Accounting, it **cannot be changed**.

Separate number ranges are established for vendor accounts. The range of possible account numbers is split into smaller **number ranges**. Each number range needs to be **defined as internal or external**. Each **number range can be assigned to one or more account groups**, and the same number range can be assigned to different account groups.

When a range is defined as **internal**, it means that **numbers are assigned systemically.** When a range is defined as **external**, the **numbers are supposed to be assigned manually**.

Information on each screen can be defined in configuration as mandatory, suppressed or optional depending on the company code.

A one-time account master record **does not store vendor specific information**, because the account is used for more than one vendor. Therefore, the **vendor-specific fields should be hidden**. Vendor-specific data for one-time vendors is **entered in the document during posting**.

Account group-specific control: normally the field status is controlled only by the **account group**. This means that all accounts that belong to the same account group will have identical screen layouts.

Transaction-specific control: sometimes the field status can be dependent on the master data transaction performed through a menu (such as "Create", "Change" or "Display").

The transaction-dependent field status should be **set to "display"** for the "change" transaction **if the field is not to be changed** after it has been created.

Company code-specific control: company code-specific **screen layouts** can also control the field status for fields in the company code segment of vendor master records. For instance, fields that are not needed in one company code can be hidden, while the same fields can be available for entry in other company codes.

The system compares the account group-specific field status, the transaction-specific field status and the company code-specific field status; then uses the field status that has the highest priority. **To avoid use of the transaction-specific or company code-specific control**, the **field status for all fields should be set to optional**. In this case the **account group-specific** control is always used, because the optional field status **has the lowest priority**.

The object pertaining to the **field status of the activity** can be used to **prevent a change of the reconciliation account in the customer's master data**.

In order to **closely track changes on certain fields**, a field in the vendor master record can be **defined as "sensitive".** In case of a field change, the corresponding vendor account will be blocked for payment until a different person from the one who changed the fields, confirms or rejects the change. The person who approves the change needs to have appropriate authorizations. This approach is referred to as **dual control**.

A **vendor can also be a customer, or vice versa** within the same company code. The payment and the dunning program can **clear open items** against each other. Clearing open items can be carried out by:
• Entering a vendor account number in the customer account and vice versa.
• Determining that each company code chooses to clear open items between customers and vendors.
• Selecting the field "Clearing with Vendor" in the customer account or the corresponding field in the vendor account, to allow clearing.

In addition, an **alternative payer/payee** can be entered in the master record (at the client and company code level), for payments to be made or received by a different party. The entry in the company code segment has higher priority than the entry at client level:

If the "**Individual Entries**" indicator is set; information about an individual payer/payee for a customer/vendor can be directly entered when creating an invoice, even if there is no previous master record for the individual in the system. If the **alternative payer/payee** is already an existing customer or vendor, the customer/vendor account number can be directly entered as a permitted payee/payer in the master record.

In the procurement process invoices can be paid centrally through a head office, or locally by each individual branch, depending on company policies and procedures. Each approach can be reflected in the SAP System design by using **head office and branch accounts**.
Items posted to a branch account can be transferred systemically to the head office account.

When a vendor master record is no longer needed it **can be marked for deletion using a deletion indicato**r. The master record will **only be deleted once all dependent data has been deleted**. In addition, master data in Financial Accounting can only be deleted if no transactions have been posted to the related accounts.

Special G/L transactions

Application Area for Special G/L Transactions

Special G/L transactions are transactions in Accounts Payable and Accounts Receivable that **need to be displayed distinctively** in the G/L and in the sub-ledgers, for particular reporting needs. For instance, there are times when Down payments may not feature in the balance sheet along with receivables and payables for goods and services.

When sub-ledger account assignments are made using a **special G/L indicator**, the postings must be performed on **alternative reconciliation accounts** (special G/L accounts) so that the transactions are **displayed distinctly**. **All Special G/L transactions are posted to G/L accounts**.

Special G/L transactions have **three main classes**:
□ Down payments
□ Bill of exchange
□ Other transactions

• **Down payments Transactions:** SAP ERP is delivered with special preconfigured entry screens and programs designed for the administration of **down payments requested, down payments received and used down payments**. Down payments processing is **integrated with the dunning and payment programs.** When **down payments** are posted **through a special G/L transaction** amounts are recorded in a reconciliation account different from the one used for regular payables and receivables.

• **Bills of Exchange Transactions:** Bills of exchange are intended to address country specific particularities. The **standard menus for the accounts receivable and payable provide options for processing bills of exchange**.

• **Other transactions:** Special G/L transactions pertain to very specific business transactions. The document entry **menu for accounts receivable and payable has an option for "Other"** which has a functionality to handle such transactions.

There are **three special G/L types** for the transfer of special general ledger entries (**noted items, automatic offsetting entries, and free offsetting postings**). The **configuration of the special G/L indicator (which supplements the special posting key)** will determine if the posting **is a free G/L account posting, a noted item or a posting with automatic offsetting**:

1. Automatic offsetting entries (statistical) must always be **posted on the same offsetting account**. They are normally covered in the notes to financial statements. **Posting of a guarantee of payment** is a typical example of an automatic offsetting entry.
If an open item is cleared in the respective account, the respective item in the offsetting account will be cleared systemically.

Automatic offsetting entries are called **statistical postings,** because they normally do not feature in the financial statements, but may feature in the notes to the financial statements.

2. Noted items are **single account assignments** (better known **as one side entries**) that merely **serve as reminders** for due payments, and are **not supposed to be displayed** in the G/L. **A down payment request** is a typical **example of a noted item**.

No figure updates occur after the entry of a noted item. Therefore, items displayed on the line item list do not affect the customer balance, and the associated special G/L account **constantly displays a zero balance**. Creating a noted item **only updates a single line item. No offsetting entry** is made. Therefore, **no zero balance check is made**, because it is not needed.

Noted items **can be accessed by the payment program and the dunning program** for further processing, as needed. On the other hand, **noted items are administered as open items in** the **accounts payable, accounts receivable and the special G/L account**. Therefore, **line item display must always be activated for these accounts**.

3. Free offsetting entries are supposed to be included in the financial statements. As implied by the name, **users can freely define offsetting entries**. An **incoming down payment** is a typical example of a free offsetting entry. A down payment made by a customer before a service is rendered becomes a payable and may therefore not change the receivables of the reconciliation account. The down payment should be transferred or written off once the invoice is generated.

Down payments in the customer area:
The **steps for a customer down payment** can be listed as follows:
1. Post the down payment request.
2. Enter the down payment made.
3. Create the vendor invoice.
4. Clear the down payment.
5. Clear the payment during the payment of the balance.

Other Example for Special G/L Transactions: The Individual Value Adjustment

Disputed or doubtful receivables are entered as individual value adjustments during the preparations of the balance statement for year-end closing. The special general ledger procedure can be handy for this, because the transaction needs to be entered in a customer account and at the same time be posted to the special G/L account - **Individual Value Adjustments for Receivables**.

The **steps for handling individual value adjustments** include:
1. **Entry of receivable** in a customer account.
2. **Entry of the individual value adjustment amount** (tax deducted) in the "Expense for Individual Value Adjustment" account.
3. **Clear the individual value adjustment** from the balance sheet after the key date, by a reversal.

4. **Make the final value adjustment** after confirming that the receivable is uncollectable.

The amount for the loss is eventually posted to the **Expenses for Uncollectable Receivables** account. No special G/L account is needed, because **adjustment postings are supposed to be made on the regular customer reconciliation accoun**t.

Bills of Exchange are handled like special G/L transactions. They are recorded systemically in the sub-ledger apart from other transactions, and posted to a special G/L account. Therefore, it is possible to get an overview of Bills of Exchange at any time.

Configuration of Special G/L Transactions

Postings for special G/L transactions are made **from the application interface using special posting keys and special G/L indicators**. Special G/L transactions of the standard system are recorded using **posting keys 09, 19, 29 and 39**. The **special G/L indicator should always be used** to show that a special G/L transaction is being posted. **Special G/L transactions post to an account stored in Customizing instead of the reconciliation account stored in the master record**. The special G/L accounts have been defined as reconciliation accounts for the K (vendor) or D (customer) account types.

The configuration of the special G/L transactions **depends on the special G/L indicator** that determines the type of transaction and the **account type** (customer or vendor account). The **account is stored based on the combination of the account type** (customer or vendor account) and the **special G/L indicator** that is used.

Set up of a **special G/L transaction with automatic offsetting entry requires**:
- An alternative special G/L account (alternative reconciliation account) for the selected special G/L indicator
- A clearing account defined in the table for "accounts for automatic (offsetting) postings, similar to the one for "guarantees of payment" special G/L transaction.

Payment Terms and Cash Discounts

Terms of payment reflect **agreed conditions** between business partners concerning payment of invoices. The conditions indicate **due dates** and the **cash discounts offered** for payment of the invoice within a certain timeframe. The **key role of a payment term** is to avail the **conditions used to calculate a cash discount** and the invoice **pay by date**. The system calculations are based on the following data:
- **Baseline date:** the date when the terms start to apply. It is used to determine the due date.
- **Cash discount terms:** conditions to meet for the allowed cash discount percentage rates
- **Cash discount percentage rates:** The percentage applicable to the cash discount.

Terms of payment can be **recorded in master data Company Code segment**, the **Sales Area segment**, and the **Purchasing Organization segment** of a customer or a vendor.

The **default terms of payment that apply** during posting depend on the module where the invoice was created:
- If the **invoice is created in Financials**, the terms of payment from the **company code segment** will apply.
- If a **customer invoice is created in Sales order Management**, the terms of payment from the **sales area segment** will apply.
- If a **vendor invoice is created in Purchasing Management**, terms of payment from the **purchasing organization segment** will apply.

Invoice related credit memos:
- Normally the **terms of payment in credit memos are invalid**. These credit memos are **due on the baseline date**. To **activate the payment** terms on these **non-invoice related credit memos,** a **"V"** is entered in the "Invoice Reference" field while recording the document.

- A c**redit memo** can be **linked** to its original invoice **by entering the invoice number in the "Invoice Reference"** field while recording the document. In such cases, **the terms of payment get copied from the invoice** so that the **invoice and the credit memo are due on the same** date.

Basic Data for Terms of Payment

General:

Inquiries: support@sapseries.com

- The **day limit** is the **calendar day up to which** the **terms of payment apply**. The day limits are used **to store several versions of terms of payment** under the same terms of payment key.
- The **description** for terms of payment includes an **explanation** that is generated systemically, but can be changed by the user, and also a **Sales and Distribution text** that prints on invoices.
- The **account type** defines the sub-ledger where the terms of payment can be used. The account type field must be **defined separately to prevent unauthorized editing.**

Payment Controls for Terms of Payment

Payment control:
- **Block keys**, entered in the line items or accounts can be used to block line items or accounts for payment or collection.
- **Payment methods** are entered in the line items or the accounts master data. Payment methods can also be entered in the terms of payment.
When the **payment method in a document line item is different from the payment method in the master data**, the **document data overrides the master data**.

Payment methods specify acceptable modes of payment, they are defined with:
- □ An allowed currency for country level
- □ Maximum and minimum payment amounts

Baseline date
The baseline date is the start date used by the system to calculate the invoice due date. Applicable rules for the calculation of the baseline date include:
- Options for determining **default values for the baseline date** are:
- □ No default
- □ Document date
- □ Posting date or entry date

- **Specifications for baseline date calculation: Fixed day** is used to override the calendar day of the baseline date.

A **percentage rate** is recorded on **the same line as the number of days** that the percentage is valid for, **to calculate the cash discount** for the terms of payment. Fixed days and months can be added as needed. Up to three cash discount periods can be stored.

When the following terms of payment are used the specification of a day limit is required:

• Documents with an **invoice date up to the 15th of the month**, are payable on the last day of the following month

• Documents with an **invoice date after the 15th of the month**, are payable on the 15th of the following month.

An **installment plan** can be used for invoices that need to be spread over several months:

  • The total invoice amount should be divided into partial amounts due on different dates.

  • The **total invoice amount will be split** systemically into separate installments, if **installment payment is defined** in the terms of payment. The percentage **rates specified must add up to 100%.**

  • Each **individual installment** of an installment plan needs to have its own terms of payment defined in the line items.

It is essential to define the **cash discount base** for **each company code** or **tax jurisdiction code** - the relevant setting is in the **Global parameters** of a company code.

Depending on the national regulations within a country, **the cash discount base amount** can be the **net value** or the **gross value.**

• In the **cash discount net procedure** a vendor invoice is posted with a **document type for the net procedure**. A **cash discount clearing account** and **cash discount loss account** are used to record the cash discount.

• In the **cash discount gross procedure**, the cash discount amount is recorded manually or systemically based on the terms of payment. A **cash discount revenue account** and a **cash discount expense account** are used to record the discount.

Days Sales Outstanding (DSO) **and the terms agreed** are evaluation types which **are only used for customers. Overdue items evaluation and due date analysis** are available for both **customer and vendor transactions**

Incoming and Outgoing Payments

A manual payment is a transaction that **will clear an open item**, such as an invoice. The clearing is done by the manual assignment of a clearing document.

Incoming payments are normally **used to clear open debit** amounts for Accounts Receivable, whereas **outgoing payments** are used to **clear open credit** amounts for Accounts Payable.
Manual payments are processed in three steps:
☐ Data is entered in the document header.
☐ Open items are selected to be cleared.
☐ The transaction is saved.

The document header for a manual payment has **three sections: The payment header, the bank data, and the open item selection**.

To process open items, first you **activate the required line items**, then you **assign a payment**.
Various options are available for activating or deactivating line items:
● Select the editing options for open items: click on "Selected Item Initially Inactive".
● Double-click on the specific amount.
● Make a selection from the action menus and function keys.

A document can be posted if the **amount entered** matches the **assigned amount**. Eventual errors can be corrected by resetting the cleared items, then reversing the document, after which the original posting can be correctly re-entered.

Reset clearing removes the clearing data from the items. The changes will be logged and can later be displayed in the change documents. Depending on the situation, the payment history and the credit limit will also be corrected in Accounts Receivable.

Payment Differences and Tolerances

Tolerances are rules used to specify acceptable differences that occur during posting. There are three types of tolerances: **Employee tolerance groups, G/L account tolerance groups, and customer/vendor tolerance groups**.

Two steps need to be completed in order to use tolerance groups:

1- **Group definition**
- The tolerance group is described by a group key, company code, and a currency code.
- The group key is described by a four character alphanumeric key.
- The key "____" **(blank) which is the minimum requirement for tolerance groups** should be **used as the standard tolerance group**.

2- **Group assignment**
- Employee tolerance groups can be assigned to employees.
- G/L account tolerance groups can be assigned to G/L account master data.
- Customer/vendor tolerance groups can be assigned to customer or vendor master data.
- When no tolerances are defined, the default tolerance group "____" (blank) applies.

Once a **user has been assigned to a specific tolerance group, tolerance maintenance for the user will be needed in every company code that the user is authorized for**. When **various tolerances simultaneously apply** to a user such as, tolerances in the customer/vendor master, **the most restrictive tolerance has prevalence**.

The particular details for **permitted payment differences** specified in both types of tolerance groups control the automatic posting of **cash discount adjustments** and **unauthorized customer deductions**. The entries in both groups are considered during clearing. The payment difference must be within both tolerances in order to be processed systemically.

Whenever a **payment difference** occurs during the clearing of an open item, **the difference is compared to the tolerance groups of the employee and the customer/vendor**. If the difference is:
- **Within tolerances** – the amount is posted systemically as a **cash discount adjustment** or an **unauthorized deduction**.
- **Outside tolerances** – the amount has to be **processed manually**.

Users can **manually process** differences by:
• Posting the payment as a **partial payment** whereby a payment is posted to an account **without clearing any of the open items**.
• Posting the payment as a **residual item** whereby the open item is fully cleared, and new line item is created based on the original open item amount minus the amount paid. The new line item will be created under a new document number that references the original documents.
• **Posting the payment difference to an alternative account** using automatic account determination and a reason code for difference postings.
• **Write off the difference** (through manual account assignment).

Reason codes that describe the reason for a payment difference can be assigned to:
□ Difference postings
□ Partial payments
□ Residual items

Reason codes are also used to analyze and post-process payment differences. Other **optional functions include**:
• Control of the payment notice type for a customer.
• Control the G/L account used to post a residual item.
• Post residual items to specific G/L accounts systemically.
• Exclude any disputed residual items from credit limit checks.

Automatic Payments

The **automatic payment program** helps users **manage payables**. Users can automatically:
• Select open invoices that need to be paid or collected.
• Post payments.
• Print the payment media, using data medium exchange (DME), or generate electronic data interchange (EDI).

The **payment program** can be used for **national payments and international** payment transactions, **for vendors and customers**, as well as **outgoing and incoming payments**.

During the automatic payment process the System performs **the following actions**:

- Vendor invoices are entered directly into the System, or are generated after invoice verification.
- Due date analysis for open invoices.
- Review preparation of Invoices due for payment.
- Approval or modification of payments.
- Payment of Invoices.

The **value date** can be defaulted **through the document date or from the posting date** depending on the payment terms of the business transaction.

The **payment process consists of four steps**:
- □ Set parameters
- □ Generate a proposal
- □ Schedule the payment run
- □ Print the payment media

1- **Set parameters**: In this step, the user specifies:

- □ The invoices to be paid
- □ The payment method(s) to be used
- □ The date for the payment
- □ The company codes to include
- □ How amounts will be paid out

The **parameters** indicate the **accounts and documents** that are to be **considered for the payment run**. It is essential to note that **company codes from varying countries cannot be processed within the same payment run**.

If **multiple payment methods** are used **in a payment run**, it is essential to **prioritize** them, because the **sequence in which the payment methods are entered** determines their priority. The payment method **entered first**, will be given the **highest priority**.

On the other hand, **the payment method recorded in the line item of a vendor document always takes precedence** over the payment method specified in the parameters of the payment run. For instance, if a payment method listed in an invoice document differs from the payment method in the related vendor master data; the payment method in the invoice line item will prevail.

It is required to enter the **next posting date** (also known as **next payment date**) for the System to determine **whether an open item has to be paid in the current payment run or in the next one**.

2- **Generate a proposal**: after the parameters have been entered, the System generates a list of open invoices due for payment. Invoices can be blocked or unblocked for payment, as needed.

3- **Schedule the payment run**: once verification of the payment list is completed, a payment run needs to be scheduled. The System creates a payment document that will update the G/L and sub-ledger accounts.

4- **Print the payment media**: at this point accounting functions have been completed and a print program will be scheduled to generate the payment media.

Payment Program Configuration

The **settings** for the **Payment Program** are directly accessible through the application's user interface. They are divided into these **six areas**:
- All company codes
- Paying company codes
- Payment method/country
- Payment method for company code
- Bank selection
- House banks

All Company Codes

Specifications pertaining to the below, need to be made for all company codes:
- Intercompany payment relationships.
- Company codes that will process payments.
- Cash discounts.
- Tolerance days for payments.
- Customer and vendor transactions that can be processed.

In regards to payments, the System has a **sending company code** and a **paying company code**. When a first company code needs to make a payment on behalf of a second company code, the **second company code is the sending company code**, while the **first one is the paying company code**. The **paying company code** is the one **in charge of handling the outgoing payments**. When a company code is not specified; **the sending company code, and the paying company code are assumed to be identical**.

Tolerance days for payables can be set for all company codes. The tolerance days for payments defers the payment up **to the date of the next payment run**. Meanwhile, the company still receives all previously granted discounts.

Activation of **Payment Method Supplements** triggers the option to **print and sort payments**.

The entries for **Vendor/Customer Sp. G/L transactions to be paid** determine which **special G/L transactions can be handled by the payment program.**

□ **Paying Company Codes**
Every company code requires a definition for the below, in the "Paying company codes" area:
- Minimum amounts for incoming and outgoing payments.
- Forms for payment advice and EDI.
- Bill of exchange specifications.

In this area, **minimum amounts for payment and the accompanying forms** need to be defined for each paying company code. The **sender** screen is used to define any **company code dependent-standard texts** needed for the payment forms.

□ **Payment Method/country**
Each country requires definitions for:
- Methods of payment, with related basic requirements and specifications.
- Creation of checks, bank transfers, bills of exchange, etc.
- Master records such as addresses, etc.
- **Document types for postings.**
- Print programs.
- Permitted currencies.

This area **stores the basic requirements and specifications** that apply **for each payment method**. There are two components for payment methods:
☐ **Country-specific settings**
☐ **Company code-specific settings**

If specific **master record requirements** apply for a payment method, such as the vendor address; invoices that have a payment method where this requirement is not met will not be paid.

This area also specifies the **document types** that will be used for posting and clearing documents. Furthermore, the **print program and the print data set** for the payment method are also defined in this area.

Payment methods can be restricted to certain currencies. The **permitted currencies** screen, is used to specify any **currency that the payment method is limited** to. If the **screen is blank** (no currency specified), the **payment method is usable with all currencies**.

☐ **Payment method for the company code**
This area defines the payment methods that can be used for a company code, along with their specifications.

Settings **for each payment method and company code** can differ depending on the company code. These include:
   ● **Minimum and maximum payment amounts** (amounts higher or lower will be excluded).
   ● Foreign business partner (allows payments to foreign customers and vendors).
   ● Payments via banks abroad (allows payments from customer/vendor banks abroad).
   ●Foreign currency allowed (select to use foreign currency with the payment method).
   ● **Postal code optimization** (makes payment from closest bank to the vendor/customer).
   ● **Bank optimization** (banks that can pay from the same clearing house System – ACH will have priority).

The **form data** area makes provision for the name of the **SAPScript for the payment media**.

☐ **Bank Selection**

The elements below are **taken into account when a House Bank is selected for payment**. These are located on the **Bank Selection screen**:
- Ranking order
- Amounts
- Accounts
- Expenses/charges
- Value date

For **each payment method** it is necessary to **indicate a ranking order**, to **determine which House Bank should be used first, second, third, etc**. The ranking order is **defined in conjunction with the payment method**. **Currencies** also need to be specified as well as a **Bill of Exchange** account. The **amount field** for the funds available in the House Bank (in the bank selection screen) is **not updated systemically after a payment run**.

Each **combination of House Bank and payment method** requires:
- The Offset account to the sub-ledger posting.
- Clearing accounts for Bills of Exchange.
- Available funds in each bank.

If a required **combination** of **house bank and payment method is missing**, it **must be created** by specifying:
- The payment method.
- The currency.
- The ranking order.
- The House Bank identifier that will be used with the payment method.

The screen for **Available Amounts** displays the **House Banks and the funds available** at each bank. In case a required House Bank is missing, define the following to add it:
- The Bank and the corresponding bank account.
- For Bills of Exchange, enter the days until the value date, or enter 999 as default.
- Currencies; **leave blank if the payment method is usable with all currencies.**
- **Amount available** for outgoing payment: indicate the funds on hand. The **amount field** is not updated systemically **after each payment run**.

When a clearing account is used in relation with the cashed checks program, it will debit the sub-account and credit the cash account after the check has cleared the bank. **Bank sub-accounts can be used as cash or cash clearing accounts**.

   □   **House Bank**

It is necessary to setup House Bank (bank accounts), and the corresponding G/L accounts that will be used by the payment program. An identifier will be needed for each House Bank.

House Banks are the banks where a company code holds accounts. The System uses:
□ A **House Bank ID** to identify each bank
□ An **account ID** to identify each account at the bank

House Bank data includes:
- Company code
- House bank ID
- House bank data (Bank country, bank key)
- House bk. Comm. Data
- DME/EDI data

Check Management

There are **three types of documents** involved **in payment processes**:
□ Vendor invoices
□ Payment documents
□ Checks

Check management
For **checks to be printed** from SAP ERP, **the System must contain a payable** such as an invoice.

The **check and payment documents are created in two** distinct steps:
- Check creation.
- The check number, bank information, and the check beneficiary are printed on the payment document and on the open invoice.

There are **three different options to pay an invoice**:
• **Automatic payment program** (RFFOUS_C or RFFOD__S): this payment option creates various payment documents and checks systemically. This is the best option for **paying multiple vendors at once**.

• **Post and print forms**: this payment option creates individual payment documents and checks. Invoices for payment must be selected manually. This option is used to pay a particular vendor or invoice. This is suitable when a specific vendor needs to be paid instantly.

• **Post**: this option creates individual payment documents after the invoices for payment have been selected manually. It makes provision for times when a check printer is not available; users can update system records, after a pre-printed or manual check has already been issued. A payment document can be created later and assigned the appropriate check number.

Voiding Checks and Reversing Payments:

Checks can be **voided before a print** run in the following circumstances:
• Accidentally damaged
• Stolen
• Destroyed

Checks can be **voided after a print run** in the following circumstances:
• No longer needed because a cash payment has been made
• Torn during printing
• Used for a test print

After a check is voided, it is always necessary to **verify whether the payment document needs to be reversed**. However, **a check can be voided without reversing the payment document**. Reversal options in the System include:
• Reverse the check.
• Reverse the check then reverse the payment document separately.
• Reverse the check and the payment document simultaneously.

It is possible to void a check and reverse the payment document at the same time. But, it is **not possible to void a check and reverse the payment document and the vendor invoice** all at the same time. The **vendor invoice reversal must be done apart** from voiding the check and reversing the payment document. **Unused checks can also be voided**.

Reasons for Voiding Checks

The System **requires a reason code entry, anytime a check is voided**. Standard Reason codes **are delivered with the System, but additional Reason codes can be defined as needed**. When defining new Reason codes, it is a **must to specify whether they are usable with the print program**.

Check Register

The Check Register program RFCHKN00 is a **dynamic report** that provides details for:

☐ All checks
☐ Outstanding checks
☐ Checks paid
☐ Voided checks

The report can be run by:

☐ Payment run
☐ Issue/creation/cashing date

Checks Cashed Online

The **cashed checks program** is used to **manually reconcile** checks that have been cashed by the bank. The process can be performed systemically with the RFEBCK00 program using data supplied from the user's bank. Once checks have been cashed, and a notification has been received from the bank, the check amount will be transferred systemically from the check clearing account to the cash account.

Steps for Running the Payment Program

The **Steps for running the payment program** involve:

☐ Parameters
☐ Proposal run
☐ Editing the Proposal
☐ Starting the payment run

- **Parameters**

Two fields are used to identify each payment program run:

☐ Run Date
☐ Identification

The **run date** is proposed as the actual date of the program run. However, the main function of the run date is to identify the program run, and does not have to be the particular date of the payment.

The **payment parameters** enable the payment program to determine when an **open item should be paid - in the current payment run or in the next payment run**.

All **company codes** involved in a payment run parameters **must be in the same country**, because payments for company codes in varying countries cannot be processed together.

If a **payment method** is missing in the account master record of an item, it **can directly be recorded in the line item**.

• Proposal run

This is when the **program picks the documents and accounts that have items pending for paymen**t. Any **item that is blocked for payment**, or that does not have **valid bank data or a payment method**, is added systemically to **the exception list**. Any selected invoice that cannot be paid for some reason will also be added to **the exception list**. Users can check the **additional log** to find out the reason an invoice or item **was not processed for payment**.

After completion of a proposal run, two reports are generated systemically: the **payment proposal list** and the **exception list**. The reports can be edited online or printed. The payment proposal **does not alter any of the values at document or master record** level.

The **exception list is part of the payment proposal**. The **proposal list** shows the vendors (or customers) and the amounts due or expected. During payment proposal editing, the key of a particular clerk can be entered to select customer or vendor payments that fall under the responsibility of the specific clerk.

In case of a problem during the **invoice verification process**, the invoice will be **blocked for payment**. If for some reason a vendor should not be paid, a **payment block** can added to the **master record**. The block can be applied to a line item in order to prevent payment of an item.

Any changes made in the line items or master data of a vendor account will not have any effect if the payment proposal has already been created; **because the records get selected as soon as the proposal was prepared.** For the changes to take effect, the payment proposal would need to be deleted and restarted. The **proposal can be changed or restarted** over and over again as needed.

Normally, **bank sub-accounts** are used for posting incoming and outgoing payments, such as accounts for **outgoing checks, outgoing transfers, incoming checks and transfers received**.

Advantages of using sub-accounts:

Inquiries: support@sapseries.com

• The bank account balance can be reconciled at any time with the corresponding G/L account.

• The sub-accounts **store all the incoming and outgoing payments** until they are **cleared** - amounts are actually withdrawn or charged to a bank account **based on the value date**.

Document types for payment documents are defined in the country-specific definitions for a payment method. Cross-company-code payments, allow **additional document types** that are used for the **clearing postings**. The **value date** of a clearing document is determined by adding the **days to value date** to the posting date.

The configuration settings for the payment program requires **payment medium forms** either **for the paying company code** or for every single **payment method assigned to each company code**.

The payment program **first runs** the print program RFFOEDI that selects all payments designated for **EDI.** Matching intermediate documents (IDocs) will be created systemically and forwarded to the EDI subsystem. The EDI subsystem transforms the IDocs into EDI data that can be processed by banks.

For **Data Medium Exchange (DME)**, the System creates a file that contains all the payment information required by the banking rules of the specific country. The DME will be stored in **Data Medium Administration** for future downloading to data medium, and forwarding to a bank.

In the check printing program RFFO "xx"_"y"; the "xx" part normally stands for the country and the "y" part usually contains additional details pertaining to the form.

Check management can be used to assign **predefined check numbers** to checks.

A **check number range** represents a batch of numbered checks, referred to in SAP ERP as a **check lot.** The check lot number ranges must be defined in Customizing, and must correspond to actual check lots. A check number range is defined by determining the length of the check numbers.

It is possible to print checks with predefined check numbers (using check management) or the document number can also be used as the check number (when check management is not in use). When using check management, **check lots** are needed in order to print checks.

Check lots are used to manage checks for both **manual and automatic payments**. The check number ranges should match pre-numbered checks to allow monitoring of the number status. Each **payment method type should be associated with a distinct check lot**.

A check number range cannot be deleted if any checks have already been printed from the related check lot.

The **print program handles**:
● Assignment of check numbers to payment documents.
● Updates of the payment documents and original invoice documents with the check details.
● Printing checks and accompanying documents.

Payment Medium Workbench (PMW)

The Payment Medium Workbench (PMW) is an extra option for payment media printing. **PMW has several benefits over the standard payment media** RFFO*, including:
 ● Formats are easily changeable without making modifications.
 ● New formats can easily be created **without any programming experience**.
 ● All the advice notes can be output in a single print file.
 ● Enhanced sort options for advice notes.
 ● Notes to payee can be defined by users during customization.
 ● The note to payee can be assigned according to origin and payment method in Customizing.
 ● Performance for mass payments is improved.

Each payment method can be converted to the PMW payment media format, and can be used interchangeably, because the standard payment media programs RFFO* and the new PMW payment media formats are usable in the same system and in the same payment run.

Payment methods are converted to PMW in six steps:
1. Make the change in the payment method definition/country by selecting the PMW radio button.
2. Select an available PMW format in the payment method definition/country.
3. Assign either general or origin specific notes to payee to the payment method definition/country
4. Assign a PMW form for the additional sheets

5. Discard the form for document-based payment medium
6. Create and assign selection variants for every single payment group.

Steps in the PMW Process
A payment media needs to be created for a **payment with a PMW payment method** in order to start payment program **SAPFPAYM_SCHEDULE**. There are two main steps including a **pre-service**, that will be followed by the launch of payment **program SAPFPAYM and advice note program RFFOAVIS_FPAYM.**
A Pre-service is first carried out to process the data specifically provided by the PMW payment. The following occurs during the pre-service:
• Payments are sorted according to PMW format and other format-specific fields.
• Payment groups are created depending on the level of granularity
• The note to payee is created.

The **granularity** is a specification in the payment medium format that determines output of payment media in **payment groups**.

Debit Balance Check

A payment run will occasionally create a payment although an account has a debit balance. To ensure that no payments are made to individuals who owe the company money, a **debit balance check** can be performed **after a payment proposal has been created**. The debit balance check can be performed by using **program RFF110SSP**. The check will offset any due debit item that does not have an incoming payment method for the proposed payment.

If a credit memo is entered against a vendor invoice, a valid payment method for incoming payments needs to be defined in the credit memo or in the vendor master record. Otherwise, the credit memo will not be taken into consideration during a payment proposal, and the vendor invoice will still be processed for payment.

The **debit balance check will offset all due debits that lack an incoming payment method for the corresponding proposed payments.**

If the debit balance or credit balance resulting from the check is less than the minimum payment amount, the payments will be added to the **exception list** and the vendor account will be placed on a list of blocked accounts. The **accounts will remain blocked** even if the payment proposal is later deleted.

Automating the Payment Process

Periodic payment runs can be scheduled to include an automatic debit balance check. **Program RFF110S** can be used to **schedule the payment program SAPF110S** in the background. The program features are very similar to the parameters in transaction F110 (used for automatic payments). The parameters can be saved in a variant that will later be scheduled to run in program RFF110S. Although, program RFF110S needs to be scheduled as a proposal run beforehand, after which **program RFF110SSP** will perform a systemic debit balance check to prevent any outgoing payments on due debit balances.

The **Schedule Manager** can be used to schedule functions for **payment processes,** or to automate other periodic recurring activities.

Four types of tasks can be created in the task plan of the Schedule Manager:
- Program with variant
- Notes
- Transaction
- Process definition

The **key components of the Schedule Manager** are:
- Flow definition
- Scheduler
- Monitor

• The **Flow definition** is used to link tasks to each other, whether they are related or simply need to be used together in a worklist.

• The **Scheduler** is used to schedule tasks in a structure tree. Drag and drop can be used to record tasks in a daily overview for execution at a specific time.

• The **Monitor** provides an overview of all scheduled tasks. It is accessible during and after processing.

Integration with Procurement

The **plant** is the central organizational unit in logistics. A plant can be an **operating area or a branc**h within a company. It can also be a **central delivery warehouse**, a **regional sales office**, a **manufacturing facility**, a **corporate headquarters**, or a **maintenance plant**.
A plant can only be assigned to a single company code. Nevertheless, **various plants can be assigned to one company code**.

The **valuation level** is an inventory setting that **applies to the entire client**. It can be set at the **company code level** or at the **plant level**: once the **valuation level** has been defined, it **cannot be changed**. A valuation level change would cause inconsistencies, and require a major conversion of the inventory accounting data and the material documents.
In a **Production Planning** context, the **valuation area needs to be at plant level**, for the program to access accounting data for materials, and to determine the cost of a production order.

The valuation level determines the definition of the **valuation area**:
● When the **valuation level is the company code**, the **valuation area is the company code**.
● When the **valuation level is the plant**, the **valuation area is the plant**.

The valuation area controls postings for the **material valuation**:
. When the **valuation area is the company code** all material stocks for all plants are **managed in a common stock account**. All plants use the **same unit price** for identical products.

. When the **valuation area is the plant**, the material stocks for individual plants are **managed in different accounts**. All plants will have **different unit prices** for identical products.

Best practice recommends the use of **valuation at plant level**.

The Material Master Record provides the views that show the **maintenance level** (a specification of the **master data level at which each field can be maintained**).
Accounting views 1 and 2 are maintained at the **valuation level**, which can either be at plant level or at company code level. These views **store the data used for integration with SAP Financials**.

Inquiries: support@sapseries.com

Each component of a material stock is associated with a **valuation type**, and **Accounting views 1 and 2**, which hold the valuation data for maintenance. The valuation data can be maintained differently for each type. **A material can only be assigned to a single division**.

A **division** is an organizational unit in Logistics that is **used in Sales Order Management** to associate sales or profits from material (or service) sales with the relevant area of responsibility.
The division is also used for systemic assignments of **logistics business area transactions** to Financials. Each material is assigned to a division by recording the right division in the material master data.

Basic Procurement process in SAP ERP

A **purchasing organization** is an organizational unit assigned to a plant for **procurement** purposes.

• **Plant-Specific Purchasing**
A **purchasing organization** can only be **assigned to a single plant**. Purchasing transactions are posted to the company code associated with this plant. **One or several purchasing organizations** can be associated with **the same plant**.

Accounts can only be assigned on a **plant-dependent basis** if the **valuation level is the plant**, the **valuation grouping code is active** and each plant is associated with a **separate valuation grouping code**.

• **Company Code-Specific Purchasing**
In this case, a single purchasing organization is **associated with multiple plants** that are **all linked to the same company code**. To enable **automatic posting of the purchasing transaction** the **purchasing organization must be associated with this company code**. The applicable company code must also be specified while posting the purchasing transaction.

• **Corporate Group-Wide Purchasing**
In this case, a purchasing organization is linked to **several plants** that are associated with **different company codes**. The applicable company code must be recorded manually while posting the purchasing transaction.

The Complete Vendor Account

Before a purchasing organization can carry out business with a vendor it must create a purchasing organization segment. The purchasing organization segment stores purchasing organization-specific data. The **purchasing organization segment created must be associated with the purchasing organization assigned to the company code**.

The account number should be associated with the vendor at the client level, to ensure that the account number for a vendor is the same for all company codes and purchasing organizations.
A complete vendor account always has three segments:
● General data at the client level.
● Company code segment.
● Purchasing organization segment.

Three-Step Reconciliation
The three-step reconciliation is a standard procedure used to post procurement transactions. As implied by the name, it has three steps:
● **Purchase order**:
The purchase order is fully processed in purchasing management – **no postings occur in Financials.**
● **Goods receipt**
A **material document** is created in **purchasing management** to **update inventory data**. An **accounting document** is created concurrently for **posting the valuated goods** to the material stock or consumption account (debit), and to the **goods receipt/invoice receipt account** (credit).
● **Invoice receipt**
When a vendor invoice is posted in purchasing management, an accounting document systemically posts the invoice amount to the **goods receipt/invoice receipt account** (debit) and the **vendor account** (credit). The order for the last two steps can be interchanged depending on the arrival order of the goods and the invoice.

The **goods receipt/invoice receipt (GR/IR) account** is always managed on an open item basis, to ensure that goods have been received for every invoice and vice versa (clearing process).

Automatic Account Determination in Logistics

Systemic postings in logistics widely rely on **automatic account determination to specify G/L accounts** without user intervention. As a precondition for automatic account determination, all relevant accounts are initially recorded in a special table in Customizing pertaining to **inventory management, invoice verification, and material valuation areas**. This manual process is performed only once, unless there is a need to change the account that will be charged systemically. Automatic account determination also applies to goods movements that are initiated by processes in manufacturing (such as a goods issue for a production order) and sales (such as a goods issue for a sales order).

The G/L accounts used for automatic posting for materials are **stored in transaction keys**. For instance, **Inventory postings** use transaction **key BSX** and **GR/IR clearing postings** use transaction **key WRX**.

Account Determination Influencing Factors

• Valuation Areas
The configuration for automatic posting can be based on the valuation area pertaining to a transaction. Certain contexts will require a **valuation at plant level**, in order to assign plant-dependent G/L accounts. Yet other contexts will require a **valuation at company code level**.

• Materials
The configuration for automatic posting can be based on a material (and corresponding material type) pertaining to a transaction. Depending on the material type, it is essential to be able to differentiate **materials produced in-house** from those **procured externally**.

• Movement Types
When a goods movement is entered in SAP ERP, a movement type (MTy) is used to specify the business process that the posting applies to.
For instance, the use of movement types helps distinguish expenses for production from expenses used for physical inventory differences in Financial Accounting and Controlling. Given that **physical inventory** is related to the Materials Management/Production Planning module transaction, **no accounting entries are made in the G/L**.

Various factors influence the accounts in an accounting document for **goods movements**. **Account determination considers the following:**

▢ The chart of accounts for the relevant company code
▢ The material pertaining to the posting
▢ The business transaction that is being posted
▢ Occasionally, the plant where a transaction is posted

A wide range of **data** is used to determine systemically all applicable **G/L accounts**:

• Organizational Level
Once a user specifies the **plant** for the **goods movement**, the System is able to identify the following:
▢ The **company code** relevant to the plant, and the corresponding chart of accounts.
▢ The **valuation area** associated with the plant, and the **valuation grouping code** that differentiates the accounts associated with each valuation area.

A **valuation grouping code** groups valuation areas with identical **assignments** to simplify automatic account determination. It also enables **valuation area-dependent differentiation** during automatic account determination.

Each **plant within a company code can be associated with the same valuation grouping code**, in which case **all plants in the company code will use the same G/L accounts.**

• Material
Once a user specifies the **materials** related to a **goods receipt**, the System is able to identify the following:
▢ The **material type** and the matching indicators used to determine the **update mode** (quantity based or value based).
▢ The **valuation class** used by **materials** to differentiate accounts assigned by material and material type.

Importance of Company Code and Valuation Area

The assignment of G/L accounts during the posting of account-relevant transactions can depend on:
• Chart of accounts

Account determination must be configured separately for each chart of accounts. Each **company code is only assigned a single chart of accounts, which can be distinct from other company chart of accounts**.

• **Valuation area**
Account determination can be configured based on the valuation area for certain transactions, (for instance consumption postings).

• **Valuation type**
Once split valuation has been used for some materials, account determination can be configured based on the valuation type.

• **Movement Type**
Movement types used for posting **goods receipts** can be **specified directly or indirectly**. Movement types **differentiate goods movements** (such as goods receipt, goods issue, and transfer posting). Each movement type symbolizes a specific business process involved in a goods movement. The system determines:
⬜ The **definitions for posting to FI accounts** (such as balance sheet accounts and consumption accounts. the **posting rule** (also called *value string*).
⬜ The **definitions for updating the stock** (inventory) and **value fields** in material master.

Role of Material and Material Type

The material type **groups materials that have identical essential properties**, such as raw materials, semi-finished products, and finished products. A material master record is associated with a material type upon creation. The material type **controls the main process flows in each application**.

The **inventory management type for a material type** is defined separately for **each valuation area**. Inventory management can be managed on a **quantity basis or on a value basis**.

Automatic account determination can be **specific to each material**, whereby the receipt of a raw material can be posted to a different stock account than the receipt of trading goods, depending on the material type. Different stock accounts can also be defined exclusively for materials, depending on the procurement type (produced in-house or procured externally).

The determination of G/L accounts can be configured identically for all materials of a material type or even for various material types. In addition, the determination of different G/L accounts can be configured for the different materials of a material type.

Valuation Classes

The **valuation class** is used for **material-dependent differentiation of automatic accounts**. It is the key used for grouping materials that have an identical account determination. The valuation class is **recorded in the accounting data of a material**.

Other functions of a valuation class key:
- Use account determination to differentiate G/L accounts based on the material.
- Group assign materials per valuation area in the accounting view.
- Restrict a material to a specific grouping key.

Account Determination Key: Material/Material Type

On one hand, a single material type may be used for various valuation classes. On the other hand, a single valuation class may be used for various material types. It all depends on needs.

The **account category reference** is the link between a **valuation class** and a **material type**. Account category references are valuation class groupings used by ERP SAP to verify that a particular valuation class is compatible with accounting data maintenance of a material master record. **A valuation class** can only associated with a **single account category reference**.

Account category references are assigned **to material types**. **A material** type can only be associated with **a single account category reference**.

However, **several material types can be assigned to the same account category reference**, as long as they have the same account category.

Every material type that is supported in inventory management on a **quantity and value** basis **must have an account category reference**.

For **materials that use split valuation**, account determination is accomplished by the **valuation class of the valuation type record**.

Effect of Business Transactions on Account Determination

Business transactions **affect account determination differently**. Materials Management postings for **account-relevant transactions** use **value strings**, as opposed to specific **G/L account numbers**.
All **inventory management movement types** and all transactions in **invoice verification** are assigned posting records that are predefined in a **value string that acts as a posting rule**.

Value strings hold the **transaction keys** for the various **systemic transaction postings.** Typically, the first transaction key in a posting key pertains to a debit. It is the transaction key that determines whether a posting applies a stock (inventory) account, or a GR/IR clearing account, etc. For instance, BSX is used for inventory posting. BSX contains **the value strings for the transaction keys** that are relevant for inventory posting.

SAP ERP **only** uses standard **predefined transaction keys**. Therefore, value strings **cannot be modified or created** at will. The assignment of the value strings to inventory movements, and their respective breakdown into transaction keys is accessible in Customizing for inventory management and physical inventory. These **value strings and their assignments cannot be changed** in any way; however, **G/L accounts from the chart of accounts can be assigned to the posting transactions** as needed.

Valuation of Goods Receipt

The purpose of a **valuation of goods** is to provide **unit cost information** for the calculation of margins between goods received and goods sold. **Goods receipts must be valuated prior to posting in Financial Accounting**.
Valuation types are defined by the entry in the **price control indicator** in the material master record. Options for the price control indicator include:

Moving average price (V)

This is the average weighted price of all goods available, whereby the **total value is divided by the total inventory** based on the purchase order price. It is used by the System as the **clearing price for goods issues**.

Standard price (S)

This is the **price that is recorded in the material master data**, and is **used to valuate the goods received**. Eventual **differences between the valuated goods received and the purchase order** amount are **posted to a price difference account**. Normally **the standard price** is the basis for the **valuation of goods received**. It is mainly used for products that are not subject to frequent fluctuations. Standard cost estimates are usually performed only once, at the beginning of a fiscal year.

Determination of the Value String for Goods Movements

Predefined settings and manual settings are used **to determine** systemically the **value string** for **each business transaction**.

Value string WE01 pertains to business transactions for materials that are managed on a value and quantity basis. The transaction keys assigned to the WE01 value string include:
- **BSX** is used for all postings to stock (inventory) accounts
- **WRX** is used for postings to the GR/IR clearing account based on the Goods Receipts and Invoice Receipts for regular orders.
- **PRD** is used for price difference postings that result from postings where the order price (or invoice price) is different from the material's standard price:
- **KDM** is used for exchange rate difference postings that result in Materials Management when orders in foreign currencies cause exchange rate differences between goods receipt and invoice receipt.

Assignment of G/L Account Number

Definable rules may be used to drive the use of automatic account assignment for G/L transactions based on:
- The valuation grouping codes.
- The account groupings (not possible for every posting key).
- The valuation class.

There is a separate indicator that is used in conjunction with individual posting transactions to assign distinct G/L accounts for credit postings and debit postings (not applicable with inventory accounts).

Account Determination Simulation

A simulation function is available under "Configure automatic postings activity" to preview settings for automatic account determination. **Configure Automatic Postings** activity displays the G/L accounts assigned for:
- The specified material or valuation class.
- The specific plant.
- The specified transaction in inventory management or invoice verification.

The simulation is also used to confirm that all accounts assigned actually exist in the parameters. Transaction keys for particular value strings should also be examined, especially the **account for the offsetting postings**.

Inquiries: support@sapseries.com

Chapter 6 - Asset Accounting

Organizational Aspects

The Chart of Depreciation

A **chart of depreciation** is used to **manage the legal requirements for the valuation and depreciation** of assets. The System is delivered with **country-specific charts of depreciation designed for the particular needs of numerous countries**. Each country-specific chart of depreciation **has predefined depreciation areas**. Authorized **must define their own chart** of depreciation by **copying and editing** an existing one, as the delivered ones are meant for reference and not direct use. Charts of depreciation **are defined at the client level**.

A chart of depreciation is **organized in three parts (depreciation area, depreciation keys, special calculation of asset values)**:

• **Depreciation Areas** are organized according to business management requirements and other characteristics that reflect a **specific type of valuation**. They are used **to calculate and store different values** in parallel using area **01** as the **leading depreciation and applies to ordinary depreciation**. A Depreciation area is always **associated with a single chart of depreciation**. Depreciation areas **can be deleted or added** according to circumstances. **Additional depreciation areas can be defined for a chart of depreciation, even after system Go-live**. Specifications must be made for all depreciation types and special valuations pertaining to a depreciation area. A maximum of **99 depreciation areas** can be managed in parallel.

A typical depreciation area handles:

Inquiries: support@sapseries.com

▢ Country-specific valuation
▢ Values or depreciation that differ from area 01 (such as for tax or cost accounting)
▢ Consolidated versions in the company code or the group currency
▢ Book depreciation in the group currency
▢ Difference between book and country-specific tax-based depreciation

Depreciation attributes can be proposed for each **depreciation area**. **Depreciation attributes can be system-specific or user-specific**. When depreciation attributes are **specified by a user, they can be changed as needed**. However, when depreciation attributes are **specified by the System they cannot be changed**.

● **Depreciation Keys** are used for systemic depreciation of assets in a chart of depreciation. Keys can be added or changed as needed.

● **Special calculations of asset values** pertain to special objects in the chart of depreciation, such as investment support keys for investment support.

A **company code** only uses **a single chart of accounts and a single chart of depreciation**, which are assigned to the company code during customization. The company code is setup prior to the assignment of the chart of accounts and the chart of depreciation. All data pertaining to asset accounting is later added to the company code. **Different company codes can be assigned to the same chart of depreciation** and vice versa, because the assignment of a company code to a chart of accounts is not tied to its assignment to a chart of depreciation.

Integration with Cost Accounting

The integration of Asset accounting with Cost Accounting is accomplished through **cost objects recorded in the asset master** data. Each object is associated with a Controlling Area that includes one or more company codes. Integration with Cost Accounting enables:
▢ **Focusing planning measures.**
▢ **Monitoring the implementation of these measures.**
▢ **Calculation and settlement of costs** incurred as a result of these measures.

When Asset Accounting is integrated with Controlling or General Ledger Accounting, the following **objects can be assigned to an asset master** record:
▢ **Business area**

- Cost center/internal order
- Real estate object
- WBS element
- Profit center/segment
- Funds center/financial budget item

Asset Classes - Naming and Assigning

All assets are **classified based** on **Asset Classes**. Default values can be defined for an asset class, for uniformity purposes. **An asset class consists of two main sections:**
- **Master data** section:
Stores control data and the default values for the administrative data within an asset master record
- **Valuation section**:
Stores control parameters and default values for depreciation terms and valuation

The **asset class is created at the client level** then is assigned to a chart of depreciation. Therefore, the **asset classes defined** in the chart of depreciation **apply to all company codes**.

Multiple charts of depreciation can be assigned to the **same asset class**. This **ensures uniformity in the asset catalog** regardless of differences between charts of depreciation.

An asset can only be assigned to a **single asset class**. An **asset class has three parts** which need definitions for the elements here below:
- Control parameters
- Default values for master data
- Default values for depreciation terms (default values for depreciation calculation).

Two special asset classes should normally be considered for:
- **Assets under construction**
- **Low value assets**

- **Assets under construction (AuC)** need a **distinct asset class** with a **matching G/L account**, because assets under construction are supposed to be displayed separately in a balance sheet. Therefore, **a distinct account determination for AuC will be setup in the asset class**.

Depreciation **Key 0000** should always be **assigned to each asset under construction** to **prevent depreciation calculation**. Nevertheless, it is acceptable to **perform special tax depreciation and investment support** on assets under construction. In addition, **down payments are possible** for assets under construction, and **credit memos can be posted to assets under construction** even after full capitalization. However, there is a **precondition – negative APC must be allowed**. The Accumulated Production Cost (APC) represents the original cost of an asset.

Monitoring details for capital investments is feasible in Financials by **integrating internal orders** and **projects** with the Asset under Construction (AuC), through **Investment Management (IM)**.

• **Low-value Assets (LVA)** can be managed on an individual basis or on a collective basis. A **separate asset class will be needed for each approach**. In order to use collective management of LVA **a base unit of quantity** should be recorded in the asset class.

On the other hand, **a check of the maximum amount** in the depreciation areas is required in the asset class for a Low-value asset (LVA).

Posting Depreciation to the G/L

The **mode for posting values** from depreciation areas to G/L accounts is based on one of the following options:
▫ Do not post any values.
▫ Post asset values online, depreciations periodically.
▫ Post asset values and depreciations periodically.
▫ Only post depreciations periodically.

Each asset class must have a **reconciliation account defined in the account determination for the depreciation are**a. Accounts that need to be specified in the depreciation area include:
• The asset cost account
• Accumulated depreciation
• Depreciation accounts

By default, only depreciation area 01 can post APC (Accumulated Production Cost) values to the G/L online in real time. Depreciation should **always be posted on a periodic basis**.

Although other depreciation areas can receive their values from depreciation area 01, they will calculate and post different depreciation values to the General Ledger.

Some depreciation areas can be defined solely for reporting purposes, in which case no values will post to the General Ledger.

Asset balance sheet values and depreciation values from a specific depreciation area can be posted to separate balance sheet accounts or income statement accounts in the General Ledger. **When multiple financial statement versions are in use, several depreciation areas will need to post to the G/L**. In this case, each balance sheet account and income statement account will need to be linked to a specific financial statement version for the underlying items to be properly displayed.

Parallel Accounting in Asset Accounting

Parallel accounting can be handled in Asset Accounting using depreciation areas. Depreciation areas will need to be defined for all relevant accounting principles.
Two approaches are available for handling parallel accounting in Asset Accounting, namely the additional **accounts approach** and the parallel **ledgers approach**. **Accounting principles in Asset Accounting mainly differ** in relation with the:
• Determination of depreciation
• Capitalization of assets produced in-house

Determination of Depreciation

Specific depreciation terms need to be recorded for each accounting principle. The recorded depreciation rules will drive the determination of depreciation in parallel for each depreciation area.
Postings will be made to additional accounts or parallel ledgers, depending on the selected approach. Based on the approach chosen for parallel accounting, the following settings are required:

● **Additional accounts approach**:
All needed additional accounts should be recorded during customization of Financial Accounting (New).

● **Parallel ledgers approach**:
The values from depreciation area 01 need to be posted to all ledgers. However, the leading ledger must be assigned to depreciation area 01.

On one hand, **a wizard can be used** to set up the depreciation areas for parallel ledgers. On the other hand, it is possible to **define depreciation areas and enter a target ledger group** for each depreciation area. In addition, a different depreciation area should be assigned for account determination, to avoid entering additional accounts for the depreciation area. Normally, this should pertain to master depreciation area 01.

Master Data

The definition of an asset class applies to **all the company codes in a client**. The asset class acts as a template for the creation of asset master records. Therefore, the default values defined for each asset class are applied systemically to all newly created asset master data.

The **main function of the asset class** is to **link the asset master records and the General Ledger accounts** to posted values and depreciation.

Additional functions of the asset class include:
● Copy of asset classes from reference (suitable for extending uniform default values – depreciation terms).
● Definition of the authorized entries for user fields (evaluation groups, reason for investment, environmental protection indicator – **all three fields can later be used as selection criteria in reporting**).
● Entry of default values for user fields (insurance values, net worth values, leasing, depreciation terms and index series).
● Linking asset classes to the material group (for Materials Management - MM integration).

In contexts with **many identical asset classes**, **different account determination keys** can be used for separation purposes, although their **respective values will be updated to a single balance sheet account**.

Inquiries: support@sapseries.com

In situations that use **multiple charts of accounts, a single account determination key is sufficient** to post asset values from all asset classes to different accounts in the different charts of accounts.

The assignment of the **number for an asset master record** is determined by the associated **number range. Number assignments** can be defined as **internal** or **external**. Each company code can be assigned a distinct **number range**, or **several company codes** can share a **single set of number ranges**.

Sub-numbers for an asset **can also be assigned internally or externally**, depending on the configuration of the asset class.

The **input fields** that are **displayed in the asset master record depend on** the associated **screen layout.** A field can be set up as:
□ A required entry
□ An optional entry
□ Display only
□ Suppressed

The selected screen layout establishes the **maintenance level** that applies for the **master data fields**. In addition, **the screen layout** determines whether a master record **can be used as a reference** for creating new assets (by copying the asset).

The input fields for asset master records are arranged on different **tab pages**. A **layout for the master data** can be designated for each asset class, where the layout defines:
● The number of tab pages.
● The description of the tab pages.
● The field groups displayed on the tab pages.

Account assignment objects must be **activated** prior to their **maintenance in the master data**.

A screen layout rule must be selected for every **depreciation area** of each **asset class**. The layout rule will affect the valuation fields in the depreciation area. **Screen layout control handles the field attributes in the asset master record and the maintenance level of the fields.**
There are **two standard screen layout rules, namely 1000 and 2000**. Each of these screen layout rules contain a **maintenance level** that ensures that depreciation is handled in the same manner, based on **three available options**:

1 - Asset class
Control of valuation is **performed at the asset class level**, whereby entries made in the asset class are passed on to the asset master record, and cannot be overwritten.

2 - Main asset number
Control of valuation is **performed at asset master record level**, whereby entries made in the asset class are used in the asset master record, and can be edited. All asset sub-numbers that are related to the specific master record will also use the values from the main number. The **sub-number values cannot be edited**.

3 - Asset sub-number
Control of valuation is **performed with flexibility**, such that **asset sub-numbers can have their own individual depreciation terms**.

Creation of Multiple Similar Assets

Multiple identical asset master records can be created simultaneously. Nevertheless, individual entries can still be made for each asset in the fields below:
▢ Description of the asset
▢ Inventory number
▢ Business area
▢ Cost center
▢ Evaluation groups 1-5

Data in an asset master record **can be managed on a time-dependent basis**, whereby asset master can be maintained for specific time intervals (the related fields will affect how depreciation is calculated).

The information in the asset master record that is managed as time-dependent data is **essential for cost accounting assignments**.
Parameters that can be changed on a time-dependent basis include absolute scrap value, variable depreciation amount, percentage scrap value, depreciation key and useful life.

Mass Changes

When many assets need to be changed concurrently, a mass change option can be used to expedite the process. An asset that comprises many components can use sub-numbers to manage each component separately.

Mass changes are best carried out with a worklist, a standard function in FI-AA. The steps below are used to process a worklist for mass changes:

Step 1 – Create a substitution rule to indicate the fields for change and specify the type of change required

Step 2 – Run a report to output the list of assets to be changed

Step 3 – Select the "Create worklist" function.

Step 4 - Enter a description for the worklist and select a purpose from the predefined standard list.

Step 5 – Identify a suitable substitution rule for the mass change.

Step 6 – Assign the worklist to a user for immediate processing, or save it for future processing

Step 7 – Preview the assets for mass change (display or run a report) to confirm that all changes were successfully made

There are **two parts in a substitution rule for Mass Changes**:

(1) **Conditions** identify the records for selection. This can be done with in Form Builder or with expert mode. The use of expert mode requires a knowledge of the fields and table descriptions.

(2) **The Substitution rules** point to the replacement values. This can be either a constant or a user exit.

Asset Accounting Transactions

Transaction types are additions to asset posting keys 70 (debit) and 75 (credit) that are used during postings to an asset account. The transaction type **distinguishes the various types of transactions and indicates where the asset posting should be displayed** in the **asset history sheet**. Asset transaction postings are **identified by the transaction type**, such as buying, selling, acquisition from internal production, retirement without revenue, etc. **Some transaction codes enable users to create an asset master record during document entry**. Transaction codes should not be confused with transaction types.

Asset Acquisition

Entries for asset acquisition can be Integrated or non-integrated. Some typical entries are:

● Asset accounting entry integrated with Accounts Payable (incoming invoice) without reference to a purchase order.

● Financials entry for asset accounting with an automatic offsetting entry, but no reference to a purchase order or any integration with accounts payable; is suitable when the **invoice has not been delivered, or the invoice was posted during a separate previous step**.

● Financials entry for asset accounting with automatic clearing of the offsetting entry: The first posting usually occurs in FI-AP, whereby the clearing account is cleared concurrently with the asset posting. Another possibility is to enter an asset with an automatic offsetting entry, followed by a credit posting for an incoming invoice to clear the clearing account.

● Asset entry directly in Materials Management (MM) - The asset is posted in MM.

● On rare occasions, an asset acquisition can be posted using a CO order.

When an acquisition is initially made, the information below is recorded systemically in the asset master record:
● Date of asset capitalization.
● Date of initial acquisition in the relevant master record.
● Acquisition year and acquisition period (derived from the posting date).

The **posting date and the asset value date** must always have a **matching fiscal year**. The date of asset capitalization and the date of initial acquisition are derived from the asset value date.

The **document type drives the posting**:
● Document type AA posts gross (without deducting a discount).
● Document type AN (KN, RN), deducts the discount from the capitalized asset amount (net).

All asset postings must have a **transaction type**, to identify acquisitions, retirements and transfers.

The transaction type is **used in the asset history sheet and other FI-AA reports** to identify the various forms of transactions and distinctly display them. For instance, the transaction type indicates how the value change appears in the asset history sheet: either as a retirement from a prior-year acquisition, or as a current-year acquisition.

When asset **acquisition postings are not integrated, a clearing account is needed**. Acquisition **postings without integration are made when**:
▫ An invoice arrives before the asset
▫ An asset has been delivered without an invoice

Asset Retirement

Options for posting retirements include:
▫ With or without revenue (scrapping)
▫ With or without customer (non-integrated)
▫ As a full or a partial retirement
▫ As a mass retirement (using a worklist)
▫ As a retirement of various assets that will be selected manually

The **reference period** for an asset retirement **depends on the asset value date** (asset retirement date) and the period control method (period control key) of the depreciation key.

Proportional value adjustments (depreciation) are handled systemically. The System identifies the period that applies to the asset being retired and posts the asset retirement, then it cancels the depreciation accordingly.

Mass retirement, with or without revenue, is a standard function in the system. Mass retirement is performed according to the following steps:
Step 1 - Create the list of the assets for retirement from an asset report
Step 2 - Create a **worklist**.
Step 3 – Choose the purpose of the worklist from the two options below:
- Retirement without revenue
- Retirement with revenue

Step 4 - Enter the revenue distribution.
Step 5 - Process the **worklist**, or edit the worklist before completion.

Intra-company and Inter-company Asset Transfers

Different types of transfers occur in Asset Accounting based on circumstances:

☐ **Intra-company transfer**, the transfers occurs within a company code.

☐ **Inter-company transfer**, the transfers occurs between different company codes.

Transfer variants contain specifications for **the transfer method and transaction types** for use **in inter-company asset transfers.** Transfer **variant 4 is the standard for intra-company** transfers.

For **intercompany** transfers, the **relationship type** needs to be considered:
• When a transfer occurs within a legal, independent unit (within a company), whereby **both company codes belong to the same company** - two company codes are considered to be part of the same legal unit, and have a **transfer of relationship type 02**.

• When a transfer occurs between legally independent organizational units (company codes), whereby each belongs to a distinct company, and the company codes are not related within a company, but still belong to a group of affiliated companies (corporate groups) - there is a **transfer of relationship type 01**.

In order to define **cross-company depreciation areas**, the context must involve company codes that have **different charts of depreciation**, with **different depreciation areas** (different keys) but with the **same actual functions**.

Cross-company depreciation areas **do not have specific control parameters**; they simply rely on a **key** that is common throughout the client, and a short description.

Assets under Construction (AuC)

There are **two Asset Accounting phases pertaining to assets produced within a company**:
☐ The under construction phase
☐ The useful life phase

The assets need to be displayed in two distinct balance sheet items during these two phases. The phase where the asset is transferred from the **under-construction phase** to a **completed asset** is known as the **capitalization of the asset under construction**.

Depending on the required functions, **the "under construction phase" can be managed as**:
• A normal asset master record (for summary settlement).
• An asset master record with line item management.

During capitalization of an asset under construction, a **distinction is made** systemically between the transactions **from the previous years** and the transactions **from the current year**. This differentiation is achieved by using **different transaction types**.

To perform a **line item settlement of an asset under construction** to one or more completed assets:
• **Select the line items** that you want to settle to a receiver.
• **Define the distribution rules** for the selected line items.
• **Post the settlement of line items to the designated receivers** using the distribution rule.

Settlements can be performed gradually , because it is not a requirement to settle all line items at once, neither is it required to distribute the 100 percent of each line item.

There are **two ways to manage expenses for assets under construction**:

1 - The application component - Investment Management, can be used to create, post and manage investment orders or investment management projects, which are reconciled with assets under construction.
Investment Management provides a wide range of functions for handling investment procedures.

2 - An **asset under construction** can receive direct postings in Asset Accounting even when Investment Management is not in use.

After **completion of an asset under construction**:
• A new master data record must be created to become the receiver for the AUC settlement.
•The values from the asset under construction account must be settled against one or more completed assets.

During settlement, the AuC costs will be distributed to one or more assets (receiver) based on the settlement rules.

Unplanned Depreciation

Besides the automatic calculation of depreciation, manual depreciation can be planned for individual assets in FI-AA. When the **appropriate transaction type** is applied, the system recognizes that the user is about to perform a manual depreciation (such as the current-value depreciation).

In order to enter depreciation, **a dialog box is needed for selection of the appropriate depreciation areas**. This pertains to the manual planning of depreciation. An FI document will not be created until the depreciation posting program is run.

Write-ups or post-capitalization can also be posted based on the above approach, combined with the selection of an appropriate transaction type and depreciation area(s) for the posting. A special report is available to display manual depreciation.

Periodic Processing

Depreciation

Depreciation handles the **posting of depreciation and the determination of the related asset values**. The following **types of direct depreciation can be processed** in the System:
- Ordinary depreciation
- Special depreciation
- Unplanned depreciation

Definition of Depreciation Areas

Depreciation areas **define the posting mode for asset balance sheet values and depreciation to the G/L accounts**. Depreciation areas **can also be defined for reporting purposes only**, whereby values can be calculated and displayed, although no postings will occur on the G/L accounts.

Specifications are also needed to indicate **how values for posting and depreciation terms should be transferred for each depreciation area**. In addition, **frequency, procedure, and CO account assignment** need to be provided for depreciation posting. The types of depreciation applicable for each depreciation area, such as ordinary, special, or unplanned depreciation also need to be determined.

• **Ordinary depreciation** applies to the planned reduction in asset value caused by normal wear and tear.

• **Special depreciation** is a purely tax-based type of depreciation for wear and tear.

• **Unplanned depreciation** is performed when unusual circumstances arise, such as a damage that causes a permanent reduction in the asset value.

• **Unit-of-production depreciation** is used to consider fluctuations in activity for the depreciation calculation.

Depreciation Terms for Depreciation Areas

All specifications and parameters for depreciation **calculations are entered in calculation methods**, which **replace the internal calculation key** of the depreciation key. **Calculation methods need to be assigned to a depreciation key**.
Individual calculation methods include:
□ Base method
□ Declining-balance methods
□ Maximum amount methods
□ Multilevel methods
□ Period control methods

Specifications can be made for **interest to be calculated for the cost-accounting depreciation area**, and for **depreciation to carry-on below zero**. These specifications are to be included in the definition of depreciation areas.

Additional possibilities include the use of index series for the indexing of replacement values, whereby specifications are made for an index series to calculate the replacement value (if revaluation/indexing is used in a depreciation area). In this case:
• The index series needs to be recorded in the asset or in the asset class.
• Only year-dependent index classes can be used.
• The index series must be assigned to an index class.
• An indexed revaluation can be calculated for accumulated depreciation and imputed interest.

In order **to calculate imputed interest on the capital tied up in assets**, specifications should be made for:
• The calculation of imputed interest for the depreciation area.
• The determination of interest posting for the company code and the corresponding depreciation area.
• The use of a depreciation key for the assignment of calculation methods for the depreciation type *Interest.*

On the other hand, there are additional **parameters that mainly pertain to the cost-accounting depreciation area**, namely:
▫ Index
▫ Variable depreciation portion
▫ Scrap value

Calculation of Depreciation

The calculation logic for depreciation is based on **period intervals** that consider the duration for which the same reference value (such as the purchase value) has been valid within a fiscal year.

In case there is **no transaction for an asset, the depreciation calculation** will be based on the same reference value for the entire year and **will be calculated with a single period interval** (=> period 1 to period 12).
In case of any transactions, the reference value will change and other periods will be used in the **calculation based on the period control**.

The System provides support for an automatic changeover method to period/months, but this is not part of the standard System. Therefore, it requires a user exit that is implemented using the BAdI *FAA_DC_CUSTOMER.*

Time-dependent intervals **enable depreciation to be calculated more accurately**. In the absence of time-dependent depreciation terms **all open and future fiscal years would be recalculated**. When a time-dependent change is made to depreciation terms, it is essential to ensure that the changes do not affect any other system dependencies or settings for the depreciation areas, particularly during **reductions** of depreciation amounts.

The parameters here below can be changed on a time-dependent basis:
□ Depreciation key
□ Useful life
□ Variable depreciation Amount
□ Absolute scrap value
□ Percentage scrap value

Analysis of Depreciation Values

Depreciation terms are stored in asset master records. The **depreciation key** and **useful life** are used to calculate the **annual depreciation**. The **depreciation start date** is based on **the asset value date** and on the **period control method**.

The **Asset Explorer** is a tool that **displays the values and the depreciation for every transaction and each area**, including the calculation of depreciation values. A change in customization settings for depreciation keys will not directly correct any depreciation values that have already been calculated. A **recalculation** of depreciation is necessary to update the figures.

Posting a Depreciation Run

The **depreciation posting program (RAPOST2000) handles** postings for:
• Ordinary depreciation (which includes book depreciation and cost-accounting).
• Tax depreciation, allocation and write-off of reserves due to special tax.
• Depreciation (ordinary).
• Unplanned depreciation (and other manually planned depreciation).

- Imputed interest.
- Revaluation of APC or accumulated depreciation.

The relevant amounts are posted systemically **to** the **G/L accounts and additional account assignment objects**. However, **only real CO account assignment objects can be posted**, whereas **statistical postings can be made to other objects**.

The following is **required in order to post depreciation:**
- Configuration of the required depreciation areas.
- Definition of the G/L accounts for depreciation postings in the account assignments.
- Assignment of the document type for depreciation postings (AF) to the company code.
- Definition of posting rules and intervals per depreciation area.
- Activation of account assignment objects.
- Specification of account assignment types for the account assignment objects.

The depreciation posting program (RAPOST2000) carries out **all essential checks** during the test run, and logs errors including:
- Incorrect account assignment objects.
- Missing account assignment types.
- Missing Accounts for depreciation posting.
- Incorrect posting period entries.
- Missing settings for the depreciation posting cycle in the depreciation area.

Fiscal Year Change and Year-End Closing

The main task of the fiscal year change program is to **open new annual value fields for each asset**:
- The fiscal year change program cannot be run before the last posting period of the current fiscal year.
- The program run must apply to the entire company code.
- A fiscal year change in a subsequent year **can only be processed if the previous year has already been closed**.

Preparations for year-end closing:
- Before posting depreciation, depreciation lists and the asset history sheet must be checked.
- The report for periodic posting (RAPERB2000) must be run beforehand, for areas that posts APC values to the general ledger periodically.

- **Re-run depreciation posting after any eventual changes.**
- Generate a balance sheet and profit and loss statement after posting depreciation.

The year-end **closing program verifies**:
- Depreciation and asset values posted completely.
- Assets are devoid of errors.

In no errors are found during the verification check, the year-end closing program updates the last closed fiscal year for each depreciation area, and concurrently locks posting in Asset Accounting for the closed fiscal year. **If a closed fiscal year is later re-opened** for posting, it **can only be closed again after the year-end closing program has been re-run**.

Periodic APC Values Posting

There should be no transactions pending for posting prior to the year-end close. Running a **periodic posting can prevent** having any asset accounting transactions pending for posting. In addition, when **a specific area is supposed to post APC values to the G/L periodically**, a periodic posting run will be needed.

The periodic posting program should be started as an update run. However, the periodic posting program cannot be run immediately, because there is a prerequisite that needs to be met; namely **defining a document type with internal number assignment for each company code**. Starting the periodic posting program without meeting this prerequisite will trigger an error. The steps for the prerequisite are listed here below:

- **Definition of a new document type** in Customizing for Asset Accounting.
- Creation of a **new number range interval**.
- Creation of a **new document type for periodic posting** in each company code.

After the three steps above have been completed, the program for the periodic posting run (RAPERB2000) can be started. An initial test run is recommended to view a comprehensive log with a simulation of individual documents.

Information System

Report Selection

The Asset Accounting standard reports are located in the area menu for reporting called **FIAA Information System Asset Accounting**, which is embedded in the Asset Accounting area menu (ASMN). The **asset class** is always available as a selection option in all the FI-AA standard reports.

Benefits of using the **Area Menu**:
- Option to display or hide columns.
- Formatting columns by double-clicking or dragging with the mouse.
- Filter.
- Sorting.
- Enable summaries and subtotals.
- Expanding/collapsing hierarchy levels.
- Saving client and user-dependent settings in variants.
- Export function in a table calculation.
- Easy display of additional fields in asset reports.

SAP List Viewer

The List Viewer is a user-friendly tool that supports dynamic creation of layouts. The **main List Viewer features** include:
- Deletion and insertion of columns.
- Sorting values in columns in ascending or descending order.
- Calculation of totals or subtotals for one or more columns of a list.
- Using layouts to save an individual report structure as a variant for future use.
- Filters.

Asset History Sheet

The **asset history sheet** is the single **most useful and comprehensive year-end standard report for Asset Accounting**, because it represents the asset portfolio in the detailed form of an asset history sheet. Sort versions and totals at various group levels can be accommodated within the report.

Country-specific versions of the asset history sheet are available to fulfill different legal requirements. Additional history sheet versions are also available to display the development of special depreciation. Personalized history sheet versions can also be defined.

Value Simulation

The **Display dep. calc**. option in the Asset Explorer can be used to display a detailed calculation of depreciation in the system. The **Posted Values** tab page displays the planned data for a fiscal year and actual amounts posted to date.

The Asset Explorer can also be used to create a **simulation of transactions** and **simulation of depreciation terms**, based on the values for individual assets. Personalized report variants can also be created.

Depreciation Simulation

A depreciation simulation is a good option to see the end result of a depreciation posting, prior to any actual posting. During the simulation of asset values **all depreciation terms can be changed** through a simulation version that will simulate the depreciation for future fiscal years. **Depreciation for planned capital investments** can be included in the forecast. However, **planned capital investments** can only be included if the planned investment amounts are **managed as planned costs on an order or project in CO**.

Simulation Versions

Simulation versions are used **to assume changes in the depreciation method for asset value/depreciation reports**. **Different simulation versions** are made by specifying the **key** and the **useful life** that apply for **each area, asset class**, and **depreciation key**. Substitution rules can be used to include additional depreciation parameters in a simulation.

Chapter 7 - Financial Closing

Month-End Activities

Before the actual month-end closing activities some pre-closing activities need to be carried out. **Pre-closing activities that begin in the old month** are listed as follows per area:

- From a technical perspective: open the new accounting period in FI.
- FI: Enter accruals/deferrals then process recurring entries and bad debt expense in AR. Post depreciation and interest expenses in Asset Accounting.
- MM: Maintain GR/IR clearing account and post material revaluations.
- HR: Post all payroll expenses.
- SD: Post goods issues for all deliveries to customers.
- Other technical step: Close old month in MM, close sub-ledgers in FI; perform a preliminary close of G/L in FI.

There is a set of managerial closing activities that cover CO allocations and re-postings, locking the old accounting period in CO, and re-opening the G/L for adjustment postings.

There are also some **closing activities for external purposes** listed as follows:
- CO: Reconciliation posting to FI for cross-organizational units.
- FI: Foreign currency valuations and financial statement adjustments.
- Technical: Final closing of the old period.
- FI-CO: Generate external and internal reports.

Year-End Activities

In the last period of a fiscal year, the month-end activities need to be performed as usual besides the year-end activities.

Before the actual month-end closing activities, the following **set of pre-closing activities** needs to be carried out:

• From a technical perspective: open the initial accounting period for the new fiscal year in FI.
• MM: perform a physical inventory count.
• PP/CO: update the product cost estimates.
• MM: use the lowest value determination method and LIFO/FIFO valuation.
• AA: Asset valuations and investment support.
• FI: carry out balance confirmation for customers and vendors.
• Other technical step: fiscal year change in AA and balance carry-forward in FI.

Closing activities for external purposes **need to be performed for the following**:
• FI - GR/IR: analyze clearing accounts, receivables and payables reclassification, reconciliation of prior year into the new-year, and other adjustment postings.
• Technical step: perform the final close of the old period in AR, AP and G/L.
• FI-CO: generate external and internal reports.

Integration with Controlling

CO - FI Reconciliation

Prior to the introduction of ECC 5.0 a program had to be run for CO to reconcile with Financial Accounting. Currently, postings in FI to an expense account charge a CO object (such as a cost center) systemically, based on the cost element that is linked with the G/L expense account.
Furthermore, CO document changes are reflected in FI in real-time.

Therefore, transaction KALC previously used for adjustment/reconciliation postings is no longer available once the new G/L is activated. In addition, users can easily move between CO and FI associated documents, because the real-time CO-FI integration creates an FI follow-on document for each activity, as opposed to a totals posting at the end of the month.

Company code validation for the related controlling area **needs to be activated** in order **to use real-time integration** in a company code.

Variants for CO and FI Real-Time Integration

Variants need to be defined during customization to handle postings in CO that will be addressed by FI objects.

Steps for Variants for CO and FI Real-Time Integration:

Step 1: Definition of variants for CO and FI real time integration during customization.
Step 2: Variant for CO are assigned to the company code(s).
Step 3: Specify characteristic changes responsible for real-time FI line items.
Step 4: Effective key date for the activation of CO–FI reconciliation.
Step 5: Define an account assignment for the transfer of secondary cost elements from CO to FI.

Real-Time Integration CO and FI: Trace/Log

The CO and FI real-time integration can be logged with a trace for analysis purposes.

The trace needs to have been active during the specific CO posting in order to analyze the posting data. Information provided includes:
- Document number of the original CO document.
- Evidence that the transaction pertained to a transfer or a test run.
- The document number of the follow-up document in FI.
- The reason for the transfer or the reason for a failed transfer.
- The posting mode: either an online posting or a subsequent transfer.
- Posting date, time and user.
- Line item data for the documents, including posted objects and partner objects.

For convenience a trace should not be activated in the real-time integration variant, because it would permanently be active for all users, and could no longer be deactivated. On the other hand, this would result in numerous undesired log entries.

However, if the trace is not activated in the real-time integration variant, there is an option to activate and deactivate it on a user-specific basis at any time.

Periodic Processing

The use of the New G/L **saves time during periodic closing and reconciliation** operations, which results into acceleration of period end activities and lower total cost of ownership (TCO).

Eliminated closing activities previously required for the Classic ledger include:

- Maintenance of the reconciliation ledger
- Balance sheet adjustments
- Profit and loss adjustments
- Maintenance of the FI-SL ledger(s)
- Other tasks related to segment reporting

The following periodic processing tasks were not eliminated with the advent of the New G/L, but were changed:

- Balance carry-forward (in FI)
- Reclassification/sorting of receivables and payables
- Flat-rate individual value adjustment

Technical Steps

The balance carry-forward program should be run at the beginning of every fiscal year, to roll over G/L account balances from the previous fiscal year.

Profit and Loss (P&L) accounts only:

• In a multi-currency environment an indicator in the master record of the P&L carry-forward account can be set for systemic translation and summarization of all currencies. The program can be run as many times as needed, and can even be run in the old fiscal year. Furthermore, when balances are carried forward to a new year, all new transactions are directly taken into consideration.

Balances for Accounts Receivable and Accounts Payables are carried forward to the following year with a different program (SAPF010). On the other hand, a separate program (SAPFGVTR) is used to carry-forward year-end balances for additional ledgers.

The purpose of the technical reconciliation is to perform consistency checks that cover the entire Financial Accounting module and its sub-modules. Checks performed include:

• Debit and credit transaction figures for customer accounts, vendor accounts, and G/L accounts are checked against the debit and credit totals of all posted documents.

• Debit and credit transaction figures for customer accounts, vendor accounts, and G/L accounts are checked against the debit and credit totals of the application index.

Posting Period Control

The posting periods available for a company code **depend on the** Fiscal **Year variant** defined during customization. The Fiscal Year variant can be used for the System settings here below:
□ Beginning and end of your fiscal year
□ Number of "normal" posting periods (01 to 16)
□ Number of special periods (up to 16 **after normal** periods)
□ Posting period length

Posting periods are managed through the posting period table that is used to close and open posting periods. There is **no limit to the number of posting periods that can be open** concurrently.

The first column in the table (labeled var.) shows the **posting period variant**; which is a code **assigned to the company codes** to handle the opening and closing for posting periods. A **single posting period variant can** be shared by **multiple company codes**.

Var.	A	From acct.	To account	Period 1			Period 2			
				From per. 1	Year	To per. 1	Year	From per. 2	Year	To per. 2

The second column in the posting periods table (labeled A) contains the account type. Account types can be designated as:

"**+**" in reference to all accounts
"**A**" in reference to assets
"**D**" in reference to customer accounts
"**K**" in reference to vendor accounts
"**S**" in reference to G/L accounts

This feature **enables control** of the open posting periods **by account type**. Accounts are open or closed as per the specification in the table. Each posting period that is supposed to be open must at least indicate account type + (valid for all account types).

The posting period table has an additional column where **authorization groups** can be assigned to selected open periods in the Period 1 interval. Authorization groups are used to enable particular groups of users to continue making postings in interval 1 even after the period has been closed.

Documentary Steps

The purpose of a balance audit trail is to:
• Display posting details for a specific fiscal year and document a status in Financial Accounting.
• Provide a statement for external auditors.

By law a company should always be able to provide support for account balances for more than one fiscal year, by tracing account balances to the relevant document items. Therefore, all relevant documents need to be retrievable.

Normally older documents are archived and deleted from the database in order to reduce system load. To explain an account balance in such a case requires that the balance audit trail is started prior to archiving any documents. As a result, the compact journal will be generated for a period, in the form of a list.

The balance audit trail provides the account balance at the beginning of a period with all related changes, followed by the resulting account balance at the end of a period.

There are three balance audit trail types based on the way the **posting data** is displayed:
- Historical Balance Audit Trail
- Open Item Balance Audit Trail
- Accumulated Balance Audit Trail

Closing Cockpit

Overview of the Closing Cockpit:
The Closing Cockpit offers the following features to support closing activities:
- **Hierarchies** that display organizational objects involved in the closing process.
- A **task list template** that portrays the organizational structure.
- A detailed view of the **characteristic values** in each hierarchy level of the task list template.
- **Task lists** based on the task list template.
- A **list display** that portrays all executable tasks from the respective task lists for processing or monitoring progress.
- A **monitor** that outlines the sequence of tasks and respective statuses, dependencies, and critical paths in a graphical form.
- **Detailed information** for the evaluation of the technical settings of tasks and the analysis of background programs (spool, job log information).
- **Dependencies** that display preconditions for processing individual tasks.

The **monitor** provides:
- Access to messages and result lists.
- Visualization of complete technical information and business information.
- The opportunity to postpone a task.
- A view of the work performed by users including the related processing sequence, and the technical and business status.
- The ability to monitor the full progress of period-end closing when several task lists are in use.

Advantages of the Closing Cockpit:
- Process Recurring periodic tasks
- Process flow determined by dependencies

- Provides uniform interface for all users
- Documentation of status of all periodic activities
- Allows shared access to tasks involving multiple responsible agents

It is essential to note that the following data **never changes in recurring entries**:
- Posting key
- Account
- Amounts

Potential Applications of the Closing Cockpit

The Closing Cockpit can be used to create a structured interface for the execution of transactions and programs related to complex processes that involve multiple organizational structures.

Particular cases where the Closing Cockpit can be used as an application tool include:
- Recurring periodic activities.
- Shared access for tasks involving multiple actors with managerial duties.
- Activities that require a fixed chronological sequence or determined by dependencies.
- Providing a common user interface for a set of shared tasks.
- Need for transparent documentation for periodic activity status.
- Providing detailed documentation for closing tasks.

Procedure for the Closing Cockpit

Step 1 – Define organizational hierarchy: define the organizational structure in the closing process.
Step 2 – Create template: create a template that will be used to schedule the entire chain process for the closing.
Step 3 – Create tasks: define all individual activities in a chronological sequence to structure transactions and programs.
Step 4 – Define dependencies: define the program and transaction sequences for each preceding task.
Step 5 – Create task list: extract the actual task list from the template after conversion
Step 6 – Release task list: transfer the configured task list into the application, and maintain the status for the task list execution.

Closing Cockpit: Task Types

Transactions and background processing for programs and flow definitions for the Closing Cockpit (CLOCO) application are directly accessible from the main interface.

There are **four types of tasks available** therein:

• **Programs**: Programs can be included in the task list template with corresponding variants to enable background processing. Programs without variants can be directly started from the Closing Cockpit (online).

• **Online transactions**: can be started manually from the task list.

• **Note**: used for documentary purposes, such as a reminder or milestone.

• **Flow definition**: represents the logical flow of programs (with variants) based on predecessor and successor relationships. The programs will run systemically in the correct sequence, and detailed processing results will be availed for analysis.

Once the task list has been released, the tasks defined in the task list are selected and scheduled in the Closing Cockpit (CLOCO) application.

Monitor: Status of Flight Destinations
The monitor shows you the processing status of the tasks:
▫ Blue: Scheduled
▫ Gray: Initial
▫ Green: Ended without errors
▫ Red: Canceled or ended with errors
▫ White: Active
▫ Yellow: Ended with warnings

Foreign Currency Valuation

Foreign currency open items and balance sheet accounts are valuated to fulfill various business and legal requirements. Exchange rates change regularly. Therefore, when a balance sheet account contains an open item in a foreign currency account, the actual value of the item is subject to change, in reference to the original exchange rate that was used when the item was posted to the balance sheet account. A **foreign currency valuation** is the means used to measure the item value change, based on the current exchange rate. The amount corresponding to the item value change will post systemically to the relevant account(s) at the end of the process.

The foreign currency valuation needs to be performed **prior to the financial statements creation**. The valuation is based on the accounts and items below:
• Foreign currency balance sheet accounts, where the G/L accounts are managed in a foreign currency.
• Open items posted in foreign currency to vendor accounts, customer accounts and G/L accounts.

Foreign Currency valuation addresses the effects of exchange rate fluctuations on business transactions. For instance, a vendor invoice is posted in foreign currency for $14,000 on January 10 at Euro/$ ROE 1.25. Assuming that the euro/dollar exchange rate later falls as of the key date of February 27, the Payables in Euro will be higher than on the posting date. Therefore, an expense corresponding to the increase or decrease of the Euro would need to be entered in order to maintain the balance. The correction posting is performed by running program FAGL_FC_VALUATION.

A Valuation run requires:
• The definition of **a valuation area** (from FI) during customization
• Assignment of **a valuation method** (not possible during the actual run)

The valuation method indicates how the valuation is run and specifies the valuation approach to be used, for instance "the maximum principle for payables".

For **overall balance valuation** (which excludes valuation of line items); the **valuation area** in Customizing must be combined with an **accounting principle**. An accounting principle is also needed for **contexts that involve multiple valuation approaches** (such as IAS and local).

In addition, **multiple valuation areas are also needed in contexts that involve parallel accounting**. In a context that only needs the local valuation approach; a single valuation area will be used. Valuation area IDs and names can be freely defined.

Note should be taken that the valuation areas mentioned above are not to be confused with the depreciation areas in Asset Accounting – these are two completely different things.

Settings made for **foreign currency (FC) Valuation** during customization cover:

• **Account determination for transaction KDF** (Exch. rate diff. open items/G/L account) for the chart of accounts.

• **Valuation area**

• Specification of a **G/L account for reconciliation accounts**: vendor payables and customer receivables.

• **Definition of valuation accounts** for expense, revenue, FS correction (balance sheet correction account).

Before a foreign currency (FC) posting can be created, **the expense and correction accounts must already be defined in the system**.

The foreign currency valuation program FAGL_FC_VALUATION normally requires a valuation area. Nevertheless, relevant **accounts can be defined without a valuation area**, whereby the valuation area field is "blank".

When document splitting is active, FI entities from vendor invoice/open items are inherited in the foreign currency valuation documents. Otherwise, the accounts are only supplied with the corresponding values, and the FI entities will not be inherited in the correction posting.

When FC pertains to the valuation of balances, it is possible to correct the valuation a second time, on the first day of the next month. This also applies for open line items.

The **revaluation amount** can be posted **online** to the original CO object that was directly charged in CO. The application of this approach **requires configuration for**:

• Document splitting must be active with expense, revenue, and correction accounts defined as item categories

• Document splitting characteristics need to be defined for CO

• Definition of a revaluation account as primary cost element

Receivables & Payables

Balance Confirmation

The balance carry-forward program is run at the very beginning of each fiscal year to rollover all balance sheet account balances from the previous fiscal year into the new one.

The posting periods pertaining to the old fiscal year need to be blocked, whereas, **the special periods** for closing postings **need to be opened**. This should be followed by a technical reconciliation to rule out any posting issues.

At this point the **account balances should be confirmed**, the foreign currency documents valuated, the values adjusted, and the receivables/payables regrouped.

There is a program that creates balance **confirmations**, a **reconciliation list** and a **results table** systemically. Balance confirmations are printed along with reply slips for that need to be sent to the selected vendors and customers.

The reports that create correspondence to check the balance of payables and receivables offer the following options:
□ Balance Confirmation
□ Balance notification
□ Balance request

Value Adjustments

Adjustment of Receivables can be **categorized in three types**:
□ Individual value adjustment (IVA)
□ Flat-rate individual value adjustment
□ Flat-rate value adjustment (FVA)

The options available for creating value adjustments for receivables include:
• Entry of individual value adjustments (IVA) as a special G/L transaction E.
• Use of program SAPF107 "Additional valuations", to carry out flat-rate individual value adjustments.

• Determine the amount of the value adjustment, followed by adjustment of the flat-rate value through a manual G/L account posting (the posting entry will be as follows: Expense from flat-rate value adjustment to value adjustment).

When an owing customer repeatedly gets behind on payments, **the debt becomes a doubtful receivable**. Doubtful receivables need to be written off as an **individual value adjustment** (IVA) during the year-end close. SAP ERP provides the ability to **perform systemic flat-rate individual value adjustments for overdue receivables**.

The **debit rate percentage** (bad debt expense percentage) **for a valuation adjustment key** and an **overdue time period in days** will need to be specified in the configuration for Accounts Receivable in order **to use the automatic adjustment** feature.
Expense accounts for the adjustment and **bad debt expense for doubtful receivables** should also need to be setup **in the account determination table**.

A **valuation adjustment key** must be assigned to the **master record of all customer accounts** that are to be affected by the flat-rate individual value adjustment posting.

Regrouping

Payables and receivables need to be displayed separately in a balance sheet. Occasionally, **some vendor accounts will have a debit balance**, and **some customer accounts will have a credit balance**. The listing on the balance sheet for these accounts needs to be changed according to the account balance, prior to producing financial statements.

Some countries require that payables be grouped in the balance sheet according to their remaining life. Receivables with extensive remaining terms need to be reposted to different accounts before the financial statements can be created.

The two types of regroupings are performed through a special program (Report SAPF101) that regroups and sorts the receivables and payables. **This functionality is used to**:
• Sort receivables and payables according to the remaining life and perform the relevant transfer postings.
• Make adjustment postings for changed reconciliation accounts.

- Determine transactions that require transfer postings.

Customization options for a sort method are used to select the cases where receivables and payables should be regrouped.

Profit and Loss

Accrual/Deferral Postings

A **deferral** is needed when an expense or revenue is **posted in the current period**, though it entirely or partly **pertains to a future period.**

An **accrual** is needed when an expense or revenue pertains to the current period, though it will be received in a future period when the invoice is received or issued.

In both cases an expense or revenue will be **posted in the current period** then **reversed in the following period**. The goal is to ensure that the final recording of the expense/revenue is performed in the period where it effectively belongs. If the following month is not the period where the amounts belongs; the postings and reversals may have to be performed for several consecutive periods.

Every accrual/deferral document must be recorded with a reversal reason. The reversal reason indicates whether:
- The reversal document **can have a different posting date.**
- The reversal document **can include negative postings.**

The Accrual Engine

The **Accrual Engine** is a standard tool that calculates accruals and posts them.

The application component is **delivered with predefined special accrual scenarios** that **customers cannot change** in any manner. **The Accrual Engine can be used for**:
- Manual Accruals in Financial Accounting
- Provisions for Awards
- Lease Accounting

◻ Intellectual Property Management

Two types of data can be stored in the Accrual Engine:
• **Basic Data**
Basic data incorporates the **description of the accrual object** and any **other relevant information** needed to perform the accruals. Basic data is **time-dependent**.

• **Accrual Engine Documents and Totals Records**
Accrual postings **create documents in the Accrual Engine** known as Accrual Engine documents, and they **update fiscal year-specific totals records**. The **Accrual Engine documents create matching documents in Financials systemically**. Any eventual errors that occur during the Financials update can be fixed by a manual re-run.

Two main processes are started from the application component:
• **Creation and change of basic data:** normally results in the immediate creation of an opening posting.
• **Periodic start of the accrual run:** results in the reversal of an accrual run.

Benefits of using the Accrual Engine:
• Automatic calculation of accrual amounts.
• Automatic performance-optimized periodic posting of accruals with mass data processing.
• Simulation of planned future accruals, and other complete simulation scenarios.
• Support for parallel accounting with different account areas or with parallel ledgers.
• Extensive Information System for planned accruals and processed accruals.

Steps **to activate an application component of the Accrual Engine** include:
• Assignment of the application component to the relevant company codes.
• Definition of the required accounting principles.
• Assignment of the application component to the correct accounting principle and company code combination.
• Opening the **current** fiscal year for the application component.

Closing Activities of the Accrual Engine:
A limited set of technical activities suffice to close the Accrual Engine:
• **Reconciliation: Accrual Engine/General Ledger**

The Accrual Engine documents are reconciled with the matching documents in the General Ledger for error prevention and consistency.

• **Balance carry-forward**

At the end of the fiscal year, the balances of the accruals objects need to be rolled over to the next fiscal year. This is entirely distinct from the balance carry-forward of the General Ledger.

Manual Accruals

The "Manual Accruals", application component is based on a **simple user interface** that is used to **manually** create the basic data.

Two **function modules** are available to import accrual objects from a database table using a batch job:
ACAC_OBJECT_CREATE_EXT is used to create an accrual object.
ACAC_OBJECT_MODIFY_EXT is used to change an accrual object or to create one.

Before the function module is called up to load data into the Accrual Engine, **a report needs to be written to select and export data, and then adjust the function module's structur**e.

The periodic posting for accruals is labeled "Expense to Other Payables" or "Provisions" and is posted to account:
▫ **Other payables**: If the accrual reason and amount are clearly known.
▫ **Provisions**: If the accrual reason or amount is uncertain, and needs to be estimated.

In manual accruals, the **subject to be accrued** is defined as an **accrual object** in the "Manual Accruals" application component. These accrual objects are uniquely identified for each company code by an accrual object number, based on a defined number range. They will later be grouped in **accrual object categories**, to summarize the subject matter for other such accrual objects.

Each accrual object can be associated with various **accrual items** that will be calculated **based on a combination of** the related **accrual type** and an **accounting principle**.

Accrual items contain the **amount** to be accrued, an **accrual method** and sometimes a quantity to be accrued. A **function module** for accrual calculation needs to be defined for the accrual method. Predefined function modules (with a ACE_DS_* prefix) are delivered with the system, and customers can also **develop their own function modules** for the accruals.

Posting Control and Account Determination

The Accrual Engine **posting control** is defined for each:
▫ Company code
▫ Accounting principle
▫ Accrual type

The specifications involved pertain to:
• The **frequency** of accruals (options available: periodic, daily, monthly, quarterly, every six months, annually).
• The **summarization** level for postings prior to the update in FI (options available: No summarization, Summarization at accrual object level, Maximum summarization).

The **purpose of account determination** for the Accrual Engine is to determine:
▫ The **document type**
▫ The **debit account**
▫ The **credit account**

Customization for **account determination** is necessary for each **accrual type used to perform systemic postings**. Options available are
• None (the accruals are still calculated in the Accrual Engine, but not posted).
• Only the opening posting.
• Only periodic postings.
• All (opening posting, periodic accruals, and premature termination, closing posting).

In the context of **Parallel Accounting, the Accrual Engine supports**:
▫ Parallel accounts
▫ Parallel ledgers

For Parallel Accounting to function, the account determination of the Accrual Engine needs to be configured in such a way that the relevant accounts can be **found based on the accounting principle**. A separate ledger should be setup for the relevant accounting principle during customization for **parallel accounting**.

The accounts are identified through **derivation rules**. These rules comprise:
- **Conditions** by which the derivation rule is executed (this is optional)
- **Fields** associated to the derivation rule. Definitions are needed for:
  - The **Source fields**
  - The Target **fields**
- **Rule entries** to derive the input for the target fields from the content of the source fields.

Derivation rules are summarized in a **set of rules**. The derivation rules are processed either in parallel or sequentially.
- **Parallel derivation** rules are processed **sequentially** to provide **independent results**.
- **Sequential derivation** rules are created in a **specific order** to provide **cumulative results**.

Chapter 8 - Reporting

Information Systems

Reports in the FI-G/L, FI-AR, and FI-AP areas normally start with RFxxx. Based on the prefix the reports can be categorized as follows:

RFK___ Accounts payable reports, for instance RFKOFW00: open items – vendor due date forecast

RFD___ Accounts receivable reports, for instance RFDABL00: displays changes to customers

RFS___ G/L accounts reports, for instance RFSKPL00: Chart of accounts, RFSKVZ00: G/L account list

RFB___ document reports, for instance RFBELJ00: compact document journal

The **program documentation** can be displayed by selecting "**I**".

The Accounts Payable information system is subdivided into various reports for vendor balances, vendor items, master data, and payment transactions. It provides all the reports that are essentially needed for accounts payable information.

Dynamic Selections is a feature that provides various selection options, such as industry, account group, country, city, etc. Selections and output control are used to restrict data displayed as needed.

Report Variants and Variables

A report variant holds different **selection criteria**. To avoid entering the same values for the selection criteria pertaining to a frequently run report, the values can be recorded a single time and then **saved as a variant**. The variant makes the selection criteria permanently available. Multiple **report variants** can be defined for a single report.

Variant attributes are recorded under a **variant name**, followed by a **description**. If the **"Only for background processing"** field is selected, the variant is only usable for background processing. If the latter is not selected, the variant is usable for background and online processing. If the **Protect variant** field is selected, then only the variant creator can modify it.

Additional properties can be assigned to certain fields; the properties include: **protect a field**, **hide a field**, or a **required entry field**.

The **Selection Variable** pushbutton, accessible in the **selection screen object** maintenance, can be used to **set report** display to certain **key dates**. There **are two types of selection variables**:
□ Table variables from TVARV
□ Dynamic date calculation

• **Table variables from TVARV**: are used to store statistical information that can be used in various reports. Parameters in TVARV can be maintained for **single values or intervals**. Saved selections are usable in any other report variants and reports.

• **Dynamic date calculations:** the corresponding selection criterion in the intended program must be a **type D** (date). If the selection variable is changed from **type T** to **type D**, the *Name of Variables* field will no longer be available for input. Values can be set by using input help.

List Viewer

The SAP List Viewer can be used to display **simple and hierarchical sequential lists**. It has various **interactive functions** such as **sorting**, **summation**, **filters**, etc. The layout of lists can be changed without selecting any data.

Functions for document display and change include:
Select detail - to get detailed information pertaining to an item.

Select items - to select a single item or multiple items. Multiple items are selected by holding **Ctrl**, and selecting the items. After the selection of multiple items, **mass change** can be carried out in the associated documents.

SAP List Viewer also includes the following generic cross-application functions: **Select columns**, **sort**, **filters**, **Summation** (for totals and subtotals).

The SAP List Viewer offers two display options:
• **ALV classic list** – this is basically the **print screen** and offers an enhanced **overview of the sorted list** when the items for multiple accounts are displayed.
• **ALV grid control** – this uses proportionate text and is very suitable to **display individual accounts online** for Internet services offered by SAP programs.

Selections

Specific **selection criteria** can be used to choose line items for evaluation, based on:
▫ Accounts in the line items of certain company codes.
▫ Other available selection criteria.
▫ Line items with a specific status and category.

The following selections can be made for the **list output**:
▫ Layout
▫ Maximum number of items

If the **Worklists Available** field is selected, the **input fields for worklists** can be activated and deactivated on the selection screen for each line item list. Worklist items are maintainable.

When items are selected using **search help**, the system provides:
▫ Input help for the G/L account line item list.
▫ Input help for the vendor line item list.
▫ Input help for the customer line item list.

Besides selecting columns, users can create or change the layout, and also define **sort criteria for sorting** and creating **subtotals**. During posting, the **assignment** field for a line item based on the **Sort Field entry** is completed systemically. The assignment field can be a combination of up to four fields with a **maximum of 18 characters**.

Changing the Screen Layout

SAP ERP is delivered with several **standard layouts** that can be supplemented with other layouts. All standard layout names begin with a **slash (/)**. A standard layout can be chosen as the **default layout**. When the indicator for a display variant is set as the **initial variant**, the variant is always used for the list output unless an alternative display variant has been specified.
A **user-specific layout** can be chosen if the required authorizations to save user-specific display variants are available.

Financial Statement Versions

Financial Statement Versions (FSV) are used to define the **format for displaying accounts**. Financial Statement Versions can be created for **different organizational structures, in any language, and for any currency** based on specific currency types.
Different outputs for financial statements can be generated with the standard report (RFBILA00) that is delivered with SAP ERP. The system predefined FSVs **can be copied and modified** to suit particular needs.

Report formats for the financial statement version are configured by specifying:
• The items to include and the sequence and hierarchy of the items.
• The description for the items.
•The specific charts of accounts and the individual accounts pertaining to the report.
• The total amounts to be displayed.

A financial statement version (FSV) is **defined at the chart of account level in two steps**:
• Make an entry for the new FSV in the directory of financial statement versions

• Define the required hierarchy levels and assign the accounts hierarchically in a tree structure.

Each version **must include the "special items"** listed below:
◻ Assets
◻ Liabilities
◻ Profit
◻ Loss
◻ Profit and loss results
◻ Accounts not assigned
◻ Notes to Financial Statement

The **net profit/loss and the profit and loss results are calculated based on the same report that is used to create the financial statement**. All accounts that were not assigned to an item in the financial statement version under the item **Non-assigned Accounts** will appear at the bottom of the report. **Any number of financial statement versions can be defined for a particular chart of accounts.**

A financial statement version can have a **maximum of 20 hierarchy levels**.
• Items need to be assigned at each level. Totals and subtotals will be calculated systemically for each item.
• A descriptive text needs to be assigned to each item (maximum allowed is four lines).
• Accounts names and balances for the lowest levels need to be assigned accordingly.

Account group assignments are used to indicate whether the balance of a certain account group should be listed in a particular financial statement item. The account group assignment will **indicate whether an account balance should be listed under assets or liabilities if the amount is a debit or a credit**.

In addition, the profit and loss statement hierarchy needs to be maintained in the same manner as assets and liabilities for a balance sheet.

Classic G/L Accounting and New G/L Accounting

Once the New Ledger has been activated, the Classic Ledger needs to be deactivated immediately after running and verifying the first period.

An option is available for comparison of the Leading Ledger to the non-leading ledgers.

> The **classic report** RFBILA00 **remains available as an option** for creating balance sheet and profit & loss statements, even after activating the New G/L. Enhancements to report RFBILA00 include:
> • A selection screen for choosing the ledger for which to run analyses.
> • Dynamic selections for the selection or restriction of additional entities.

There are different methods of calculating profits in Profit Center Accounting, based on the:
□ **Time** reference (this can be periodic or transaction-oriented).
□ **Content** (period costs or cost-of-sales).
□ **Valuation** base or form of representation (account-based or costing-based).

Basically, profit is calculated using the **period accounting method** or the **cost-of-sales method**.

In **period accounting**, the profit and loss statement is organized based on income types and expenses.

In **Cost of sales accounting**, the sales revenues for the accounting period are set against the resulting costs of goods manufactured for the deducted service. In addition, expenses are assigned with priority to the functional areas within a company. In New General Ledger Accounting, the totals table (FAGLFLEXT) updates the functional areas if the Cost—of-Sales scenario is assigned to a ledger.

Drilldown Reporting in the New G/L

A **drilldown report** located directly above RFBILA00 is offered as an **alternative to the conventional financial statements**. The drilldown report can be run in a classic or graphical layout.

The drilldown report has the following benefits over RFBILA00:
• Drilldown reports offer much more flexibility then the "old" ABAP programs.

• Drilldown reports allow direct selection based on characteristics such profit center, business area, functional area, segment, company code, account number, partner objects.

However, **it is highly suggested to use classic drilldown** reporting to **display the G/L account balances.** There are three important facts about G/L account balance display:
• The appropriate ledger can be selected from the selection screen.
• Characteristics for dynamic selections can be defined during customization.
• Double-clicking on a balance value displays the line item with the general ledger view.

The **Profit Center** and the **Segmen**t are the G/L **account assignments** of the **standard drilldown**.

For analysis purposes, the **object list** can be used to display payables sorted by profit center or payables per vendor. The object list provides a wider range of results in comparison with other output types, because the values are issued in combination with a document number.

Drilldown Reporting Architecture

Drilldown reporting is an information system tool for navigating in a dataset, and for interactively processing reports. It also evaluates FI, G/L, AR, AP databases, **but mainly** analyzes **G/L account transaction figures** and **financial statements**. Drilldown lists are **also suitable for variance analyses** such as plan/actual comparisons, fiscal year comparisons, etc.

SAP Graphics, SAPmail, Microsoft Word for Windows and Microsoft Excel are all linked to drilldown reporting. A **report definition** may include **characteristics, key figures, and forms**.

Using the Report Painter

Report types that are **usable for G/L account evaluations** include:
• Reports for financial statement analysis - based on the **financial statement versions** defined in Financial Accounting, **any number of variance analysis can be performed on actual and planned data.**

• **Key figure reports** - where the System only considers **the financial statement items** in the financial statement version **that are needed for the calculation of specific key figures**.
• **Balance display** - for account **Balance display and Line item analysis.**

The graphic interface of the **Report Painter can be used to define Report Writer reports, drilldown forms, and planning layouts**.

A **form** provides the **basic content and formal structure of report lists.** A form is like a half finished product for a report; that needs characteristics and key figures to become a complete report.

Characteristics and Key Figures

Characteristics describe classification alternatives for the dataset. Typical characteristics include: **company code**, **business area**, and **plan/actual indicator**. Characteristics from a time perspective include: **fiscal year**, **period**.
Characteristic values represent actual characteristics. Potential values for the **company code** characteristic are 0004, 0006 3030.
When a **characteristic** is combined with the corresponding **characteristic values** it becomes an **object** in drilldown reporting.

Key figures are combinations of **values, quantities** and the resulting **calculations** based on user-defined formulas.
Here below are some typical key figures:
□ **Value**: Balance sheet value, debit total, sales/purchases.
□ **Quantity**: Number of items, sales quantity.
□ **Calculation**: Sales per division, plan/actual variance.

Drilldown List/Detail List

Each drilldown report is based on various lists. The number of lists that form the report depends on the number of selected characteristics and related values. Information is displayed using **two types of lists**:
□ **Detail list**
□ **Drilldown list**

Inquiries: support@sapseries.com

• A **drilldown list** is **a** set of **several objects** that are formatted using a selection of key figures. **Key figures** are normally represented by **the columns** of the list, whereas **characteristic values** are represented by **the row**.

• A **detail list** is an **individual object** that is formatted for all key figures depending on the form. **Key figures** are normally represented by **the rows** of the detail list.

Form Types

A form is created by **defining a name** and the **type of form** that needs to be processed.

• **Single-axis form without key figure**
To use a single-axis form without key figures, **define the form rows or the columns for characteristics**. Proceed to the initial screen to display an **empty list of columns**. Then make **selections in the characteristics columns** only.

• **Single-axis form with key figure**
To use a single-axis form with key figures, define **either the form rows or the columns** with **key figures and characteristics**. Proceed to the initial screen to display an **empty list of rows**.
The key figures will be integrated with **characteristics in the rows** of the form.

• **Dual-axis form with key figure**
To use a dual-axis form with key figures, define **the form rows and the columns** with **key figures and characteristics**. The rows can contain key figures while the columns can contain the characteristics, or vice versa. To define the corresponding **report**, you only need to select the **drilldown characteristics**.

The elements needed **to create a customer-specific drilldown** report are **a form** and **characteristics.**

Navigating in Reports

There are options to switch back and forth between lists:

To switch from the drilldown list to the **detail list** select the Detail list symbol. To return to the basic list select the XX symbol in red. To switch from the detail list to the drilldown list, select Drilldown list.

Form and Report Definition

SAP ERP is delivered with some standard forms that can be used as templates for the creation of personal forms. These standard forms range from name 0SAPBLNCE-01 to 0SAPBLNCE-NN.

To define the characteristics for a form, first define the general characteristics that apply to all the columns of the form. Then define the characteristics for each distinct column. Characteristics should be selected wisely, in order to limit the quantity of data selected and to enhance system time response.

Report-Report Interface and Report Assignment

A **report-report interface** is an option that is usable when a **report on a large number of characteristics or changing combinations of characteristics** is needed. The use of this option is meant to avoid the limitations that occur when reporting on a very large volume of data online.
A report-report interface can connect several individual reports, each containing a limited number of characteristics. Typical uses include:
• Connecting reports that contain different characteristics in an application.
• Connecting reports created in different application classes.

SAP Query

SAP Query is a tool that can **create personalized queries**. It is intended for users who have no knowledge or little knowledge of the SAP ABAP programming language.
SAP Query provides various ways to define reporting programs and to create **different types of** reports such as basic lists, statistics, and ranked lists.
SAP Query has several subareas including:

• **InfoSets** are the foundation of a query and are assembled from one or more database tables

Inquiries: support@sapseries.com

• **Queries and InfoSet Queries** are used to rapidly generate simple classic reports such as lists, statistics, and ranked lists for prepared datasets, namely the InfoSets.

• **User groups** are used to differentiate application and to assign the required datasets as needed.

• **Translations** are text modules of stored queries provided for the application in different countries.

• **QuickViewer** is a tool used to display simple but very restricted datasets.

Defining a report requires entries for individual texts, such as titles, fields and options which determine the report layout.

Creating reports with **SAP Query** starts with the creation of infosets, followed by the designation of a name for the infoset. The relevant tables will later need to be selected and joined based on the reporting needs.
Creating reports with the **Quickviewer** starts the designation of a quickviewer name. Relevant tables will later need to be selected and joined, and the fields needed in the report should be selected from the tables. The report layout name can be changed when needed, using **"layout mode"**.
The main advantage of SAP Query over QuickViewer is that a query **can be shared with a group of users**.

Business Intelligence

SAP BW can be used to analyze data from SAP ERP applications or any other business application. It can also be used to extract and analyze data from external sources such as databases, online services, and the Internet.

BW runs on separate data-warehouse servers to process reporting activities as an independent business component. It has its own database and SAP System known as SAP Business Information Warehouse.

Essential Business Intelligence terminology includes:

InfoObject

InfoObjects are Business analysis-objects in BW, such as companies, sales volumes, that can be divided into characteristics and key figures.

- **Characteristics** can be divided into units, time characteristics, and technical characteristics.
- **Key figures** are represented by data fields used to store values or quantities.
- **Characteristics** are the descriptive connection with key figures.

InfoCube

InfoCubes are the central data containers that form the basis for reports and analyses.
They store key figures (such as sales volumes, actual costs) and are related to the characteristics (master data of the SAP BW system such as cost centers, customers).

- Key figures and characteristics are **InfoObjects**.
- Each distinct **InfoCube** normally stores a self-contained dataset.

Master data in BW comprises:
- Attributes of a characteristic (such as the person responsible for a cost center).
- Hierarchies and texts of a characteristic.

An **InfoCube** consists of several database tables that are linked according to the star schema. They include a fact table that contains the InfoCube key figures, as well as several surrounding dimension tables that store the links to the characteristics.

InfoCubes are stored in structures in the SAP BW. A new folder or an existing one can be used to store an **InfoCube.** These folders are called **InfoAreas** in SAP BW.

InfoProvider

InfoProvider is a generic term for objects that can be used to create reports in Business Explorer (BEx). InfoProviders include a wide range of database **metaobjects** that provide data for query definitions. Data from InfoProviders can be analyzed using a query.

There are **two types of data stores**: physical stores and operational data stores.
- **Physical stores** include:

□ BasicCubes
□ ODS Objects
□ InfoObjects

• **Logical views of physical data** stores include:
□ InfoSets
□ RemoteCubes
□ VirtualInfoCubes
□ MultiProviders

The BEx view only gives access to **InfoProviders**. The way data is modeled does not have any effect on the BEx toolset.

• **Operational Data Store** (ODS):
An ODS is a data store used for data at the basic level (document level). It is suitable to resolve and consolidate datasets from various data sources and source systems.

The **Administrator Workbench** (AWB) is a workplace for SAP BW administrators. It provides the functions needed to configure, control, and administer SAP BW, besides monitoring and maintaining all data procurement processes.

Business Intelligence Architecture

Information staging for large amounts of operative and historical data can be done in BW with Online Analytical Processing (OLAP). OLAP technology can perform multi-dimensional analyses based on various business perspectives.

• The BW server is preconfigured by Business Content for core areas and processes. It is able to examine the relationships in every area within a company.
• Business Content provides companies with targeted information divided into roles to help employees carry out their tasks, as well as roles.
• Business Content includes other preconfigured objects such as InfoCubes, queries, key figures, and characteristics that facilitate the implementation of SAP BW.
• The Business Explorer (known as BEx) component enables users to make extensive analyses.

Reporting in Business Warehouse

BEx is the key component in SAP BW that provides flexible reporting and analysis for strategic analysis and decision-making support for a company.

BEx allows a wide range of users to access information in SAP BW, using Enterprise Portal from an **iView** to extract data from applications on the Internet or Intranet (Web Application Design), or using a mobile device (such as WAP-enabled mobile telephones).

Possibilities for **Query, Reporting and Analysis include**:
(1) Query design using the BEx Analyzer
(2) Multi-dimensional (OLAP) analysis
(3) Geographical analysis
(4) Ad-hoc reporting
(5) Alerts

The SAP BW reporting functions can be used to evaluate a dataset from an **InfoProvider** based on various characteristics and key figures. Main steps for the evaluation:
• Definition of a query for a chosen InfoProvider in the **BEX Query Designer**.
• Selection and combination of the **InfoObjects in a query** (to determine how data in the InfoProvider should be evaluated).

SAP Certification Practice Tests

The practice tests hereafter are designed to test SAP FI knowledge for the associate level.

The duration of the actual test is **180 minutes** to cover **80 questions**. The purpose of the practice tests is to enable candidates to get a feel for the type of questions that will appear in the actual test, and to practice time management effectively in preparation for the actual test. These are not actual SAP tests, but are written in a similar manner so candidates can understand how their SAP knowledge will be tested, and prepare accordingly.

A passing score of 64% is required to earn the certification. There is no penalty for wrong answers; therefore, it is to your advantage to always attempt a wise guess when you don't know the answer. Read all questions carefully, and eliminate as many incorrect ones as possible, then try to choose the ones that appear correct.

As a suggestion, take a blank paper and number it from 1 to 80. Use it to mark your answers. Time yourself as you do the test. After completion, check for all correct answers and score yourself. It is advisable to not take all the practice tests consecutively. Pace yourself; read through the preparation material, then take the first practice test. Read through the material a second time, then take the second practice test, and so forth. By the time you do the last practice test you should score at least 85% or more. To compute your score, use the following formula:

Number of correct answers x 100
_____
                80

After completion of a test always review your incorrect answers. Refer to the answer page to find answers and understand the questions that you missed. Review the material again before attempting the next practice test. This approach will enable you to strengthen acquired knowledge and perform better on the next practice test. In addition, it will enable you to assess your performance improvement. Do not rush to go for the actual certification test if by the time you do the last practice test, your score does not reflect a high level of knowledge.

We all have different learning styles, and the above is a general suggestion. Tailor the preparation methodology to your own learning style. Preparation time will vary for every individual, but the book has been written to prepare candidates to pass the certification test within 30 days.

Practice Test 1

QUESTION NO: 1

Select here below the steps for defining a financial statement version (FSV): (Choose two)

A. Define the required hierarchy levels then assign the accounts.

B. Make an entry for the new FSV in the directory of financial statement versions.

C. Choose a form, then select characteristics for profit and loss accounts.

D. Define columns for the required periods, actual values, budget values and variance.

QUESTION NO: 2

Identify the correct statements in relation with Account Groups (Choose Three):

A. Needs to be defined for every company code.

B. Defines the number range for a master record.

C. Determines the fields for a data entry screen based on the field status given to each account group.

D. They are always chart of account dependent.

QUESTION NO: 3

Identify the correct statements pertaining to the creation of customer master records (Choose Four):

A. The company code is not always a required entry.

B. Information on each screen can be defined in configuration as mandatory, suppressed or optional depending on the company code.

C. An account group does not always need to be assigned to a customer.

D. The account number may be assigned by the user externally.

E. Information on each screen can be defined in configuration as mandatory, suppressed or optional, depending on the account group.

QUESTION NO: 4

True or False?

A Chart of Accounts can be modified to fit a company's requirements, but a Chart of Depreciation is always Country-specific.

A. True

B. False

QUESTION NO: 5

True or False?
Document number ranges can be freely defined for each company code.
A. True

B. False

QUESTION NO: 6

True or False?
A Controlling area can include one or more company codes.
A. True

B. False

QUESTION NO: 7

Identify the correct statements pertaining to Debit Balance Check (Choose Three):
A. The debit balance check can be maintained in a vendor's line items.

B. When a vendor account has a debit balance all line items are shown in the exception list.

C. Accounts blocked as the result of a debit check, will remain blocked even if the payment proposal is later deleted.

D. A Debit balance check can be performed after a payment proposal has been created.

E. Debit Balance check is required to prevent payments to a vendor who has a debit balance.

F. A Debit balance check is always carried out after a payment run.

QUESTION NO: 8

True or False?

Depreciation attributes can be proposed for each depreciation area.
A. True

B. False

QUESTION NO: 9

True or False?

When you choose depreciation key 0000 for an AuC; depreciation will not be calculated.

A. True

B. False

QUESTION NO: 10

True or False?

It is possible to define any number of financial statement versions per chart of accounts.

A. True

B. False

QUESTION NO: 11

Select the correct statements (Choose Two):

A. The numeric keys represent depreciation terms that cannot be entered in the asset master record or in the asset classes.

B. Each company code is assigned to exactly one chart of depreciation.

C. The system uses depreciation area 01 to calculate ordinary depreciation. The depreciation is then posted to G/L accounts.

QUESTION NO: 12

What types of lists are used in reports to display information? (Choose Two):

A. Detail list

B. Drilldown list

C. Drop-down list

D. Search list

QUESTION NO: 13

True or False?

A report definition can contain characteristics, key figures and forms.

A. True

B. False

QUESTION NO: 14

True or False?

In a detail list Key figures are normally represented by the rows of the detail list.

A. True

B. False

QUESTION NO: 15

Identify here below the sort criteria used to group dunning notices (Choose Two):

A. The different dunning levels

B. Grouping key

C. Dunning Key

QUESTION NO: 16

Paying and sending company codes balance by generating cross company postings:

A. Automatically

B. Manually

C. It depends on the user's preference.

QUESTION NO: 17

The Payment program lets you automatically:

A. print payment media

B. Post payment documents

C. Select open invoices for payment

D. all of the above

QUESTION NO: 18

True or False?

The automatic payment program is a tool that helps users manage payables.

A. True

B. False

QUESTION NO: 19

Identify the steps for the Payment process (Choose Four):

A. Generation of a proposal

B. Generation of the exception list

C. Setting parameters

D. Printing payment media

E. Scheduling the payment run

QUESTION NO: 20

Select the correct statements pertaining to foreign currency valuation (Choose Two):

A. Foreign currency valuation is required if vendor accounts contain open items in foreign currency.

B. Foreign currency valuation can be used for GL account balances in foreign currency.

C. Foreign currency valuation is required for vendor Account open items in local currency.

D. Foreign currency valuation can be used for customer open items in local and foreign currency.

E. Foreign currency valuation is required if vendor accounts contain cleared items in foreign currency.

QUESTION NO: 21

What is the advantage of using different account groups?

A. Similar type of accounts will be in the same number range.

B. Accounts of same type are scattered.

C. None of the above.

QUESTION NO: 22

Chart of accounts can be assigned to:

A. Client

B. Company code

C. Business area

D. G/L accounts

QUESTION NO: 23

Which lists here below can be printed to assist in editing a dunning proposal? (Choose two)

A. Blocked accounts

B. Blocked line items

C. Sales statistics

D. Condensed customer master data

QUESTION NO: 24

If a vendor is also a customer within the same company code, is it possible to clear their outstanding payables against their outstanding receivables? If this is the case, what settings would be needed to make this work?

A. The vendor and the customer have to be assigned to the same group account.

B. The vendor number has to be entered in the customer account or the customer number has to be entered in the vendor account.

C. The "Clearing with Vendor" field has to be selected in the customer account, and the corresponding field has to be selected in the vendor account.

D. The payment program has to be set up to enable debit checks for vendors and credit checks for customers.

E. Outstanding payables cannot be cleared against outstanding receivables.

QUESTION NO: 25

What special feature becomes available when external number assignments are usable for specific document types?

A. The number ranges can overlap.

B. The number ranges are usable across all company codes.

C. The numbers can be alphanumeric.

D. The system will issue the numbers automatically.

QUESTION NO: 26

What preconditions allow the use of cross-company cost accounting? (Choose two)

A. Use of the same variant for open periods in all company codes.

B. Use of the same currency in all company codes.

C. Use of the same chart of accounts for all company codes.

D. Use of the same fiscal year for all company codes.

QUESTION NO: 26

What are the different types of Special G/L transactions? (Choose three)

A. Free offsetting entry

B. Automatic offsetting entry

C. Document parking

D. Noted item

E. Interest

QUESTION NO: 28

Segments can automatically be derived from a:

A. G/L account

B. Functional area

C. Profit center

D. Cost center

QUESTION NO: 29

Which situations below will result in inter-company posting documents? (Choose two)

A. Central currency valuation

B. Central payment

C. Central procurement

D. Central cash journal

QUESTION NO: 30

At what level is the vendor account number assigned?

A. The company code segment level.

B. A combination of client and purchasing organization segment level.

C. A combination of client and company code segment level.

D. The client level.

QUESTION NO: 31

Which of the below are standard SAP ERP Year-specific predefined fiscal year variants? (Choose three)

A. K2

B. K3

C. R1

D. UL

E. WK

F. K4

QUESTION NO: 32

True or False?

In SAP ERP currencies are defined using a currency flag.

A. True

B. False

QUESTION NO: 33

True or false?

Reconciliation accounts can be updated between one and twelve times a day.

A. True

B. False

QUESTION NO: 34

True or False?

When a G/L account is managed in a local currency, it cannot be posted to in a foreign currency.

A. True

B. False

QUESTION NO: 35

True of False?

Reconciliation accounts contain the total of the transaction figures that are used to automatically reconcile FI and CO.

A. True

B. False

QUESTION NO: 36

True or False?

The same segment cannot be assigned to multiple profit centers.

A. True

B. False

QUESTION NO: 37

A complete customer account normally has the following parts (Choose three):

A. General data

B. Terms of payment

C. Company code segment

D. Sales area segment

E. Purchasing organization segment

QUESTION NO: 38

True or False?

The same number range can be assigned to different account groups.

A. True

B. False

QUESTION NO: 39

The document type is mainly responsible for (choose two):

A. Specifying that the amount is either a debit or a credit.

B. Determining the length of the text in the document description field.

C. Account types permitted for postings.

D. Tolerances for exchange rate variation in the document.

E. Number ranges for document numbers.

QUESTION NO: 40

What are the most important control functions of a posting key? (Choose three)

A. It controls entries in the document header.

B. It determines the exchange rate type that can be used while posting documents.

C. Definition of the account types that can be posted to.

D. Indicate the account side (debit or credit).

E. Field status of the additional account assignment.

QUESTION NO: 41

True or False?

Posting keys are always defined at the client level.

A. True

B. False

QUESTION NO: 42

Select here below the values that can be defaulted by the system for document entry (Choose four):

A. User master records

B. Parameter memory

C. System data

D. User menu

E. Accounting functions

QUESTION NO: 43

Identify the correct statements (Choose three):

A. Credit memos can be linked to invoices so they can become due on the same date.

B. The day limits define the dates of the cash discount periods.

C. Each installment in an installment plan must have its own terms of payment.

D. The baseline date is the date that the system uses to determine the due date of an invoice.

E. "Terms of Payment" is a field in the general data segment of a customer master record.

QUESTION NO: 44

Identify the data required in automatic account determination for tax amounts (Choose three):

A. Rules

B. Tax code

C. Posting key

D. Tax accounts

E. Tax indicator

QUESTION NO: 45

Identify the incorrect statement here below (Choose one):

A. Cross-company code clearing accounts are always G/L accounts.

B. The company codes of a cross-company code transaction can have different local currencies.

C. The cross-company code transaction number is a combination of the document number in the first company code, the first company code number, and the fiscal year.

D. Documents with open items cannot be archived because open items represent incomplete transactions.

E. All statements above are correct

QUESTION NO: 46

True or False?

The SAP ERP generates the exchange rate differences automatically.

A. True

B. False

QUESTION NO: 47

Identify the correct list sequence for the steps in of a payment program:

A. Maintain parameters, Execute a payment run, Proposal run, Printing payment media.

B. Proposal run, Maintain parameters, Execute a payment run, Printing payment media.

C. Maintain parameters, Proposal run, Execute a payment run, Printing payment media.

D. Proposal run, Execute a payment run, Maintain parameters, Printing payment media.

QUESTION NO: 48

True or False?

The payment program uses the "next posting date" to determine if an open item has to be paid in the current or next payment run.

A. True

B. False

QUESTION NO: 49

True or False?

A payment method can be entered in the account master record or in the line item.

A. True

B. False

QUESTION NO: 50

Identify the correct sequence for the four steps taken by the dunning program to perform an automatic dunning procedure:

A. Maintain parameters, Proposal run, Edit dunning proposal, Print dunning notices.

B. Maintain parameters, Print dunning notices, Edit proposal, Proposal run.

C. Maintain parameters, Edit dunning proposal, Proposal run, Print dunning notices.

D. Proposal run, Maintain parameters, Edit dunning notices, Print dunning notices.

QUESTION NO: 51

True or False?

The run date does not have to be the date when the dunning run is actually performed.

A. True

B. False

QUESTION NO: 52

True or False?

An account is not dunned until all overdue items have exceeded the set minimum days in arrears.

A. True

B. False

QUESTION NO: 53

True or false?

Once the dunning proposal has been created, any subsequent changes to the dunning data in items or master records will be ignored in the current dunning run.

A. True

B. False

QUESTION NO: 54

True or False?

Text module 616 is used for dunning level 6.

A. True

B. False

QUESTION NO: 55

True or False?

On a given account, SAP ERP cannot charge different interest rates based on the dollar amounts of balances or items.

A. True

B. False

QUESTION NO: 56

True or False?

In order to create a new interest calculation indicator, a two-character interest indicator is needed along with an interest calculation type.

A. True

B. False

QUESTION NO: 57

True or False?

It is possible to void a check and reverse the payment document at the same time.

A. True

B. False

QUESTION NO: 58

True or False?
In the Lockbox process a check can have one of the three statuses below:

1. Assigned:
2. Partially assigned
3. On account

A. True

B. False

QUESTION NO: 59

True or False?

Different company codes can be assigned to the same chart of depreciation.

A. True

B. False

QUESTION NO: 60

True or False?
SAP ERP supports the following direct types of depreciation:
- Ordinary depreciation
- Special depreciation
- Unplanned depreciation

A. True

B. False

QUESTION NO: 61

True or False?

Calculation methods can be assigned to a depreciation key.

A. True

B. False

QUESTION NO: 62

True or False?

If Scenarios in the New GL do not meet your company requirements, you can copy and edit an existing one to create your own scenario.

A. True

B. False

QUESTION NO: 63

Identify the correct statements pertaining to organizational structures (Choose three):

A. A client can have more than one company code.

B. A company code can be part of a company.

C. The definition of a company code includes country, currency, and address.

D. A business area can be created to exclusively produce financial statements for a company code

E. The country installation program is limited to the creation of a country template and a country –specific template for controlling areas.

QUESTION NO: 64

Select the correct statement here below (Choose one):

A. The tax procedure for a company is assigned at the company code chart level.

B. A currency must be assigned at the general chart of accounts level.

C. Account groups are chart of account dependent.

D. Postings can be made directly to a reconciliation account.

E. General data for a G/L account must be updated every time an account is extended from the general Chart of Accounts to a company code.

QUESTION NO: 65

Which of the following statements are correct about customer data?

A. General data is valid for all company code and sales areas.

B. The company code data must be created before you can record customer entries.

C. Sales Area data is needed for the Sales & Distribution system.

D. An Account Group is required to create customer master data.

E. The account group controls the field status for customer data.

QUESTION NO: 66

Which of the following statements are correct? (Choose three)

A. A primary cost element is supposed to be related to a G/L expense account.

B. Secondary cost elements are only used in controlling.

C. Operational accounts are mapped to group accounts at the company code level.

D. All P&L accounts must have an associated cost element.

E. G/L Account blocking is only possible at account level.

QUESTION NO: 67

Which of the following statements are correct? (Choose two)

A. A G/L account has 3 segments.

B. Country accounts are mapped at the client level.

C. It is possible to have more than one retained earnings account.

D. A G/L account number cannot be configured to have 12 digits.

E. Account groups are company code dependent.

QUESTION NO: 68

Which of the following statements are correct? (Choose three)

A. Posting period variants control posting periods by using a range of G/L accounts.

B. The special periods are mainly used to record Special G/L transactions.

C. Authorization groups can only be assigned to the first period interval.

D. The number of posting periods depends on settings defined in the fiscal year variant.

E. Any number of period intervals can be open at the same time.

QUESTION NO: 69

Which of the following statements are correct? (Choose four)

A. Changes can be made in a document header or line items.

B. Amounts for posted transactions can be changed only if the appropriate settings have been configured accordingly.

C. The document change rules are based on the account type, transaction class, and company code.

D. Negative postings are not possible unless they are configured for the company code and include reason codes for negative reversals.

E. If a System is not configured for negative postings, a normal reversal posting will need to be made.

QUESTION NO: 70

The Accrual Engine is characterized by which if the following? (Choose three)

A. Stores accrual engine documents that have matching documents in Financials.

B. Allows customers to change its components so it can be tailored for particular needs.

C. The application components must be activated in order to run.

D. It can be configured to automatically accrue any type of transaction in all SAP modules.

E. Two main processes are triggered from its application component.

QUESTION NO: 71

Identify the correct statements here below? (Choose three)

A. Tax calculation procedures need to be associated with the relevant company codes.

B. The tax calculation procedure contains the order of the steps, conditions of tax, and the account keys for posting.

C. Tax codes are valid for specific date ranges.

D. For postings to the revenue account, account keys can be associated with condition types in the calculation procedures.

E. Tax codes can be used to calculate an additional tax portion.

QUESTION NO: 72

Which of the following is incorrect regarding payments? (Choose one)

A. Partial payments leave an open item on the account.

B. Require the use of reason codes for auditing purposes.

C. Can be charged off to a G/L account or back to the customer account.

D. Reason codes cannot be used to automatically post residual items to a G/L account.

E. Residual items create a new invoice and clear the old item.

QUESTION NO: 73

Which of the following statements is correct regarding special G/L indicators? (Choose two)

A. They are used to post Special G/L transactions from the application interface.

B. Automatic offsetting entries are recorded in the body of the financial statements.

C. Noted items are one-sided and therefore aren't considered by the payment program.

D. Special G/L indicators show that a posting key is being used to record a special G/L transaction.

E. Free offsetting entries are recorded as a note to the financial statements.

QUESTION NO: 74

Which of the following statements are correct regarding tax codes? (Choose three)

A. They are used to verify the tax amount.

B. They are needed to correctly display tax on the tax forms.

C. A separate tax code is needed for each tax rate and each tax type.

D. Tax codes are date independent.

E. Tax code properties are needed for countries that have special tax requirements.

QUESTION NO: 75

Which of the following statements on payments are incorrect? (Choose one)

A. Payments can be optimized based on postal codes.

B. The selection of banks can be currency dependent or currency independent.

C. Incoming payments clear open debits in Accounts Payable and outgoing payments clear open credits for Accounts Receivable.

D. Available amounts are automatically updated after each payment run.

E. All the above are incorrect

QUESTION NO: 76

Identify the incorrect statements regarding check management. (Choose three)

A. When a check is voided the accounting entry always reverses automatically.

B. Canceling a payment can void the check and simultaneously reverse the accounting entry.

C. There is no need to void unused checks therefore the option is not available.

D. A reversal reason code is an option used to explain why a check was voided.

E. If you create a new void reason code you must indicate whether it is used by the print program.

QUESTION NO: 77

Which statements here below are incorrect? (Choose two)

A. Interest can be calculated for a specific item in an account or for the entire balance of an account.

B. Balance interest can be evaluated on customer and vendor accounts as well as G/L accounts.

C. Different interest rates cannot be applied on line items in a given customer or vendor account.

D. Interest calculation indicators are entered into the master record for the calculation of interest to take place.

E. Interest rates for customers cannot be date dependent.

QUESTION NO: 78

Identify the correct statements on Correspondence here below. (Choose four)

A. A correspondence type is a class of letter sent out by a company.

B. Required settings in the type include requiring a document number, account number, and the number of date fields.

C. Each correspondence always has a correspondence type.

D. A reason code can be used to create a particular correspondence.

E. A correspondence type can be linked to a transaction in order to be launched automatically.

QUESTION NO: 79

Identify the incorrect statements about dunning. (Choose two)

A. A dunning procedure must be entered into the master record for a customer or vendor to be considered.

B. Dunning keys determine the number of letters will be sent out.

C. Each company code is required to send out its own correspondence.

D. Dunning areas are organizational entities that handle dunning for company codes.

E. Charges for dunning can be based on a fixed amount or a percentage of the dunned amount.

QUESTION NO: 80

Why does the accrual engine need to use account determination? (Choose two)

A. To determine the CO object.

B. To determine the correct posting period.

C. To determine the document type.

D. To determine debit and credit accounts.

Practice Test 1 - Answers

QUESTION NO: 1

Select here below the steps for defining a financial statement version (FSV): (Choose two)

A. Define the required hierarchy levels then assign the accounts.

B. Make an entry for the new FSV in the directory of financial statement versions.

C. Choose a form, then select characteristics for profit and loss accounts.

D. Define columns for the required periods, actual values, budget values and variance.

Answer: A, B

Page(s): 188

QUESTION NO: 2

Identify the correct statements in relation with Account Groups (Choose Three):

A. Needs to be defined for every company code.

B. Defines the number range for a master record.

C. Determines the fields for a data entry screen based on the field status given to each account group.

D. They are always chart of account dependent.

Answer: B, C, D

Page(s): 52, 91, 92, 111

QUESTION NO: 3

Identify the correct statements pertaining to the creation of customer master records (Choose Four):

A. The company code is not always a required entry.

B. Information on each screen can be defined in configuration as mandatory, suppressed or optional depending on the company code.

C. An account group does not always need to be assigned to a customer.

D. The account number may be assigned by the user externally.

E. Information on each screen can be defined in configuration as mandatory, suppressed or optional, depending on the account group.

Answer: A, B, D, E

Page(s): 91, 92

QUESTION NO: 4

True or False?

A Chart of Accounts can be modified to fit a company's requirements, but a Chart of Depreciation is always Country-specific.

A. True

B. False

Answer: A

Page(s): 49, 51, 145

QUESTION NO: 5

True or False?
Document number ranges can be freely defined for each company code.
A. True

B. False

Answer: A

Page(s): 42

QUESTION NO: 6

True or False?
A Controlling area can include one or more company codes.
A. True

B. False

Answer: A

Page(s): 35

QUESTION NO: 7

Identify the correct statements pertaining to Debit Balance Check (Choose Three):

A. The debit balance check can be maintained in a vendor's line items.

B. When a vendor account has a debit balance all line items are shown in the exception list.

C. Accounts blocked as the result of a debit check, will remain blocked even if the payment proposal is later deleted.

D. A Debit balance check can be performed after a payment proposal has been created.

E. Debit Balance check is required to prevent payments to a vendor who has a debit balance.

F. A Debit balance check is always carried out after a payment run.

Answer: C, D, E

Page(s): 133, 134

QUESTION NO: 8

True or False?

Depreciation attributes can be proposed for each depreciation area.
A. True

B. False

Answer: A

Page(s): 145

QUESTION NO: 9

True or False?

When you choose depreciation key 0000 for an AuC; depreciation will not be calculated.

A. True

B. False

Answer: A

Page(s): 148

QUESTION NO: 10

True or False?

It is possible to define any number of financial statement versions per chart of accounts.

A. True

B. False

Answer: A

Page(s): 189

QUESTION NO: 11

Select the correct statements (Choose Two):

A. The numeric keys represent depreciation terms that cannot be entered in the asset master record or in the asset classes.

B. Each company code is assigned to exactly one chart of depreciation.

C. The system uses depreciation area 01 to calculate ordinary depreciation. The depreciation is then posted to G/L accounts.

Answer: B, C

Page(s): 145, 146

QUESTION NO: 12

What types of lists are used in reports to display information? (Choose Two):

A. Detail list

B. Drilldown list

C. Drop-down list

D. Search list

Answer: A, B
Page(s): 192

QUESTION NO: 13

True or False?

A report definition can contain characteristics, key figures and forms.

A. True

B. False

Answer: A

Page(s): 191

QUESTION NO: 14

True or False?

In a detail list Key figures are normally represented by the rows of the detail list.

A. True

B. False

Answer: A

Page(s): 192

QUESTION NO: 15

Identify here below the sort criteria used to group dunning notices (Choose Two):

A. The different dunning levels

B. Grouping key

C. Dunning Key

Answer: A, B

Page(s): 99

QUESTION NO: 16

Paying and sending company codes balance by generating cross company postings:

A. Automatically

B. Manually

C. It depends on the user's preference.

Answer: A

Page(s): 124

QUESTION NO: 17

The Payment program lets you automatically:

A. print payment media

B. Post payment documents

C. Select open invoices for payment

D. all of the above

Answer: D

Page(s): 122

QUESTION NO: 18

True or False?

The automatic payment program is a tool that helps users manage payables.

A. True

B. False

Answer: A

Page(s): 122

QUESTION NO: 19

Identify the steps for the Payment process (Choose Four):

A. Generation of a proposal

B. Generation of the exception list

C. Setting parameters

D. Printing payment media

E. Scheduling the payment run

Answer: A, C, D, E

Page(s): 122, 123

QUESTION NO: 20

Select the correct statements pertaining to foreign currency valuation (Choose Two):

A. Foreign currency valuation is required if vendor accounts have open items in foreign currency.

B. Foreign currency valuation can be used for GL account balances in foreign currency.

C. Foreign currency valuation is required for vendor Account open items in local currency.

D. Foreign currency valuation can be used for customer open items in local and foreign currency.

E. Foreign currency valuation is required if vendor accounts have cleared items in foreign currency.

Answer: A, B

Page(s): 176

QUESTION NO: 21

What is the advantage of using different account groups?

A. Similar type of accounts will be in the same number range.

B. Accounts of same type are scattered.

C. None of the above.

Answer: C

Page(s): 52, 92

QUESTION NO: 22

Chart of accounts can be assigned to:

A. Client

B. Company code

C. Business area

D. G/L accounts

Answer: B

Page(s): 36, 49, 50

QUESTION NO: 23

Which lists here below can be printed to assist in editing a dunning proposal? (Choose two)

A. Blocked accounts

B. Blocked line items

C. Sales statistics

D. Condensed customer master data

Answer: A, B

Page(s): 97, 98

QUESTION NO: 24

If a vendor is also a customer within the same company code, is it possible to clear their outstanding payables against their outstanding receivables? If this is the case, what settings would be needed to make this work?

A. The vendor and the customer have to be assigned to the same group account.

B. The vendor number has to be entered in the customer account or the customer number has to be entered in the vendor account.

C. The "Clearing with Vendor" field has to be selected in the customer account, and the corresponding field has to be selected in the vendor account.

D. The payment program has to be set up to enable debit checks for vendors and credit checks for customers.

E. Outstanding payables cannot be cleared against outstanding receivables.

Answer: B, C

Page(s): 92, 93, 112

QUESTION NO: 25

What special feature becomes available when external number assignments are usable for specific document types?

A. The number ranges can overlap.

B. The number ranges are usable across all company codes.

C. The numbers can be alphanumeric.

D. The system will issue the numbers automatically.

Answer: C

Page(s): 42

QUESTION NO: 26

What preconditions allow the use of cross-company cost accounting? (Choose two)

A. Use of the same variant for open periods in all company codes.

B. Use of the same currency in all company codes.

C. Use of the same chart of accounts for all company codes.

D. Use of the same fiscal year for all company codes.

Answer: C, D

Page(s): 35, 36, 49

QUESTION NO: 26

What are the different types of Special G/L transactions? (Choose three)

A. Free offsetting entry

B. Automatic offsetting entry

C. Document parking

D. Noted item

E. Interest

Answer: A, B, D

Page(s): 114, 115

QUESTION NO: 28

Segments can automatically be derived from a:

A. G/L account

B. Functional area

C. Profit center

D. Cost center

Answer: C

Page(s): 56, 77

QUESTION NO: 29

Which situations below will result in inter-company posting documents? (Choose two)

A. Central currency valuation

B. Central payment

C. Central procurement

D. Central cash journal

Answer: B, C

Page(s): 83, 84

QUESTION NO: 30

At what level is the vendor account number assigned?

A. The company code segment level.

B. A combination of client and purchasing organization segment level.

C. A combination of client and company code segment level.

D. The client level.

Answer: A

Page(s): 91, 109

QUESTION NO: 31

Which of the below are standard SAP ERP Year-specific predefined fiscal year variants? (Choose three)

A. K2

B. K3

C. R1

D. UL

E. WK

F. K4

Answer: A, B, F

Page(s): 38

QUESTION NO: 32

True or False?

In SAP ERP currencies are defined using a currency flag.

A. True

B. False

Answer: B

Page(s): 38

QUESTION NO: 33

True or false?

Reconciliation accounts can be updated between one and twelve times a day.

A. True

B. False

Answer: B

Page(s): 53

QUESTION NO: 34

True or False?

When a G/L account is managed in a local currency, it cannot be posted to in a foreign currency.

A. True

B. False

Answer: B

Page(s): 54

QUESTION NO: 35

True of False?

Reconciliation accounts contain the total of the transaction figures that are used to automatically reconcile FI and CO.

A. True

B. False

Answer: B

Page(s): 53

QUESTION NO: 36

True or False?

The same segment cannot be assigned to multiple profit centers.

A. True

B. False

Answer: B

Page(s): 56, 77

QUESTION NO: 37

A complete customer account normally has the following parts (Choose three):

A. General data

B. Terms of payment

C. Company code segment

D. Sales area segment

E. Purchasing organization segment

Answer: A, C, D

Page(s): 90, 91

QUESTION NO: 38

True or False?

The same number range can be assigned to different account groups.

A. True

B. False

Answer: A

Page(s): 92

QUESTION NO: 39

The document type is mainly responsible for (choose two):

A. Specifying that the amount is either a debit or a credit.

B. Determining the length of the text in the document description field.

C. Account types permitted for postings.

D. Tolerances for exchange rate variation in the document.

E. Number ranges for document numbers.

Answer: C, E

Page(s): 41, 42

QUESTION NO: 40

What are the most important control functions of a posting key? (Choose three)

A. It controls entries in the document header.

B. It determines the exchange rate type that can be used while posting documents.

C. Definition of the account types that can be posted to.

D. Indicate the account side (debit or credit).

E. Field status of the additional account assignment.

Answer: C, D, E

Page(s): 42, 43

QUESTION NO: 41

True or False?

Posting keys are always defined at the client level.

A. True

B. False

Answer: A

Page(s): 42

QUESTION NO: 42

Select here below the values that can be defaulted by the system for document entry (Choose four):

A. User master records

B. Parameter memory

C. System data

D. User menu

E. Accounting functions

Answer: A, B, C, E

Page(s): 61

QUESTION NO: 43

Identify the correct statements (Choose three):

A. Credit memos can be linked to invoices so they can become due on the same date.

B. The day limits define the dates of the cash discount periods.

C. Each installment in an installment plan must have its own terms of payment.

D. The baseline date is the date that the system uses to determine the due date of an invoice.

E. "Terms of Payment" is a field in the general data segment of a customer master record.

Answer: A, C, D

Page(s): 115, 116, 117

QUESTION NO: 44

Identify the data required in automatic account determination for tax amounts (Choose three):

A. Rules

B. Tax code

C. Posting key

D. Tax accounts

E. Tax indicator

Answer: A, C, D

Page(s): 82, 83

QUESTION NO: 45

Identify the incorrect statement here below (Choose one):

A. Cross-company code clearing accounts are always G/L accounts.

B. The company codes of a cross-company code transaction can have different local currencies.

C. The cross-company code transaction number is a combination of the document number in the first company code, the first company code number, and the fiscal year.

D. Documents with open items cannot be archived because open items represent incomplete transactions.

E. All statements above are correct

Answer: A

Page(s): 84, 85, 86

QUESTION NO: 46

True or False?

The SAP ERP generates the exchange rate differences automatically.

A. True

B. False

Answer: A

Page(s): 63

QUESTION NO: 47

Identify the correct list sequence for the steps in of a payment program:

A. Maintain parameters, Execute a payment run, Proposal run, Printing payment media.

B. Proposal run, Maintain parameters, Execute a payment run, Printing payment media.

C. Maintain parameters, Proposal run, Execute a payment run, Printing payment media.

D. Proposal run, Execute a payment run, Maintain parameters, Printing payment media.

Answer: C

Page(s): 129

<u>QUESTION NO: 48</u>

True or False?

The payment program uses the "next posting date" to determine if an open item has to be paid in the current or next payment run.

A. True

B. False

Answer: A

Page(s): 123

<u>QUESTION NO: 49</u>

True or False?

A payment method can be entered in the account master record or in the line item.

A. True

B. False

Answer: A

Page(s): 123, 130

<u>QUESTION NO: 50</u>

Identify the correct sequence for the four steps taken by the dunning program to perform an automatic dunning procedure:

A. Maintain parameters, Proposal run, Edit dunning proposal, Print dunning notices.

B. Maintain parameters, Print dunning notices, Edit proposal, Proposal run.

C. Maintain parameters, Edit dunning proposal, Proposal run, Print dunning notices.

D. Proposal run, Maintain parameters, Edit dunning notices, Print dunning notices.

Answer: A

Page(s): 93

QUESTION NO: 51

True or False?

The run date does not have to be the date when the dunning run is actually performed.

A. True

B. False

Answer: A

Page(s): 96, 130

QUESTION NO: 52

True or False?

An account is not dunned until all overdue items have exceeded the set minimum days in arrears.

A. True

B. False

Answer: B

Page(s): 93, 94, 95

QUESTION NO: 53

True or false?

Once the dunning proposal has been created, any subsequent changes to the dunning data in items or master records will be ignored in the current dunning run.

A. True

B. False

Answer: A

Page(s): 97, 98

QUESTION NO: 54

True or False?

Text module 616 is used for dunning level 6.

A. True

B. False

Answer: A

Page(s): 99

QUESTION NO: 55

True or False?

On a given account, SAP ERP cannot charge different interest rates based on the dollar amounts of balances or items.

A. True

B. False

Answer: B

Page(s): 70

QUESTION NO: 56

True or False?

In order to create a new interest calculation indicator, a two-character interest indicator is needed along with an interest calculation type.

A. True

B. False

Answer: A

Page(s): 70

QUESTION NO: 57

True or False?

It is possible to void a check and reverse the payment document at the same time.

A. True

B. False

Answer: A

Page(s): 129

QUESTION NO: 58

True or False?
In the Lockbox process a check can have one of the three statuses below:

1. Assigned:
2. Partially assigned
3. On account

A. True

B. False

Answer: B

Page(s): 106, 107

QUESTION NO: 59

True or False?

Different company codes can be assigned to the same chart of depreciation.

A. True

B. False

Answer: A

Page(s): 146

QUESTION NO: 60

True or False?
SAP ERP supports the following direct types of depreciation:
- Ordinary depreciation
- Special depreciation
- Unplanned depreciation

A. True

B. False

Answer: A

Page(s): 158

QUESTION NO: 61

True or False?

Calculation methods can be assigned to a depreciation key.

A. True

B. False

Answer: A

Page(s): 159

QUESTION NO: 62

True or False?

If scenarios in the New GL do not meet your company requirements, you can copy and edit an existing one to create your own scenario.

A. True

B. False

Answer: B

Page(s): 75

QUESTION NO: 63

Identify the correct statements pertaining to organizational structures (Choose three):

A. A client can have more than one company code.

B. A company code can be part of a company.

C. The definition of a company code includes country, currency, and address.

D. A business area can be created to exclusively produce financial statements for a company code

E. The country installation program is limited to the creation of a country template and a country –specific template for controlling areas.

Answer: A, B, C,

Page(s): 33, 34

QUESTION NO: 64

Select the correct statement here below (Choose one):

A. The tax procedure for a company is assigned at the company code chart level.

B. A currency must be assigned at the general chart of accounts level.

C. Account groups are chart of account dependent.

D. Postings can be made directly to a reconciliation account.

E. General data for a G/L account must be updated every time an account is extended from the general Chart of Accounts to a company code.

Answer: C

Page(s): 34, 50, 51, 52, 53, 81

QUESTION NO: 65

Which of the following statements are correct about customer data?

A. General data is valid for all company code and sales areas.

B. The company code data must be created before you can record customer entries.

C. Sales Area data is needed for the Sales & Distribution system.

D. An Account Group is required to create customer master data.

E. The account group controls the field status for customer data.

Answer: A, B, C, D, E

Page(s): 90, 91, 92

QUESTION NO: 66

Which of the following statements are correct? (Choose three)

A. A primary cost element is supposed to be related to a G/L expense account.

B. Secondary cost elements are only used in controlling.

C. Operational accounts are mapped to group accounts at the company code level.

D. All P&L accounts must have an associated cost element.

E. G/L Account blocking is only possible at account level.

Answer: A, B, D

Page(s): 36, 50, 55, 56

QUESTION NO: 67

Which of the following statements are correct? (Choose two)

A. A G/L account has 3 segments.

B. Country accounts are mapped at the client level.

C. It is possible to have more than one retained earnings account.

D. A G/L account number cannot be configured to have 12 digits.

E. Account groups are company code dependent.

Answer: C, D

Page(s): 50, 51, 52

QUESTION NO: 68

Which of the following statements are correct? (Choose three)

A. Posting period variants control posting periods by using a range of G/L accounts.

B. The special periods are mainly used to record Special G/L transactions.

C. Authorization groups can only be assigned to the first period interval.

D. The number of posting periods depends on settings defined in the fiscal year variant.

E. Any number of period intervals can be open at the same time.

Answer: A, C, D

Page(s): 40

QUESTION NO: 69

Which of the following statements are correct? (Choose four)

A. Changes can be made in a document header or line items.

B. Amounts for posted transactions can be changed only if the appropriate settings have been configured accordingly.

C. The document change rules are based on the account type, transaction class, and company code.

D. Negative postings are not possible unless they are configured for the company code and include reason codes for negative reversals.

E. If a System is not configured for negative postings, a normal reversal posting will need to be made.

Answer: A, C, D, E

Page(s): 62, 63

QUESTION NO: 70

The Accrual Engine is characterized by which if the following? (Choose three)

A. Stores accrual engine documents that have matching documents in Financials.

B. Allows customers to change its components so it can be tailored for particular needs.

C. The application components must be activated in order to run.

D. It can be configured to automatically accrue any type of transaction in all SAP modules.

E. Two main processes are triggered from its application component.

Answer: A, C, E

Page(s): 180, 181

QUESTION NO: 71

Identify the correct statements here below? (Choose three)

A. Tax calculation procedures need to be associated with the relevant company codes.

B. The tax calculation procedure contains the order of the steps, conditions of tax, and the account keys for posting.

C. Tax codes are valid for specific date ranges.

D. For postings to the revenue account, account keys can be associated with condition types in the calculation procedures.

E. Tax codes can be used to calculate an additional tax portion.

Answer: B, D, E

Page(s): 81, 82, 103

QUESTION NO: 72

Which of the following is incorrect regarding payments? (Choose one)

A. Partial payments leave an open item on the account.

B. Require the use of reason codes for auditing purposes.

C. Can be charged off to a G/L account or back to the customer account.

D. Reason codes cannot be used to automatically post residual items to a G/L account.

E. Residual items create a new invoice and clear the old item.

Answer: D

Page(s): 121

QUESTION NO: 73

Which of the following statements is correct regarding special G/L indicators? (Choose two)

A. They are used to post Special G/L transactions from the application interface.

B. Automatic offsetting entries are recorded in the body of the financial statements.

C. Noted items are one-sided and therefore aren't considered by the payment program.

D. Special G/L indicators show that a posting key is being used to record a special G/L transaction.

E. Free offsetting entries are recorded as a note to the financial statements.

Answer: A, D

Page(s): 114, 115, 116

QUESTION NO: 74

Which of the following statements are correct regarding tax codes? (Choose three)

A. They are used to verify the tax amount.

B. They are needed to correctly display tax on the tax forms.

C. A separate tax code is needed for each tax rate and each tax type.

D. Tax codes are date independent.

E. Tax code properties are needed for countries that have special tax requirements.

Answer: A, B, D

Page(s): 80, 81, 82, 83

QUESTION NO: 75

Which of the following statements on payments are incorrect? (Choose one)

A. The best way to optimize payments is based on postal codes.

B. The selection of banks can be currency dependent or currency independent.

C. Incoming payments clear open debits in Accounts Payable and outgoing payments clear open credits for Accounts Receivable.

D. Available amounts are automatically updated after each payment run.

E. All the above are incorrect

Answer: D

Page(s): 119, 126, 127

QUESTION NO: 76

Identify the incorrect statements regarding check management. (Choose three)

A. When a check is voided the accounting entry always reverses automatically.

B. Canceling a payment can void the check and simultaneously reverse the accounting entry.

C. There is no need to void unused checks therefore the option is not available.

D. A reversal reason code is an option used to explain why a check was voided.

E. If you create a new void reason code you must indicate whether it is used by the print program.

Answer: A, C, D

Page(s): 128, 129

QUESTION NO: 77

Which statements here below are incorrect? (Choose two)

A. Interest can be calculated for a specific item in an account or for the entire balance of an account.

B. Balance interest can be evaluated on customer and vendor accounts as well as G/L accounts.

C. Different interest rates cannot be applied on line items in a given customer or vendor account.

D. Interest calculation indicators are entered into the master record for the calculation of interest to take place.

E. Interest rates for customers cannot be date dependent.

Answer: C, E

Page(s): 69, 70, 71

QUESTION NO: 78

Identify the correct statements on Correspondence here below. (Choose four)

A. A correspondence type is a class of letter sent out by a company.

B. Required settings in the type include requiring a document number, account number, and the number of date fields.

C. Each correspondence always has a correspondence type.

D. A reason code can be used to create a particular correspondence.

E. A correspondence type can be linked to a transaction in order to be launched automatically.

Answer: A, C, D, E

Page(s): 100, 101

QUESTION NO: 79

Identify the incorrect statements about dunning. (Choose two)

A. A dunning procedure must be entered into the master record for a customer or vendor to be considered.

B. Dunning keys determine the number of letters will be sent out.

C. Each company code is required to send out its own correspondence.

D. Dunning areas are organizational entities that handle dunning for company codes.

E. Charges for dunning can be based on a fixed amount or a percentage of the dunned amount.

Answer: B, C

Page(s): 94, 95

QUESTION NO: 80

Why does the accrual engine need to use account determination? (Choose two)

A. To determine the CO object.

B. To determine the correct posting period.

C. To determine the document type.

D. To determine debit and credit accounts.

Answer: C, D

Page(s): 183

Inquiries: support@sapseries.com

Practice Test 2

QUESTION NO: 1

Which statement below regarding financial reporting is correct? (Choose one)

A. The system can translate a financial statement into any currency for reporting purposes.

B. During display of a financial statement, the system can automatically calculate the profit and loss statement result.

C. A summarized financial statement can be generated for any hierarchy level in the financial statement version.

D. A financial statement version cannot include more than one company code, unless FI-LC is used.

E. A financial statement version displays either a balance sheet or a profit and lost statement, but not both.

QUESTION NO: 2

Which of the following statements about vendor transactions are correct? (Choose Two)

A. A vendor down payment request cannot be included in the payment program.

B. A vendor down payment is cleared after a final invoice is received from the vendor.

C. Vendor down payments are shown on balance sheets under a normal reconciliation account for payables.

D. A special G/L transaction is a transaction included in the Special Purpose Ledger under a coding block in G/L account.

E. A vendor down payment request is a noted item.

QUESTION NO: 3

Select the correct statement regarding Cross-company code transactions.

A. No configuration needs to be performed for cross-company code transactions.

B. A cross-company code document transaction number contains the company code of the second company number, the document number of the first company code and the fiscal year.

C. None of the above is correct.

QUESTION NO: 4

True or False?

The asset class is a selection option in all FI-AA standard reports.

A. True

B. False

QUESTION NO: 5

Screen layout rules are used to control which of the following? (Choose two)

A. Maintenance level

B. references/copies

C. Field attributes

D. All are correct

QUESTION NO: 6

True or False?

The Chart of Depreciation is a catalog of country-specific depreciation areas based on various business aspects.

A. True

B. False

QUESTION NO: 7

True or False?

When an asset master record is created the default values defined for each asset class are automatically applied to the new asset.

A. True

B. False

QUESTION NO: 8

True or False?

Various charts of depreciation can be assigned to the same asset class.

A. True

B. False

QUESTION NO: 9

The layout of the master data in each asset class defines:

A. The number of tab pages.

B. The specific field groups that appear on tab pages.

C. The names of tab pages.

D. All are correct.

QUESTION NO: 10

True or False?

The Segment field is a standard account assignment object.

A. True

B. False

QUESTION NO: 11

A specific type of depreciation valuation is represented by which of the following?

A. The chart of depreciation

B. The chart of accounts

C. The depreciation area

QUESTION NO: 12

Which of the following statements pertain to a Detail List? (choose two):

A. Key figures are normally in the rows of the list.

B. An individual object is formatted for all key figures depending on the form.

C. The rows contain characteristic values.

D. Key figures are normally in the columns of the list.

E. Various objects are formatted using a selection of key figures.

QUESTION NO: 13

Identify the correct statement related to Financial Statement versions (FSV). (Choose one):

A. The best way to create a Financial Statement Version is to start from scratch, because the copy function can cause errors that are difficult to edit.

B. A Financial Statement Version is defined at company code level.

C. You can define a maximum of 999 financial statement versions.

D. A Financial Statement Version is defined at chart of account level.

E. You can define a maximum of 99 financial statement versions.

QUESTION NO: 14

True or False?

When defining a dual-axis form the rows can be used for key figures while the columns can be used for the characteristics, or vice versa.

A. True

B. False

QUESTION NO: 15

Any number of variance analyses based on actual and planned data can be performed for which of the below?

A. Balance display

B. Key figure reports

C. Reports for financial statement analysis

QUESTION NO: 16

Payment method supplement is a functionality that allows printing payments with additional vouchers.

A. True

B. False

QUESTION NO: 17

The steps in a Dunning run follow the sequence below:

A. Dun accounts, Select accounts, Dun line items.

B. Dun accounts, Dun line items, Select accounts.

C. Select accounts, Dun line items, Dun accounts.

D. Dun line items, Select accounts, Dun accounts.

QUESTION NO: 18

True or False?

The Payment Program is designed to handle national and international transactions.

A. True

B. False

QUESTION NO: 19

False or True?

Settings for the Payment Program are normally accessible through the user interface.

A. True

B. False

QUESTION NO: 20

What is the highest dunning level attainable by item in a customer master record?

A. Level 10

B. Level 9

C. Level 7

D. Level 12

QUESTION NO: 21

True or False?

Exchange rate differences in SAP ERP are gathered automatically in a worklist that needs to be posted manually

A. True

B. False

QUESTION NO: 22

True or False?

It is possible for hidden fields to contain values that will be used by the system.

A. True

B. False

QUESTION NO: 23

What are the three types of chart of accounts in SAP ERP?

A. Consolidation chart of accounts

B. Company chart of accounts

C. Group chart of accounts

D. Country-specific chart of accounts

E. Operating chart of accounts

F. International chart of accounts

QUESTION NO: 24

Posting keys are used to control (Choose three):
A. Account type

B. Document type

C. Field status

D. Number range

E. Debit/credit indicator

QUESTION NO: 25

What happens when the payment method in a document is different from the payment method in the master data?

A. The payment run will stop and then the system will issue an error message.

B. The payment run will temporarily stop then the system will prompt the user to correct the data. After correction of the data, the payment run will continue.

C. The document data will override the master data.

D. The master data will override the document data.

QUESTION NO: 26

Which objects here below can be posted to from a cash journal? (Choose two)

A. Customer

B. One-time customer

C. Asset master

D. Accrual Engine

E. Material master

QUESTION NO: 27

Which parameters below are required to execute a payment run? (Choose two)

A. The payment method

B. The company code

C. The currency

D. The bank account

QUESTION NO: 28

Select here below one of the benefits of document parking?

A. It enables the use of a principle known as dual control.

B. It enables the posting of technically incomplete documents.

C. It provides a user friendly option to change posted documents.

D. It enables the assignment of individual document numbers.

QUESTION NO: 29

Parking documents is better than holding documents for the following reasons (Choose two):

A. Parked documents can be posted through automatic speech recognition.

B. Parked documents can be posted using a cross-client approach to increase efficiency.

C. Workflows can be used to post parked documents.

D. Parked documents can be changed and posted by a different user, in order to support the dual control principle.

QUESTION NO: 30

What is the main benefit of posting a down payment using a special G/L transaction?

A. Down-payment requests are automatically cleared.

B. The down-payments posts to a reconciliation account that is different from the one normally used for payables and receivables.

C. The data will show in the appendix of the balance sheet.

D. Down-payments are automatically cleared by the final invoice.

QUESTION NO: 31

Which transactions in the procurement process with valuated goods receipt lead to the creation of documents in FI? (Choose two):

A. Create purchase requisition

B. Enter invoice receipt

C. Post valuated goods receipt

D. Create purchase order

QUESTION NO: 32

True or false?

Year-specific fiscal year variants can be used if:

The start and end date of the posting periods are different every year.

A. True

B. False

QUESTION NO: 33

What are the commonly used exchange rate types and their respective uses? (Choose three):

A. Average rate for posting and clearing (M).

B. Daily rate for current entries (S).

C. Buying rate (G).

D. Selling rate (B).

E. Forecast rate for budgeting (P).

QUESTION NO: 34

Line items of a G/L account should always be set for display.

A. True

B. False

QUESTION NO: 35

When a G/L account is managed in a foreign currency, it can only be posted to in the specific foreign currency.

A. True

B. False

QUESTION NO: 37

True of False?

Company codes for different countries can use the same chart of accounts.

A. True

B. False

QUESTION NO: 38

True or False?

Segments have a time reference that determines their validity dates.

A. True

B. False

QUESTION NO: 39

An accounting manager wants to ensure that changes to certain fields in customer and vendor data are always confirmed by a second person who has the appropriate authorization. This dual control principle can be made required by defining particular fields as a (choose one):

A. Confirmation field

B. Required field

C. Sensitive field

D. Management field

E. Authorization field

F. Dual control field

QUESTION NO: 40

A complete vendor account normally has the following parts:

A. Sales area segment

B. General data

C. Company code segment

D. Purchasing organization segment

E. Terms of payment

QUESTION NO: 41

True of False?

Internal number assignments enable SAP ERP users to assign numbers manually.

A. True

B. False

QUESTION NO: 42

Choose the incorrect statements: (Choose two)

A. If a user can assign document numbers manually, external number assignment is allowed.

B. External numbers may be alphanumeric.

C. Every company code may define its own document types.

D. Every company code may define its own document number ranges.

E. Document number assignment is defined at the client level.

QUESTION NO: 43

What influences the field status of document fields? (Choose two):

A. Account-dependent field status

B. Field status group

C. Posting key

D. Key-dependent field status

E. Account group

QUESTION NO: 44

Choose the correct statement: (Choose one)

A. The field status group controls the field display during document entry.

B. Each G/L account has a field status group.

C. The posting period variant is assigned to the company code.

D. All statements are correct.

E. All the above statements are incorrect.

QUESTION NO: 45

Identify the incorrect statements (Choose two):

A. There are two ways to reverse a document in SAP ERP Financials.

B. A reversal reason code needs to be entered before a document is reversed.

C. Reversal by negative posting is used to reverse documents with cleared items.

D. In normal reversal posting the posted amount is not added to the transaction figures.

QUESTION NO: 46

Which cash discount accounts are used in the net procedure? (Choose two):

A. Cash discount clearing account

B. Cash discount revenue account

C. Cash discount expense account

D. Cash discount loss account

QUESTION NO: 47

Which of the below are examples for cross-company code transactions in SAP ERP? (Choose two)

A. Central purchasing

B. Central master data

C. Central payment

D. Central management

QUESTION NO: 48

True of False?
There are two basic transactions for clearing open items: account clearing and post with clearing

A. True

B. False

QUESTION NO: 49

G/L accounts must be defined for exchange rate losses or gains.

A. True

B. False

QUESTION NO: 50

True or False?

Configuration of the payment program is divided in the following five areas:

• All company codes

• Paying company codes

• Payment method/country

• Payment method for company code

• House banks

A. True

B. False

QUESTION NO: 51

The sequence in which the payment methods are entered in the payment parameters does not matter.

A. True

B. False

QUESTION NO: 52

True or False?

A payment proposal can only be edited, deleted, and recreated once. After this the user will need to start a new payment proposal if more changes are needed.

A. True

B. False

QUESTION NO: 53

True or false?

Customers without a dunning procedure in the master record cannot be dunned.

A. True

B. False

QUESTION NO: 54

True or False?

Dunning parameters are only used to specify what needs to be included in the dunning run.

A. True

B. False

QUESTION NO: 55

True or false?

Payment terms for credit memos usually do not apply, and the due date is typically the due date of the associated invoice or the baseline date of the document.

A. True

B. False

QUESTION NO: 56

The dunning data is not updated until the dunning notices are printed.

A. True

B. False

QUESTION NO: 57

True or False?

A dunning proposal can be changed, deleted, and redone as many times as needed.

A. True

B. False

QUESTION NO: 58

The last dunning level leads to the manual dunning procedure

A. True

B. False

QUESTION NO: 59

SAP ERP can be configured to calculate interest for customers or vendors who owe a company. Interest will be calculated for all customers and vendors including the ones owed money by the company.

A. True

B. False

QUESTION NO: 60

True or False?

Payment processes only use three types of documents.

A. True

B. False

QUESTION NO: 61

True or False?

Voiding a check and reversing the payment document and the vendor invoice is a process that requires two different steps.

A. True

B. False

QUESTION NO: 62

True or false?

The chart of depreciation is defined at company code level.

A. True

B. False

QUESTION NO: 63

True or False?

The sub-number for an asset can be assigned internally or externally, depending on the configuration of the asset class.

A. True

B. False

QUESTION NO: 64

Identify the incorrect statements: (Choose two)

A. Ordinary depreciation is the planned reduction in asset value due to normal wear and tear.

B. Special depreciation is a purely tax-based type of depreciation for wear and tear.

C. Unplanned depreciation is used for calculation of depreciation on assets that were not in the original budget.

D. Unit-of-production depreciation is not an option in SAP ERP.

QUESTION NO: 65

Messages for validations can have different meanings. Each message is represented by a symbol (letter): Select the number where the symbol has an incorrect meaning.

1. I = Information

2. W = Warning

3. E = Error

4. C = Cancel

QUESTION NO: 66

Which of the following statements are incorrect in relation with the fiscal year functionality? (Choose two):

A. Year independent assumes there are only regular opening and closing dates.

B. The fiscal year variant specifies if a period is open or closed.

C. Special periods are associated with calendar dates.

D. A year shift can only be used for non-calendar years.

QUESTION NO: 67

Which of the following is correct about documents? (Choose three):

A. A document type controls the document header data.

B. The account group dictates number ranges and the screen layout for document entry.

C. The document type controls the number assignment for a document.

D. The document type controls the account types allowed for posting.

E. The document type controls the posting rules for documents.

QUESTION NO: 68

Which of the following statements are correct? (Choose three):

A. Accounts managed in a foreign currency can only be posted to in that currency.

B. Open item management must be used for all P&L accounts.

C. Line item display should always be set for reconciliation accounts.

D. The three charts of accounts are called operating, group, and tailored.

E. The group chart of accounts is used for consolidation purposes.

QUESTION NO: 69

Which of the following statements are correct? (Choose three)

A. Boolean classes specify which message classes can be used for validation messages.

B. Validations can be tailored using unlimited field combinations to generate a user defined message as a warning, error or information message when required conditions are not met.

C. PC Profit Center Accounting and GA Allocations (FI-SL) cannot use validations.

D. You can substitute a cost center based on pre-defined conditions in the substitution rule.

E. PS Project System and CS Consolidation only accept validations.

F. Validation and substitution rules are only performed when manually initiated in the transaction.

QUESTION NO: 70

With regard to tolerances, which of the following is correct? (Choose four):

A. Tolerances are managed at the client level.

B. Tolerance group blank has the lowest limits and applies to anyone not assigned to a specific tolerance group.

C. After a user has been assigned to a specific tolerance group, they need to be maintained in every company code for which they have access.

D. Tolerances have settings for limits that apply at the document level and to permitted payment differences.

E. When tolerances for the user and tolerances in the customer/vendor master are jointly related to a transaction, the most restrictive takes precedence.

QUESTION NO: 71

Which of the following is correct regarding the Cash Journal? (Choose two):

A. Cash journals can be used instead of standard A/P and A/R transactions.

B. Can have any needed business transactions created at the time of document entry.

C. Allows new business transactions to be defined in two places.

D. Cannot be used to process entries for one-time accounts.

E. Cannot record financial transactions related to checks.

QUESTION NO: 72

Which of the following is incorrect regarding reason codes? (Choose three):

A. Reason codes can be configured to point to automatic charge-off accounts.

B. Can automatically generate letters based on reason code.

C. Is independent of credit management.

D. Are exclusively used for partial payments and residual items.

E. Can extend the customer discount to an unapplied account if within tolerance.

QUESTION NO: 73

Which of the following statements is correct regarding document parking? (Choose three):

A. When posting a parked document, a new document number is created.

B. Held documents have no document number assigned by the system.

C. Held and parked documents can be evaluated in reports.

D. Workflow can be used to post parked documents.

E. Held documents are only available to the user who created them.

QUESTION NO: 74

Which of the following statements are correct? (Choose two):

A. The paying company code is the one that identifies intercompany payment relationships.

B. Activation of the payment method supplements provides additional print and sort options.

Inquiries: support@sapseries.com

C. All company code specifications pertain to the amounts for incoming and outgoing payments.

D. Payment method/country specifies the print program to be used.

E. A Payment Medium Workbench (PMW) only requires basic ABAP skills in order to configure enhanced payment media.

QUESTION NO: 75

Which of the following statements on payments are incorrect? (Choose one)

A. Each payment run is restricted to company codes in one country.

B. Next payment date considers discounts to be taken based on configuration.

C. A proposal must be generated before the payment run can be executed.

D. You can use multiple payment methods in the same payment run, in which case they need to be prioritized.

E. All the above are incorrect

QUESTION NO: 76

At which level is the vendor account number assigned?

A. At the client level.

B. At a combination of client and purchasing organization segment level.

C. At the company code segment level.

D. At a combination of client and company code segment level.

QUESTION NO: 77

True or False?

Segment reporting can be carried out by using business areas.

A. True

B. False

QUESTION NO: 78

Down payments can be posted using a special G/L transaction. What is the main benefit of this functionality?

A. It posts down-payments to a reconciliation account that is different from the one used for ordinary payables and receivables.

B. It shows data in the appendix of the balance sheet.

C. It automatically creates the final invoice and clears down-payments against it.

D. It automatically clears down-payment requests.

QUESTION NO: 79

Identify the correct statements here below. (Choose two)

A. Asset classes are configured at the company code level.

B. Depreciation Areas hold the values calculated by different depreciation keys.

C. In some cases an asset can be created at the time of document entry.

D. Cross-system transfer variants hold transfer values

QUESTION NO: 80

Which are correct in the following statements? (Choose three)

A. Classic drilldown reporting remains a good option for the evaluation of G/L account balances.

B. Report Painter is a basic reporting tool that is not compatible with Report Writer.

C. Report-report interfaces are suitable for reporting on large numbers of characteristics and changing combinations.

D. Forms can be a framework for reports.

E. The different types of forms always need key figures in their definition.

Practice Test 2 - Answers

QUESTION NO: 1

Which statement below regarding financial reporting is correct? (Choose one)

A. The system can translate a financial statement into any currency for reporting purposes.

B. During display of a financial statement, the system can automatically calculate the profit and loss statement result.

C. A summarized financial statement can be generated for any hierarchy level in the financial statement version.

D. A financial statement version cannot include more than one company code, unless FI-LC is used.

E. A financial statement version displays either a balance sheet or a profit and lost statement, but not both.

Answer: A

Page(s): 188, 189

QUESTION NO: 2

Which of the following statements about vendor transactions are correct? (Choose Two)

A. A vendor down payment request cannot be included in the payment program.

B. A vendor down payment is cleared after a final invoice is received from the vendor.

C. Vendor down payments are shown on balance sheets under a normal reconciliation account for payables.

D. A special G/L transaction is a transaction included in the Special Purpose Ledger under a coding block in G/L account.

E. A vendor down payment request is a noted item.

Answer: B, E

Page(s): 113, 114, 115

QUESTION NO: 3

Select the correct statement regarding Cross-company code transactions.

A. No configuration needs to be performed for cross-company code transactions.

B. A cross-company code document transaction number contains the company code of the second company number, the document number of the first company code and the fiscal year.

C. None of the above is correct.

Answer: C

Page(s): 84

QUESTION NO: 4

True or False?

The asset class is a selection option in all FI-AA standard reports.

A. True

B. False

Answer: A

Page(s): 163

QUESTION NO: 5

Screen layout rules are used to control which of the following? (Choose two)

A. Maintenance level

B. references/copies

C. Field attributes

D. All are correct

Answer: A, C

Page(s): 91, 92, 111, 151

QUESTION NO: 6

True or False?

The Chart of Depreciation is a catalog of country-specific depreciation areas based on various business aspects.

A. True

B. False

Answer: A

Page(s): 145

QUESTION NO: 7

True or False?

When an asset master record is created the default values defined for each asset class are automatically applied to the new asset.

A. True

B. False

Answer: A

Page(s): 147

QUESTION NO: 8

True or False?

Various charts of depreciation can be assigned to the same asset class.

A. True

B. False

Answer: A

Page(s): 147

QUESTION NO: 9

The layout of the master data in each asset class defines:

A. The number of tab pages.

B. The specific field groups that appear on tab pages.

C. The names of tab pages.

D. All are correct.

Answer: D

Page(s): 151

QUESTION NO: 10

True or False?

The Segment field is a standard account assignment object.

A. True

B. False

Answer: A

Page(s): 35, 76

QUESTION NO: 11

A specific type of depreciation valuation is represented by which of the following?

A. The chart of depreciation

B. The chart of accounts

C. The depreciation area

Answer: C

Page(s): 145

QUESTION NO: 12

Which of the following statements pertain to a Detail List? (choose two):

A. Key figures are normally in the rows of the list.

B. An individual object is formatted for all key figures depending on the form.

C. The rows contain characteristic values.

D. Key figures are normally in the columns of the list.

E. Various objects are formatted using a selection of key figures.

Answer: A, B

Page(s): 192

QUESTION NO: 13

Identify the correct statement related to Financial Statement versions (FSV). (Choose one):

A. The best way to create a Financial Statement Version is to start from scratch, because the copy function can cause errors that are difficult to edit.

B. A Financial Statement Version is defined at company code level.

C. You can define a maximum of 999 financial statement versions.

D. A Financial Statement Version is defined at chart of account level.

E. You can define a maximum of 99 financial statement versions.

Answer: D

Page(s): 188, 189

QUESTION NO: 14

True or False?

When defining a dual-axis form the rows can be used for key figures while the columns can be used for the characteristics, or vice versa.

A. True

B. False

Answer: A

Page(s): 193

QUESTION NO: 15

Any number of variance analyses based on actual and planned data can be performed for which of the below?

A. Balance display

B. Key figure reports

C. Reports for financial statement analysis

Answer: C

Page(s): 190, 191

QUESTION NO: 16

Payment method supplement is a functionality that allows printing payments with additional vouchers.

A. True

B. False

Answer: B

Page(s): 124

QUESTION NO: 17

The steps in a Dunning run follow the sequence below:

A. Dun accounts, Select accounts, Dun line items.

B. Dun accounts, Dun line items, Select accounts.

C. Select accounts, Dun line items, Dun accounts.

D. Dun line items, Select accounts, Dun accounts.

Answer: C

Page(s): 96

QUESTION NO: 18

True or False?

The Payment Program is designed to handle national and international transactions.

A. True

B. False

Answer: A

Page(s): 122

QUESTION NO: 19

False or True?

Settings for the Payment Program are normally accessible through the user interface.

A. True

B. False

Answer: A

Page(s): 123

QUESTION NO: 20

What is the highest dunning level attainable by item in a customer master record?

A. Level 10

B. Level 9

C. Level 7

D. Level 12

Answer: B

Page(s): 96

QUESTION NO: 21

True or False?

Exchange rate differences in SAP ERP are gathered automatically in a worklist that needs to be posted manually

A. True

B. False

Answer: B

Page(s): 63, 64

QUESTION NO: 22

True or False?

It is possible for hidden fields to contain values that will be used by the system.

A. True

B. False

Answer: A

Page(s): 52

QUESTION NO: 23

What are the three types of chart of accounts in SAP ERP?

A. Consolidation chart of accounts

B. Company chart of accounts

C. Group chart of accounts

D. Country-specific chart of accounts

E. Operating chart of accounts

F. International chart of accounts

Answer: C, D, E

Page(s): 49

QUESTION NO: 24

Posting keys are used to control (Choose three):
A. Account type

B. Document type

C. Field status

D. Number range

E. Debit/credit indicator

Answer: A, C, E

Page(s): 42, 43

QUESTION NO: 25

What happens when the payment method in a document is different from the payment method in the master data?

A. The payment run will stop and then the system will issue an error message.

B. The payment run will temporarily stop then the system will prompt the user to correct the data. After correction of the data, the payment run will continue.

C. The document data will override the master data.

D. The master data will override the document data.

Answer: C

Page(s): 118

QUESTION NO: 26

Which objects here below can be posted to from a cash journal? (Choose two)

A. Customer

B. One-time customer

C. Asset master

D. Accrual Engine

E. Material master

Answer: A, B

Page(s): 67, 68

QUESTION NO: 27

Which parameters below are required to execute a payment run? (Choose two)

A. The payment method

B. The company code

C. The currency

D. The bank account

Answer: A, B

Page(s): 122, 123

QUESTION NO: 28

Select here below one of the benefits of document parking?

A. It enables the use of a principle known as dual control.

B. It enables the posting of technically incomplete documents.

C. It provides a user friendly option to change posted documents.

D. It enables the assignment of individual document numbers.

Answer: A

Page(s): 44, 45

QUESTION NO: 29

Parking documents is better than holding documents for the following reasons (Choose two):

A. Parked documents can be posted through automatic speech recognition.

B. Parked documents can be posted using a cross-client approach to increase efficiency.

C. Workflows can be used to post parked documents.

D. Parked documents can be changed and posted by a different user, in order to support the dual control principle.

Answer: C, D

Page(s): 44, 45

QUESTION NO: 30

What is the main benefit of posting a down payment using a special G/L transaction?

A. Down-payment requests are automatically cleared.

B. The down-payments posts to a reconciliation account that is different from the one normally used for payables and receivables.

C. The data will show in the appendix of the balance sheet.

D. Down-payments are automatically cleared by the final invoice.

Answer: B

Page(s): 113, 115

QUESTION NO: 31

Which transactions in the procurement process with valuated goods receipt lead to the creation of documents in FI? (Choose two):

A. Create purchase requisition

B. Enter invoice receipt

C. Post valuated goods receipt

D. Create purchase order

Answer: B, C

Page(s): 137

QUESTION NO: 32

True or false?

Year-specific fiscal year variants can be used if:

The start and end date of the posting periods are different every year.

A. True

B. False

Answer: A

Page(s): 38

QUESTION NO: 33

What are the commonly used exchange rate types and their respective uses? (Choose three):

A. Average rate for posting and clearing (M).

B. Daily rate for current entries (S).

C. Buying rate (G).

D. Selling rate (B).

E. Forecast rate for budgeting (P).

Answer: A, C, D

Page(s): 39

QUESTION NO: 34

Line items of a G/L account should always be set for display.

A. True

B. False

Answer: B

Page(s): 53

QUESTION NO: 35

When a G/L account is managed in a foreign currency, it can only be posted to in the specific foreign currency.

A. True

B. False

Answer: A

Page(s): 54

QUESTION NO: 37

True of False?

Company codes for different countries can use the same chart of accounts.

A. True

B. False

Answer: A

Page(s): 49

QUESTION NO: 38

True or False?

Segments have a time reference that determines their validity dates.

A. True

B. False

Answer: B

Page(s): 34, 35, 76

QUESTION NO: 39

An accounting manager wants to ensure that changes to certain fields in customer and vendor data are always confirmed by a second person who has the appropriate authorization. This dual control principle can be made required by defining particular fields as a (choose one):

A. Confirmation field

B. Required field

C. Sensitive field

D. Management field

E. Authorization field

F. Dual control field

Answer: C

Page(s): 92, 112

QUESTION NO: 40

A complete vendor account normally has the following parts:

A. Sales area segment

B. General data

C. Company code segment

D. Purchasing organization segment

E. Terms of payment

Answer: B, C, D

Page(s): 110

QUESTION NO: 41

True of False?

Internal number assignments enable SAP ERP users to assign numbers manually.

A. True

B. False

Answer: B

Page(s): 42

QUESTION NO: 42

Choose the incorrect statements: (Choose two)

A. If a user can assign document numbers manually, external number assignment is allowed.

B. External numbers may be alphanumeric.

C. Every company code may define its own document types.

D. Every company code may define its own document number ranges.

E. Document number assignment is defined at the client level.

Answer: C, E

Page(s): 41, 42

QUESTION NO: 43

What influences the field status of document fields? (Choose two):

A. Account-dependent field status

B. Field status group

C. Posting key

D. Key-dependent field status

E. Account group

Answer: B, C

Page(s): 41

QUESTION NO: 44

Choose the correct statement: (Choose one)

A. The field status group controls the field display during document entry.

B. Each G/L account has a field status group.

C. The posting period variant is assigned to the company code.

D. All statements are correct.

E. All the above statements are incorrect.

Answer: D

Page(s): 43, 44

QUESTION NO: 45

Identify the incorrect statements (Choose two):

A. There are two ways to reverse a document in SAP ERP Financials.

B. A reversal reason code needs to be entered before a document is reversed.

C. Reversal by negative posting is used to reverse documents with cleared items.

D. In normal reversal posting the posted amount is not added to the transaction figures.

Answer: C, D

Page(s): 63

QUESTION NO: 46

Which cash discount accounts are used in the net procedure? (Choose two):

A. Cash discount clearing account

B. Cash discount revenue account

C. Cash discount expense account

D. Cash discount loss account

Answer: A, D

Page(s): 119

QUESTION NO: 47

Which of the below are examples for cross-company code transactions in SAP ERP? (Choose two)

A. Central purchasing

B. Central master data

C. Central payment

D. Central management

Answer: A, C

Page(s): 83

QUESTION NO: 48

True of False?
There are two basic transactions for clearing open items: account clearing and post with clearing

A. True

B. False

Inquiries: support@sapseries.com

Answer: A

Page(s): 85

QUESTION NO: 49

G/L accounts must be defined for exchange rate losses or gains.

A. True

B. False

Answer: A

Page(s): 64

QUESTION NO: 50

True or False?

Configuration of the payment program is divided in the following five areas:

- All company codes
- Paying company codes
- Payment method/country
- Payment method for company code
- House banks

A. True

B. False

Answer: B

Page(s): 123, 124

QUESTION NO: 51

The sequence in which the payment methods are entered in the payment parameters does not matter.

Inquiries: support@sapseries.com

A. True

B. False

Answer: B

Page(s): 123

QUESTION NO: 52

True or False?

A payment proposal can only be edited, deleted, and recreated once. After this the user will need to start a new payment proposal if more changes are needed.

A. True

B. False

Answer: B

Page(s): 131

QUESTION NO: 53

True or false?

Customers without a dunning procedure in the master record cannot be dunned.

A. True

B. False

Answer: A

Page(s): 94

QUESTION NO: 54

True or False?

Dunning parameters are only used to specify what needs to be included in the dunning run.

A. True

B. False

Answer: B

Page(s): 93, 96

QUESTION NO: 55

True or false?
Payment terms for credit memos usually do not apply, and the due date is typically the due date of the associated invoice or the baseline date of the document.

A. True

B. False

Answer: A

Page(s): 97

QUESTION NO: 56

The dunning data is not updated until the dunning notices are printed.

A. True

B. False

Answer: A

Page(s): 95

QUESTION NO: 57

True or False?

A dunning proposal can be changed, deleted, and redone as many times as needed.

A. True

B. False

Answer: A

Page(s): 97

QUESTION NO: 58

The last dunning level leads to the manual dunning procedure

A. True

B. False

Answer: A

Page(s): 97

QUESTION NO: 59

SAP ERP can be configured to calculate interest for customers or vendors who owe a company. Interest will be calculated for all customers and vendors including the ones owed money by the company.

A. True

B. False

Answer: B

Page(s): 69,70

QUESTION NO: 60

True or False?

Payment processes only use three types of documents.

A. True

B. False

Inquiries: support@sapseries.com

Answer: A

Page(s): 127

QUESTION NO: 61

True or False?

Voiding a check and reversing the payment document and the vendor invoice is a process that requires two different steps.

A. True

B. False

Answer: A

Page(s): 129

QUESTION NO: 62

True or false?

The chart of depreciation is defined at company code level.

A. True

B. False

Answer: B

Page(s): 145

QUESTION NO: 63

True or False?

The sub-number for an asset can be assigned internally or externally, depending on the configuration of the asset class.

A. True

B. False

 Inquiries: support@sapseries.com

Answer: A

Page(s): 151

QUESTION NO: 64

Identify the incorrect statements: (Choose two)

A. Ordinary depreciation is the planned reduction in asset value due to normal wear and tear.

B. Special depreciation is a purely tax-based type of depreciation for wear and tear.

C. Unplanned depreciation is used for calculation of depreciation on assets that were not in the original budget.

D. Unit-of-production depreciation is not an option in SAP ERP.

Answer: C, D

Page(s): 157, 158, 159

QUESTION NO: 65

Messages for validations can have different meanings. Each message is represented by a symbol (letter): Select the number where the symbol has an incorrect meaning.

1. I = Information

2. W = Warning

3. E = Error

4. C = Cancel

Answer: 4

Page(s): 46

QUESTION NO: 66

Which of the following statements are incorrect in relation with the fiscal year functionality? (Choose two):

A. Year independent assumes there are only regular opening and closing dates.

B. The fiscal year variant specifies if a period is open or closed.

C. Special periods are associated with calendar dates.

D. A year shift can only be used for non-calendar years.

Answer: B, C

Page(s): 37, 38, 40

QUESTION NO: 67

Which of the following is correct about documents? (Choose three):

A. A document type controls the document header data.

B. The account group dictates number ranges and the screen layout for document entry.

C. The document type controls the number assignment for a document.

D. The document type controls the account types allowed for posting.

E. The document type controls the posting rules for documents.

Answer: A, C, D

Page(s): 41, 42, 52

QUESTION NO: 68

Which of the following statements are correct? (Choose three):

A. Accounts managed in a foreign currency can only be posted to in that currency.

B. Open item management must be used for all P&L accounts.

C. Line item display should always be set for reconciliation accounts.

D. The three charts of accounts are called operating, group, and tailored.

E. The group chart of accounts is used for consolidation purposes.

Answer: A, D, E

Page(s): 49, 53, 54

QUESTION NO: 69

Which of the following statements are correct? (Choose three)

A. Boolean classes specify which message classes can be used for validation messages.

B. Validations can be tailored using unlimited field combinations to generate a user defined message as a warning, error or information message when required conditions are not met.

C. PC Profit Center Accounting and GA Allocations (FI-SL) cannot use validations.

D. You can substitute a cost center based on pre-defined conditions in the substitution rule.

E. PS Project System and CS Consolidation only accept validations.

F. Validation and substitution rules are only performed when manually initiated in the transaction.

Answer: A, C, D

Page(s): 45, 46, 47

QUESTION NO: 70

With regard to tolerances, which of the following is correct? (Choose four):

A. Tolerances are managed at the client level.

B. Tolerance group blank has the lowest limits and applies to anyone not assigned to a specific tolerance group.

C. After a user has been assigned to a specific tolerance group, they need to be maintained in every company code for which they have access.

D. Tolerances have settings for limits that apply at the document level and to permitted payment differences.

E. When tolerances for the user and tolerances in the customer/vendor master are jointly related to a transaction, the most restrictive takes precedence.

Answer: B, C, D, E

Page(s): 60, 61, 120, 121

QUESTION NO: 71

Which of the following is correct regarding the Cash Journal? (Choose two):

A. Cash journals can be used instead of standard A/P and A/R transactions.

B. Can have any needed business transactions created at the time of document entry.

C. Allows new business transactions to be defined in two places.

D. Cannot be used to process entries for one-time accounts.

E. Cannot record financial transactions related to checks.

Answer: A, C

Page(s): 67, 68

QUESTION NO: 72

Which of the following is incorrect regarding reason codes? (Choose three):

A. Reason codes can be configured to point to automatic charge-off accounts.

B. Can automatically generate letters based on reason code.

C. Is independent of credit management.

D. Are exclusively used for partial payments and residual items.

E. Can extend the customer discount to an unapplied account if within tolerance.

Answer: C, D, E

Page(s): 63, 101, 121, 129

QUESTION NO: 73

Inquiries: support@sapseries.com

Which of the following statements is correct regarding document parking? (Choose three):

A. When posting a parked document, a new document number is created.

B. Held documents have no document number assigned by the system.

C. Held and parked documents can be evaluated in reports.

D. Workflow can be used to post parked documents.

E. Held documents are only available to the user who created them.

Answer: B, D, E

Page(s): 44, 45

QUESTION NO: 74

Which of the following statements are correct? (Choose two):

A. The paying company code is the one that identifies intercompany payment relationships.

B. Activation of the payment method supplements provides additional print and sort options.

C. All company code specifications pertain to the amounts for incoming and outgoing payments.

D. Payment method/country specifies the print program to be used.

E. The Payment Medium Workbench (PMW) only requires basic ABAP skills in order to configure enhanced payment media.

Answer: B, D

Page(s): 124, 125, 126, 133

QUESTION NO: 75

Which of the following statements on payments are incorrect? (Choose one)

A. Each payment run is restricted to company codes in one country.

B. Next payment date considers discounts to be taken based on configuration.

C. A proposal must be generated before the payment run can be executed.

D. You can use multiple payment methods in the same payment run, in which case they need to be prioritized.

E. All the above are incorrect

Answer: B

Page(s): 123, 124, 130

QUESTION NO: 76

At which level is the vendor account number assigned?

A. At the client level.

B. At a combination of client and purchasing organization segment level.

C. At the company code segment level.

D. At a combination of client and company code segment level.

Answer: A

Page(s): 109, 110

QUESTION NO: 77

True or False?

Segment reporting can be carried out by using business areas.

A. True

B. False

Answer: A

Page(s): 104

QUESTION NO: 78

Down payments can be posted using a special G/L transaction. What is the main benefit of this functionality?

A. It posts down-payments to a reconciliation account that is different from the one used for ordinary payables and receivables.

B. It shows data in the appendix of the balance sheet.

C. It automatically creates the final invoice and clears down-payments against it.

D. It automatically clears down-payment requests.

Answer: A

Page(s): 113

QUESTION NO: 79

Identify the correct statements here below. (Choose two)

A. Asset classes are configured at the company code level.

B. Depreciation Areas hold the values calculated by different depreciation keys.

C. In some cases an asset can be created at the time of document entry.

D. Cross-system transfer variants hold transfer values

Answer: B, C

Page(s): 145, 147, 153, 155

QUESTION NO: 80

Which are correct in the following statements? (Choose three)

A. Classic drilldown reporting remains a good option for the evaluation of G/L account balances.

B. Report Painter is a basic reporting tool that is not compatible with Report Writer.

C. Report-report interfaces are suitable for reporting on large numbers of characteristics and changing combinations.

D. Forms can be a framework for reports.

E. The different types of forms always need key figures in their definition.

Answer: A, C, D

Page(s): 190, 191, 192, 193, 194

Inquiries: support@sapseries.com

Practice Test 3

QUESTION NO: 1

Payment methods are defined with (Choose Two):

A. Currency for the company code.

B. A House Bank link.

C. A currency for the country level.

D. Maximum and minimum payment amounts.

QUESTION NO: 2

True or False?

Drilldown reporting is a tool that enables users to analyze G/L account transaction figures and financial statements.

A. True

B. False

QUESTION NO: 3

True or False?

Once a Chart of depreciation has been assigned to a company code, the required data for asset accounting should be added to the company code.

A. True

B. False

QUESTION NO: 4

All reconciliation accounts and all G/L accounts with open item transactions in foreign currency must be assigned to a G/L account for realized losses and gains. Which of the following options are usable for this assignment (Choose two)?

A. A single G/L account can be used for all currencies and currency types.

B. A single G/L account cannot be used for currencies and currency types.

C. A single G/L account can be used per currency.

D. A single G/L account cannot be used per currency type.

QUESTION NO: 5

Which statements are relevant for the Payment Medium Workbench (PMW)? (Choose three):

A. New formats can be created with little programming experience.

B. Payment groups are created depending on the level of granularity.

C. Performance for mass payments is improved.

D. PMW can only be used with certain payment methods.

E. There are four steps in the PMW process.

QUESTION NO: 6

Identify the correct statements regarding a Chart of Depreciation (Choose Three):

A. Needs to be assigned to a company code.

B. Depreciation areas can be added or deleted according to needs.

C. New depreciation areas can be opened even after system Go-live.

D. The fact that a Chart of depreciation is country-specific implies that it meets all requirements for the defined country, and cannot be changed.

QUESTION NO: 7

Which statements are correct in regards to Asset classes? (Choose five):

A. It has two main sections: a master data section and a depreciation area section.

B. For flexibility purposes an asset can be assigned to multiple asset classes.

C. An asset class is assigned to at least one chart of depreciation.

D. It only has a single section for master data.

E. Asset classes are created at the client level.

F. Assets under construction and low value assets are special asset classes.

G. Many different charts of depreciation can be assigned to the same asset class.

H. Asset classes are created at the company code level.

QUESTION NO: 8

True or False?

Number assignment for fixed assets can be defined as internal or external

A. True

B. False

QUESTION NO: 9

True or False?

SAP ERP delivers standard depreciation areas; therefore additional areas cannot be defined.

A. True

B. False

QUESTION NO: 10

True or False?

When multiple financial statement versions are in use, multiple depreciation areas need to post to the G/L.

A. True

B. False

QUESTION NO: 11

True or False?

If necessary, dunning notices can automatically be printed out right after a dunning run.

A. True

B. False

QUESTION NO: 12

True or False?

When company codes use the same chart of accounts, they cannot have different charts of depreciation.

A. True

B. False

QUESTION NO: 13

Identify the correct statements regarding drilldown lists (Choose three):

A. An individual object is formatted for all key figures according to the form.

B. Usually key figures are in rows of a list.

C. Key figures are represented by the columns of a list.

D. Characteristic values are represented by the row.

E. Several objects are formatted using a selection of key figures.

QUESTION NO: 14

Which Report painter report only takes into consideration financial statement items needed for the calculation of specific key figures?

A. Balance display

B. Reports for financial statement analysis

C. Key figure reports

QUESTION NO: 15

Reports for financial statement analysis, key figure reports and balance display are report types usable for (Choose one):

A. Business area evaluations

B. Client evaluation

C. G/L account evaluations

QUESTION NO: 16

Exception lists can contain any of the items here below (Choose Three):

A. No payment block indicator.

B. Blocked items.

C. Vendor accounts with credit balances.

D. Items with invalid payment methods.

E. Items with missing payment methods in the master data and in the line item.

QUESTION NO: 17

True or False?

The Payment process consists of five steps.

A. True

B. False

QUESTION NO: 18

Identify the incorrect options pertaining to main settings for the Payment program (Choose two):

A. All company codes

B. Payment method/country

C. Bank currencies

D. Company codes

E. Bank selection

F. payment method for company code

G. Accounts and Amounts

QUESTION NO: 19

When no particular company code is mentioned in Automatic payments for all company codes:

A. The system displays an error message.

B. The system automatically considers the sending company code as the paying company code.

C. The system will automatically derive the paying company code.

QUESTION NO: 20

Tolerance days for payments will defer payment to the (Choose the correct option):

A. Next transaction

B. Next month

C. Next posting period

D. Next payment run

QUESTION NO: 21

True or False?

The Payment program is designed to process incoming payments as well as outgoing payments.

A. True

B. False

QUESTION NO: 22

True or False?

The Paying company code is responsible for handling outgoing payments.

A. True

B. False

QUESTION NO: 23

How are exchange rate differences posted?

A. Manually in a profit and loss account.

B. Manually as realized gains or losses.

C. Automatically as unrealized gains or losses.

D. Automatically as realized gains or losses.

QUESTION NO: 24

True or False?

In SAP ERP, the strict lowest value allows write-ups as an alternative valuation method.

A. True

B. False

QUESTION NO: 25

In SAP ERP, the length of a G/L account number ranges between:

A. One and six digits

B. One and seven digits

C. One and eight digits

D. One and nine digits

E. One and ten digits

QUESTION NO: 26

What must be done if a customer wants Profit Center updates to be included in the General Ledger, in an environment that is running the New G/L (Choose one)?

A. Assign the Profit Center update scenario to the ledger.

B. Activation of transfer prices in Profit Center Accounting.

C. Setting up the same group currency for all company codes and profit centers.

D. Deactivation of document splitting for profit centers.

QUESTION NO: 27

What is the maximum number of line items that can be entered in a FI document?

A. Unlimited

B. 99

C. 9999

D. 999

QUESTION NO: 28

What definition is essential in the configuration of a dunning procedure (Choose one)?

A. The dunning levels and the language of the dunning note.

B. The dunning levels and the dunning charges for each dunning level.

C. The dunning levels and the account determination to post dunning interest.

D. The dunning charges for each dunning level and the customers to be dunned.

QUESTION NO: 29

How can a user change the short text field of a G/L account?

A. By making the change at the beginning of a new fiscal year.

B. By ensuring that the field status of the chart of accounts segment allows it.

C. On a central basis in the chart of accounts segment.

D. On an individual basis in the company code segment.

QUESTION NO: 30

Which option below provides the call-up points for validations in FI?

A. Document header, document type, and complete document.

B. Basic data section, detailed data section, and line item.

C. Basic data section, line item, and complete document.

D. Document header, line item, and complete document.

QUESTION NO: 31

A company decides to merge two cost centers, and wants all future postings to go to a single cost center. If a posting is made to the wrong cost center in FI, SAP ERP should automatically replace it by the correct one. How can this be implemented?

A. By defining two substitutions for the Line Item call-up point.

B. By creating a user-specific program that will automatically substitute incorrect cost centers overnight.

C. By defining a substitution in FI with the incorrect cost center as a prerequisite and the correct one as the substituted value.

D. By defining a validation in CO to ensure that the functional area is filled in the cost center master.

QUESTION NO: 32

What determines the field status for a vendor?

A. Account group, transaction, and the chart of accounts.

B. Account group, chart of accounts, and the company code.

C. Account group, transaction, and the company code.

D. Transaction, chart of accounts, and the company code.

QUESTION NO: 33

True or false?

A business area can be directly assigned to a company code.

A. True

B. False

QUESTION NO: 34

Which tools here below are used for maintaining exchange rates (Choose three):

A. Direct quotation

B. Inversion

C. Indirect quotation

D. Base currency

E. Exchange rate spreads

QUESTION NO: 35

True or False?

A G/L account has the following segments?

• Chart of accounts segment

• Corporate segment

A. True

B. False

QUESTION NO: 36

True or False?

All G/L accounts with open item management are required to have line item display.

A. True

B. False

QUESTION NO: 37

If company codes use different operational charts of accounts, you cannot carry out cross-company code controlling.

A. True

B. False

QUESTION NO: 38

True or False?

The options for field status definitions have the following priority, starting with the highest:

1. Required entry

2. Display

3. Hide

4. Optional entry

A. True

B. False

QUESTION NO: 39

True or false?

Segments are assigned to a hierarchy similar to the hierarchy of the profit centers from which they can be derived.

A. True

B. False

QUESTION NO: 40

True or False?

The definition of sensitive fields is not company code-specific.

A. True

B. False

QUESTION NO: 41

True or False?

Maintenance for Customer and Vendor accounts must be decentralized by company code.

A. True

B. False

QUESTION NO: 42

True of False?

General Ledger accounts always use external number assignment .

A. True

B. False

QUESTION NO: 43

Choose the correct statement:

A. At the beginning of each year the system always restarts the document number assignment at the start of the number range.

B. Document number ranges can overlap if needed.

C. Several number ranges can be assigned to a single document type simultaneously.

D. The same number range cannot be used for several document types.

E. All the above statements are incorrect.

QUESTION NO: 44

What are the standard posting keys for G/L accounts and on which side of the account do they post to? (Choose two)

A. Debit, posting key 70

B. Credit, posting key 75

C. Credit, posting key 50

D. Debit, posting key 40

E. Credit, posting key 39

QUESTION NO: 45

Identify the incorrect statements (Choose three):

A. The authorization group in the posting period variant only pertains to authorization for posting in special periods.

B. A posting period variant must contain at least one line with the entry valid for all accounts.

C. The account range in the posting period variant consists of G/L accounts.

D. Posting periods are opened and closed automatically.

E. It is not possible for more than two periods to be open at the same time.

QUESTION NO: 46

Select the preconditions for processing negative postings? (Choose two)

A. Negative reversal postings need to be included in the company's business process.

B. The company code must allow negative postings.

C. The user wants to set the transaction figures back to the initial state prior to the incorrect posting.

D. The reversal reason must be defined for handling negative reversals.

QUESTION NO: 47

What are the types of taxation that can be mapped in the SAP ERP system? (Choose two)

A. Taxation at national level.

B. Taxation at international level.

C. Taxation at regional/jurisdictional level.

D. Input tax.

E. Output tax.

QUESTION NO: 48

What are the correct statements regarding tax in cross-company code transactions? (Choose three)

A. A cross-company code transaction involves at least two documents.

B. Tax amounts in a cross-company code transaction cannot automatically be distributed to the company codes in which the expenses/revenues occurred.

C. A custom report needs to be configured to distribute tax to the company codes in which the expenses/revenues occurred.

D. Cross-company code transactions are not supposed to involve tax.

E. By default, the tax calculated is entirely posted to the first company code.

QUESTION NO: 49

Identify the incorrect statements here below (Choose two):

A. Account clearing occurs when a credit memo is cleared with an open invoice.

B. Posting with clearing involves posting a payment for an open invoice with a resulting zero balance.

C. A partial payment clears the invoice and the payment; then creates a new open item.

D. A residual item results in an open invoice and an incoming payment remaining in the customer account as open items.

QUESTION NO: 50

Which statements indicate the correct ways a G/L account can be determined for exchange rate differences?

A. A single G/L account can be used for all currencies and currency types.

B. A single G/L account can be used for every currency and currency type.

C. A single G/L account can be used for every currency.

D. A single G/L account can be used for every currency type.

E. All statements above are correct

QUESTION NO: 51

True or False?

The parameters indicate the accounts and documents for inclusion in a payment run.

A. True

B. False

QUESTION NO: 52

True or false?

The company codes entered in payment run parameters can pertain to multiple countries.

A. True

B. False

QUESTION NO: 53

True or False?

The exception list is the confirmation for a successful payment proposal.

A. True

B. False

QUESTION NO: 54

True or False?

Dunning notices should only be sent to customers.

A. True

B. False

QUESTION NO: 55

Identify the incorrect reasons for an overdue item to not be dunned (Choose two):

A. The account is not included in the parameters.

B. The items or accounts are blocked for dunning.

C. The items exceed the grace period.

D. The overdue amount is greater than the minimum amount.

E. The dunning data has not been updated since the last dunning run and *Always*

dun? is not checked.

QUESTION NO: 56

How many steps are in a dunning run?

A. 5

B. 6

C. 3

D. 4

QUESTION NO: 54

True or False?

A dunning procedure can have between 1 and 9 dunning levels.

A. True

B. False

QUESTION NO: 55

True or False?

If *Always dun* is selected a dunning notice will be sent, regardless of any dunning data updates since the last dunning run.

A. True

B. False

QUESTION NO: 56

True or False?

A single dunning form can be used for all dunning levels.

A. True

B. False

QUESTION NO: 57

True or False?

Calculation of interest automatically starts on overdue customer accounts, even if the account master data has no interest calculation indicator.

A. True

B. False

QUESTION NO: 58

True or False?

SAP ERP can be configured to perform interest calculation on account balances and on arrears.

A. True

B. False

QUESTION NO: 59

True or False?

You cannot void a check unless you reverse the payment document.

A. True

B. False

QUESTION NO: 60

True or False?

In the Lockbox process, payment advice notes contain the information used to clear open items on vendor accounts.

A. True

B. False

QUESTION NO: 61

The sample chart of accounts provided by SAP can be tailored to meet the requirements of a specific company.

A. True

B. False

QUESTION NO: 62

True or False?

The standard mass retirement function in asset accounting uses a worklist.

A. True

B. False

QUESTION NO: 63

SAP ERP offers different depreciation calculation methods. Identify the incorrect individual calculation method here below:

A. Base method.

B. Declining-balance methods.

C. Maximum amount methods.

D. Straight-line method.

E. Period control methods.

QUESTION NO: 64

Identify the incorrect New GL scenario here below:

A. Cost center update (FIN_CCA)

B. Preparation for consolidation (FIN_CONS)

C. Business area (FIN_GSBER)

D. Profit center update (FIN_PCA)

E. Segmentation (FIN_SEGM)

F. Cost element accounting (FIN_UKV)

QUESTION NO: 65

Select the correct statements regarding G/L Account Groups (Choose two):

A. They are used to assign number ranges.

B. They are used to assign accounts to the controlling area.

C. They are used to assign accounts to the company code.

D. They are used to assign accounts to business areas.

E. They assign the status of the fields in the chart of accounts segment.

QUESTION NO: 66

Select the correct answer (Choose one):

A. A business area can be assigned to a company code.

B. A company code may be assigned to multiple controlling areas.

C. A company code may have more than one chart of accounts.

D. A plant can be assigned to more than one company code.

E. All answers above are incorrect.

QUESTION NO: 67

Which of the following statements is correct regarding currencies? (Choose three)

A. The relationship between currencies is maintained by exchange rate type.

B. Currency relationships are date independent.

C. Using direct quotation, a unit of local currency is quoted for the foreign currency.

D. Worklists can streamline and secure currency maintenance.

E. A currency key must be assigned to every currency used.

QUESTION NO: 68

Special G/L transactions are unique business events characterized by which of the following? (Choose four)

A. They pertain to noted items, automatic offsetting entries, and free offsetting postings.

B. Free offsetting entries are considered to be statistical postings.

C. Special posting key settings must be used to enter special G/L postings.

D. Postings are mapped to an account stored in Customizing.

E. Noted items are one sided entries.

QUESTION NO: 69

Which of the following is correct regarding payment terms? (Choose one)

A. They are valid in customer invoices, vendor invoices, and non-invoice related credit memos.

B. Payment terms have four different date options based on the document, the system, posting and clearing dates.

C. Can be recorded in a company code segment, a sales area segment, or a purchasing organization segment.

D. A special indicator in installment plans can be used for the terms to apply to each individual installment.

E. All statements above are incorrect.

QUESTION NO: 70

Which of the following is correct regarding exchange rate differences? (Choose two)

A. Exchange rate differences are immediately recognized after completion of a transaction.

B. There is an option for users to choose the difference account manually.

C. Can be differentiated by account, currency, and currency type.

D. Are directly posted to the relevant reconciliation account.

E. Are recognized during month end operations and reporting.

QUESTION NO: 71

Which of the following reflects the benefits of using Workflow to post parked documents? (Choose three)

A. It supports all company processes within the System.

B. The users have access to all details that are needed to perform consecutive steps.

C. Authorized users can customize the standard Workflow templates as needed.

D. It automatically displays messages that spell out the corrections needed in a document.

QUESTION NO: 72

Which of the following statements are correct?

A. SAP Business Workflow has three layers.

B. Tasks are implemented in the Business Object Repository as methods of a business object type.

C. Each task can be performed by a group of potential processors.

D. The workflow builder is needed to maintain the process level.

E. All Statements above are correct.

QUESTION NO: 73

Which of the following statements regarding payments are correct?

A. Payment method for the company code specifies which master record fields will be checked during the payment process.

B. Settings in the Payment method/country area indicate the document types for posting.

C. A separate payment method is required for each currency.

D. Payment methods must be defined at the company code level for accuracy purposes.

E. All the above are incorrect.

QUESTION NO: 74

Identify the correct statement regarding the Application Area:

A. The application area identifies the place where a validation is used.

B. The application area identifies the place where a substitution is used.

C. The application area identifies the place where a rule is used.

D. All the above are incorrect.

QUESTION NO: 75

True or False?

A foreign currency cannot be designated as the G/L account.

A. True

B. False

QUESTION NO: 76

Identify the correct statement about a currency (Choose one):

A. Every currency key can have a validity date.

B. A currency does not need a validity date.

C. Every currency can have a validity date.

D. Currency keys don't need validity dates.

QUESTION NO: 77

Which statements are incorrect about the Field Status? (Choose one)

A. Sub-ledger accounts do not have a field status group.

B. The fields for Account Currency and Field Status Group can be optional or required.

C. Fields that are not in use can be assigned the "hide" status.

D. Hidden fields may contain values that will be used by the System.

E. The fields for Account Currency and Field Status Group are not always required.

F. All the above are incorrect.

QUESTION NO: 78

Possible definitions for a year-independent fiscal year variant include (Choose two):

A. Non-calendar year

B. Calendar year

C. Statutory calendar year

D. Fiscal calendar year

QUESTION NO: 79

Identify the correct statement pertaining to Company Code configuration in the IMG.

A. An existing company code can be copied.

B. A new company code can be created without a reference company code.

C. A new company code can be created from a country template.

D. Best practice recommends copying an existing company.

E. All the above are correct.

QUESTION NO: 80

True or False?

The asset classes defined in the chart of depreciation apply to all company codes.

A. True

B. False

Inquiries: support@sapseries.com

Practice Test 3 - Answers

QUESTION NO: 1

Payment methods are defined with (Choose Two):

A. Currency for the company code.

B. A House Bank link.

C. A currency for the country level.

D. Maximum and minimum payment amounts.

Answer: C, D

Page(s): 126

QUESTION NO: 2

True or False?

Drilldown reporting is a tool that enables users to analyze G/L account transaction figures and financial statements.

A. True

B. False

Answer: A

Page(s): 191

QUESTION NO: 3

True or False?

Once a Chart of depreciation has been assigned to a company code, the required data for asset accounting should be added to the company code.

A. True

B. False

Answer: A

Page(s): 146

QUESTION NO: 4

All reconciliation accounts and all G/L accounts with open item transactions in foreign currency must be assigned to a G/L account for realized losses and gains. Which of the following options are usable for this assignment (Choose two)?

A. A single G/L account can be used for all currencies and currency types.

B. A single G/L account cannot be used for currencies and currency types.

C. A single G/L account can be used per currency.

D. A single G/L account cannot be used per currency type.

Answer: A, C

Page(s): 64

QUESTION NO: 5

Which statements are relevant for the Payment Medium Workbench (PMW)? (Choose three):

A. New formats can be created with little programming experience.

B. Payment groups are created depending on the level of granularity.

C. Performance for mass payments is improved.

D. PMW can only be used with certain payment methods.

E. There are four steps in the PMW process.

Answer: A, B, C

Page(s): 133, 134

QUESTION NO: 6

Identify the correct statements regarding a Chart of Depreciation (Choose Three):

A. Needs to be assigned to a company code.

B. Depreciation areas can be added or deleted according to needs.

C. New depreciation areas can be opened even after system Go-live.

D. The fact that a Chart of depreciation is country-specific implies that it meets all requirements for the defined country, and cannot be changed.

Answer: A, B, C

Page(s): 145, 146

QUESTION NO: 7

Which statements are correct in regards to Asset classes? (Choose five):

A. It has two main sections: a master data section and a depreciation area section.

B. For flexibility purposes an asset can be assigned to multiple asset classes.

C. An asset class is assigned to at least one chart of depreciation.

D. It only has a single section for master data.

E. Asset classes are created at the client level.

F. Assets under construction and low value assets are special asset classes.

G. Many different charts of depreciation can be assigned to the same asset class.

H. Asset classes are created at the company code level.

Answer: A, C, E, F, G

Page(s): 147, 148

QUESTION NO: 8

True or False?

Number assignment for fixed assets can be defined as internal or external

A. True

B. False

Answer: A

Page(s): 151

QUESTION NO: 9

True or False?

SAP ERP delivers standard depreciation areas; therefore additional areas cannot be defined.

A. True

B. False

Answer: B

Page(s): 145

QUESTION NO: 10

True or False?

When multiple financial statement versions are in use, multiple depreciation areas need to post to the G/L.

A. True

B. False

Answer: A

Page(s): 149

QUESTION NO: 11

True or False?

If necessary, dunning notices can automatically be printed out right after a dunning run.

A. True

B. False

Answer: A

Page(s): 94

QUESTION NO: 12

True or False?

When company codes use the same chart of accounts, they cannot have different charts of depreciation.

A. True

B. False

Answer: B

Page(s): 146

QUESTION NO: 13

Identify the correct statements regarding drilldown lists (Choose three):

A. An individual object is formatted for all key figures according to the form.

B. Usually key figures are in rows of a list.

C. Key figures are represented by the columns of a list.

D. Characteristic values are represented by the row.

E. Several objects are formatted using a selection of key figures.

Answer: C, D, E

Page(s): 192, 193

QUESTION NO: 14

Which Report painter report only takes into consideration financial statement items needed for the calculation of specific key figures?

A. Balance display

B. Reports for financial statement analysis

C. Key figure reports

Answer: C

Page(s): 192

QUESTION NO: 15

Reports for financial statement analysis, key figure reports and balance display are report types usable for (Choose one):

A. Business area evaluations

B. Client evaluation

C. G/L account evaluations

Answer: C

Page(s): 191, 192

QUESTION NO: 16

Exception lists can contain any of the items here below (Choose Three):

A. No payment block indicator.

B. Blocked items.

C. Vendor accounts with credit balances.

D. Items with invalid payment methods.

E. Items with missing payment methods in the master data and in the line item.

Answer: B, D, E

Page(s): 130, 134

QUESTION NO: 17

True or False?

The Payment process consists of five steps.

A. True

B. False

Answer: B

Page(s): 123

QUESTION NO: 18

Identify the incorrect options pertaining to main settings for the Payment program (Choose two):

A. All company codes

B. Payment method/country

C. Bank currencies

D. Company codes

E. Bank selection

F. payment method for company code

G. Accounts and Amounts

Answer: C, G

Page(s): 124

QUESTION NO: 19

When no particular company code is mentioned in Automatic payments for all company codes:

A. The system displays an error message.

B. The system automatically considers the sending company code as the paying company code.

C. The system will automatically derive the paying company code.

Answer: B

Page(s): 124

QUESTION NO: 20

Tolerance days for payments will defer payment to the (Choose the correct option):

A. Next transaction

B. Next month

C. Next posting period

D. Next payment run

Answer: D

Page(s): 125

QUESTION NO: 21

True or False?

The Payment program is designed to process incoming payments as well as outgoing payments.

A. True

B. False

Answer: A

Page(s): 122

QUESTION NO: 22

True or False?

The Paying company code is responsible for handling outgoing payments.

A. True

B. False

Answer: A

Page(s): 124

QUESTION NO: 23

How are exchange rate differences posted?

A. Manually in a profit and loss account.

B. Manually as realized gains or losses.

Inquiries: support@sapseries.com

C. Automatically as unrealized gains or losses.

D. Automatically as realized gains or losses.

Answer: D

Page(s): 64

QUESTION NO: 24

True or False?

Manual depreciation can be used as an approach for posting write-ups.

A. True

B. False

Answer: A

Page(s): 157, 158

QUESTION NO: 25

In SAP ERP, the length of a G/L account number ranges between:

A. One and six digits

B. One and seven digits

C. One and eight digits

D. One and nine digits

E. One and ten digits

Answer: E

Page(s): 50

QUESTION NO: 26

What must be done if a customer wants Profit Center updates to be included in the General Ledger, in an environment that is running the New G/L (Choose one)?

A. Assign the Profit Center update scenario to the ledger.

B. Activation of transfer prices in Profit Center Accounting.

C. Setting up the same group currency for all company codes and profit centers.

D. Deactivation of document splitting for profit centers.

Answer: A

Page(s): 75, 76

QUESTION NO: 27

What is the maximum number of line items that can be entered in a FI document?

A. Unlimited

B. 99

C. 9999

D. 999

Answer: D

Page(s): 41

QUESTION NO: 28

What definition is essential in the configuration of a dunning procedure (Choose one)?

A. The dunning levels and the language of the dunning note.

B. The dunning levels and the dunning charges for each dunning level.

C. The dunning levels and the account determination to post dunning interest.

D. The dunning charges for each dunning level and the customers to be dunned.

Answer: B

Page(s): 94

QUESTION NO: 29

How can a user change the short text field of a G/L account?

A. By making the change at the beginning of a new fiscal year.

B. By ensuring that the field status of the chart of accounts segment allows it.

C. On a central basis in the chart of accounts segment.

D. On an individual basis in the company code segment.

Answer: C

Page(s): 50

QUESTION NO: 30

Which option below provides the call-up points for validations in FI?

A. Document header, document type, and complete document.

B. Basic data section, detailed data section, and line item.

C. Basic data section, line item, and complete document.

D. Document header, line item, and complete document.

Answer: D

Page(s): 46

QUESTION NO: 31

A company decides to merge two cost centers, and wants all future postings to go to a single cost center. If a posting is made to the wrong cost center in FI, SAP ERP should automatically replace it by the correct one. How can this be implemented?

A. By defining two substitutions for the Line Item call-up point.

B. By creating a user-specific program that will automatically substitute incorrect cost centers overnight.

C. By defining a substitution in FI with the incorrect cost center as a prerequisite and the correct one as the substituted value.

D. By defining a validation in CO to ensure that the functional area is filled in the cost center master.

Answer: C

Page(s): 45, 46

QUESTION NO: 32

What determines the field status for a vendor?

A. Account group, transaction, and the chart of accounts.

B. Account group, chart of accounts, and the company code.

C. Account group, transaction, and the company code.

D. Transaction, chart of accounts, and the company code.

Answer: C

Page(s): 89

QUESTION NO: 33

True or false?

 A business area can be directly assigned to a company code.

A. True

B. False

Answer: B

Page(s): 34

QUESTION NO: 34

Which tools here below are used for maintaining exchange rates (Choose three):

A. Direct quotation

B. Inversion

C. Indirect quotation

D. Base currency

E. Exchange rate spreads

Answer: B, D, E

Page(s): 38, 39

QUESTION NO: 35

True or False?

A G/L account has the following segments?

• Chart of accounts segment

• Corporate segment

A. True

B. False

Answer: B

Page(s): 50

QUESTION NO: 36

True or False?

All G/L accounts with open item management are required to have line item display.

A. True

B. False

Answer: A

Page(s): 53

QUESTION NO: 37

If company codes use different operational charts of accounts, you cannot carry out cross-company code controlling.

A. True

B. False

Answer: A

Page(s): 36, 84

QUESTION NO: 38

True or False?

The options for field status definitions have the following priority, starting with the highest:

1. Required entry

2. Display

3. Hide

4. Optional entry

A. True

B. False

Answer: B

Page(s): 52, 53

QUESTION NO: 39

True or false?

Segments are assigned to a hierarchy similar to the hierarchy of the profit centers from which they can be derived.

A. True

B. False

Answer: B

Page(s): 34, 76, 77

QUESTION NO: 40

True or False?

The definition of sensitive fields is not company code-specific.

A. True

B. False

Answer: A

Page(s): 92, 112

QUESTION NO: 41

True or False?

Maintenance for Customer and Vendor accounts must be decentralized by company code.

A. True

B. False

Answer: B

Page(s): 90, 110

QUESTION NO: 42

True of False?

General Ledger accounts always use external number assignment .

A. True

B. False

Answer: A

Page(s): 50

QUESTION NO: 43

Choose the correct statement:

A. At the beginning of each year the system always restarts the document number assignment at the start of the number range.

B. Document number ranges can overlap if needed.

C. Several number ranges can be assigned to a single document type simultaneously.

D. The same number range cannot be used for several document types.

E. All the above statements are incorrect.

Answer: E

Page(s): 42

QUESTION NO: 44

What are the standard posting keys for G/L accounts and on which side of the account do they post to? (Choose two)

A. Debit, posting key 70

B. Credit, posting key 75

C. Credit, posting key 50

D. Debit, posting key 40

E. Credit, posting key 39

Answer: C, D

Page(s): 44

QUESTION NO: 45

Identify the incorrect statements (Choose three):

A. The authorization group in the posting period variant only pertains to authorization for posting in special periods.

B. A posting period variant must contain at least one line with the entry valid for all accounts.

C. The account range in the posting period variant consists of G/L accounts.

D. Posting periods are opened and closed automatically.

E. It is not possible for more than two periods to be open at the same time.

Answer: A, D, E

Page(s): 40, 171

QUESTION NO: 46

Select the preconditions for processing negative postings? (Choose two)

A. Negative reversal postings need to be included in the company's business process.

B. The company code must allow negative postings.

C. The user wants to set the transaction figures back to the initial state prior to the incorrect posting.

D. The reversal reason must be defined for handling negative reversals.

Answer: B, D

Page(s): 63

QUESTION NO: 47

What are the types of taxation that can be mapped in the SAP ERP system? (Choose two)

A. Taxation at national level.

B. Taxation at international level.

C. Taxation at regional/jurisdictional level.

D. Input tax.

E. Output tax.

Answer: A, C

Page(s): 80

QUESTION NO: 48

What are the correct statements regarding tax in cross-company code transactions? (Choose three)

A. A cross-company code transaction involves at least two documents.

B. Tax amounts in a cross-company code transaction cannot automatically be distributed to the company codes in which the expenses/revenues occurred.

C. A custom report needs to be configured to distribute tax to the company codes in which the expenses/revenues occurred.

D. Cross-company code transactions are not supposed to involve tax.

E. By default, the tax calculated is entirely posted to the first company code.

Answer: A, B, E

Page(s): 84

QUESTION NO: 49

Identify the incorrect statements here below (Choose two):

A. Account clearing occurs when a credit memo is cleared with an open invoice.

B. Posting with clearing involves posting a payment for an open invoice with a resulting zero balance.

C. A partial payment clears the invoice and the payment; then creates a new open item.

D. A residual item results in an open invoice and an incoming payment remaining in the customer account as open items.

Answer: C, D

Page(s): 85, 122

QUESTION NO: 50

Which statements indicate the correct ways a G/L account can be determined for exchange rate differences?

A. A single G/L account can be used for all currencies and currency types.

B. A single G/L account can be used for every currency and currency type.

C. A single G/L account can be used for every currency.

D. A single G/L account can be used for every currency type.

E. All statements above are correct

Answer: E

Page(s): 64

QUESTION NO: 51

True or False?

The parameters indicate the accounts and documents for inclusion in a payment run.

A. True

B. False

Answer: A

Page(s): 123, 130

QUESTION NO: 52

True or false?

The company codes entered in payment run parameters can pertain to multiple countries.

A. True

B. False

Answer: B

Inquiries: support@sapseries.com

Page(s): 130

QUESTION NO: 53

True or False?

The exception list is the confirmation for a successful payment proposal.

A. True

B. False

Answer: B

Page(s): 130

QUESTION NO: 54

True or False?

Dunning notices should only be sent to customers.

A. True

B. False

Answer: B

Page(s): 94

QUESTION NO: 55

Identify the incorrect reasons for an overdue item to not be dunned (Choose two):

A. The account is not included in the parameters.

B. The items or accounts are blocked for dunning.

C. The items exceed the grace period.

D. The overdue amount is greater than the minimum amount.

E. The dunning data has not been updated since the last dunning run and *Always dun?* is not checked.

Answer: C, D

Page(s): 93, 94, 95

QUESTION NO: 56

How many steps are in a dunning run?

A. 5

B. 6

C. 3

D. 4

Answer: C

Page(s): 94

QUESTION NO: 54

True or False?

A dunning procedure can have between 1 and 9 dunning levels.

A. True

B. False

Answer: A

Page(s): 96

QUESTION NO: 55

True or False?

If *Always dun* is selected a dunning notice will be sent, regardless of any dunning data updates since the last dunning run.

A. True

B. False

Answer: A

Page(s): 95

QUESTION NO: 56

True or False?

A single dunning form can be used for all dunning levels.

A. True

B. False

Answer: A

Page(s): 99

QUESTION NO: 57

True or False?

Calculation of interest automatically starts on overdue customer accounts, even if the account master data has no interest calculation indicator.

A. True

B. False

Answer: B

Page(s): 70

QUESTION NO: 58

True or False?

SAP ERP can be configured to perform interest calculation on account balances and on arrears.

A. True

B. False

Answer: A

Page(s): 69, 70

QUESTION NO: 59

True or False?

You cannot void a check unless you reverse the payment document.

A. True

B. False

Answer: B

Page(s): 129

QUESTION NO: 60

True or False?

In the Lockbox process, payment advice notes are used to store the information needed to clear open items on vendor accounts.

A. True

B. False

Answer: B

Page(s): 106

QUESTION NO: 61

The sample chart of accounts provided by SAP can be tailored to meet the requirements of a specific company.

A. True

B. False

Answer: A

Page(s): 49

QUESTION NO: 62

True or False?

The standard mass retirement function in asset accounting uses a worklist.

A. True

B. False

Answer: A

Page(s): 155

QUESTION NO: 63

SAP ERP offers different depreciation calculation methods. Identify the incorrect individual calculation method here below:

A. Base method.

B. Declining-balance methods.

C. Maximum amount methods.

D. Straight-line method.

E. Period control methods.

Answer: D

Page(s): 159

QUESTION NO: 64

Identify the incorrect New GL scenario here below:

A. Cost center update (FIN_CCA)

B. Preparation for consolidation (FIN_CONS)

C. Business area (FIN_GSBER)

D. Profit center update (FIN_PCA)

E. Segmentation (FIN_SEGM)

F. Cost element accounting (FIN_UKV)

Answer: F

Page(s): 75, 76

QUESTION NO: 65

Select the correct statements regarding G/L Account Groups (Choose two):

A. They are used to assign number ranges.

B. They are used to assign accounts to the controlling area.

C. They are used to assign accounts to the company code.

D. They are used to assign accounts to business areas.

E. They assign the status of the fields in the chart of accounts segment.

Answer: A, E

Page(s): 52

QUESTION NO: 66

Select the correct answer (Choose one):

A. A business area can be assigned to a company code.

B. A company code may be assigned to multiple controlling areas.

C. A company code may have more than one chart of accounts.

D. A plant can be assigned to more than one company code.

E. All answers above are incorrect.

Answer: C

Page(s): 34, 35, 36, 49, 135

QUESTION NO: 67

Which of the following statements is correct regarding currencies? (Choose three)

A. The relationship between currencies is maintained by exchange rate type.

B. Currency relationships are date independent.

C. Using direct quotation, a unit of local currency is quoted for the foreign currency.

D. Worklists can streamline and secure currency maintenance.

E. A currency key must be assigned to every currency used.

Answer: A, D, E

Page(s): 38, 39

QUESTION NO: 68

Special G/L transactions are unique business events characterized by which of the following? (Choose four)

A. They pertain to noted items, automatic offsetting entries, and free offsetting postings.

B. Free offsetting entries are considered to be statistical postings.

C. Special posting key settings must be used to enter special G/L postings.

D. Postings are mapped to an account stored in Customizing.

E. Noted items are one sided entries.

Answer: A, C, D, E

Page(s): 114, 115, 116

QUESTION NO: 69

Which of the following is correct regarding payment terms? (Choose one)

Inquiries: support@sapseries.com

A. They are valid in customer invoices, vendor invoices, and non-invoice related credit memos.

B. Payment terms have four different date options based on the document, the system, posting and clearing dates.

C. Can be recorded in a company code segment, a sales area segment, or a purchasing organization segment.

D. A special indicator in installment plans can be used for the terms to apply to each individual installment.

E. All statements above are incorrect.

Answer: C

Page(s): 117, 118

QUESTION NO: 70

Which of the following is correct regarding exchange rate differences? (Choose two)

A. Exchange rate differences are immediately recognized after completion of a transaction.

B. There is an option for users to choose the difference account manually.

C. Can be differentiated by account, currency, and currency type.

D. Are directly posted to the relevant reconciliation account.

E. Are recognized during month end operations and reporting.

Answer: A, C

Page(s): 63, 64

QUESTION NO: 71

Which of the following reflects the benefits of using Workflow to post parked documents? (Choose three)

A. It supports all company processes within the System.

B. The users have access to all details that are needed to perform consecutive steps.

C. Authorized users can customize the standard Workflow templates as needed.

D. It automatically displays messages that spell out the corrections needed in a document.

Answer: A, B, C

Page(s): 57, 58

QUESTION NO: 72

Which of the following statements are correct?

A. SAP Business Workflow has three layers.

B. Tasks are implemented in the Business Object Repository as methods of a business object type.

C. Each task can be performed by a group of potential processors.

D. The workflow builder is needed to maintain the process level.

E. All Statements above are correct.

Answer: E

Page(s): 58

QUESTION NO: 73

Which of the following statements regarding payments are correct?

A. Payment method for the company code specifies which master record fields will be checked during the payment process.

B. Settings in the Payment method/country area indicate the document types for posting.

C. A separate payment method is required for each currency.

D. Payment methods must be defined at the company code level for accuracy purposes.

E. All the above are incorrect.

Answer: B

Page(s): 125

QUESTION NO: 74

Identify the correct statement regarding the Application Area:

A. The application area identifies the place where a validation is used.

B. The application area identifies the place where a substitution is used.

C. The application area identifies the place where a rule is used.

D. All the above are incorrect.

Answer: D

Page(s): 45

QUESTION NO: 75

True or False?

A foreign currency cannot be designated as the G/L account.

A. True

B. False

Answer: B

Page(s): 54

QUESTION NO: 76

Identify the correct statement about a currency (Choose one):

A. Every currency key can have a validity date.

B. A currency does not need a validity date.

C. Every currency can have a validity date.

D. Currency keys don't need validity dates.

Answer: A

Page(s): 38

QUESTION NO: 77

Which statements are incorrect about the Field Status? (Choose one)

A. Sub-ledger accounts have a field status group similar to G/L accounts.

B. The fields for Account Currency and Field Status Group can be optional or required.

C. Fields that are not in use should be assigned the "optional" status.

D. Hidden fields cannot contain any values, because they are invisible.

E. The "hide" status field cannot be used in combination with the "required" entry field.

F. All the above are incorrect.

Answer: E

Page(s): 43, 44, 52

QUESTION NO: 78

Possible definitions for a year-independent fiscal year variant include (Choose two):

A. Non-calendar year

B. Calendar year

C. Statutory calendar year

D. Fiscal calendar year

Answer: A, B

Page(s): 37

QUESTION NO: 79

Identify the correct statement pertaining to Company Code configuration in the IMG.

A. An existing company code can be copied.

B. A new company code can be created without a reference company code.

C. A new company code can be created from a country template.

D. Best practice recommends copying an existing company.

E. All the above are correct.

Answer: E

Page(s): 33, 34

QUESTION NO: 80

True or False?

The asset classes defined in the chart of depreciation apply to all company codes.

A. True

B. False

Answer: A

Page(s): 147

www.ingramcontent.com/pod-product-compliance
Lightning Source LLC
Chambersburg PA
CBHW080150060326
40689CB00018B/3929